The Holocaust

Also by Frank McDonough

The British Empire, 1815–1914
The Origins of the First World and Second World Wars
Hitler and Nazi Germany
Neville Chamberlain, Appeasement and the British Road to War
Opposition and Resistance in Nazi Germany
Conflict, Communism and Fascism: Europe, 1890–1945
Hitler, Chamberlain and Appeasement
Hitler and the Rise of the Nazi Party
The Conservative Party and Anglo-German Relations, 1905–1914

The Holocaust

Frank McDonough

with John Cochrane

First published 2008 by
PALGRAVE MACMILLAN

Palgrave Macmillan in the UK is an imprint of Macmillan Publishers Limited,
registered in England, company number 785998, of Houndmills, Basingstoke,
Hampshire RG21 6XS.

Palgrave Macmillan in the US is a division of St Martin's Press LLC,
175 Fifth Avenue, New York, NY 10010.

Palgrave Macmillan is the global academic imprint of the above companies
and has companies and representatives throughout the world.

Palgrave® and Macmillan® are registered trademarks in the United States,
the United Kingdom, Europe and other countries.

ISBN-13: 978 0 230 20386 0 hardback
ISBN-10: 0 230 20386 8   hardback
ISBN-13: 978 0 230 20387 7 paperback
ISBN-10: 0 230 20387 6   paperback

This book is printed on paper suitable for recycling and made from fully
managed and sustained forest sources. Logging, pulping and manufacturing
processes are expected to conform to the environmental regulations of the
country of origin.

A catalogue record for this book is available from the British Library.

A catalog record for this book is available from the Library of Congress.

10 9 8 7 6 5 4 3 2 1
17 16 15 14 13 12 11 10 09 08

Printed and bound in China

For Ann, with love
F.M.

For Eileen, with love
J.C.

Contents

Acknowledgements

The Holocaust is one of the most complex and difficult events to comprehend and understand. After spending several years grappling with this subject, I would have to conclude that it is something of a minefield of conflicting evidence and divergent interpretations. It is also a very harrowing subject. It taxes the human emotions and the 'objective' training of the historian more fully than any other subject I have ever written about. Luckily, I have not been alone on this difficult journey. In the early stages of research, I asked John Cochrane to collaborate with me on this project. His contribution both in important research assistance and in providing detailed input throughout the completion of the book is very gratefully acknowledged. This is a much better book because of John's very important contribution to it. I would also like to take this opportunity to thank a number of people who have helped along the way. I would especially like to thank Professor Richard Evans who made some useful comments on the book. I would like to thank Christopher Wheeler for getting me energised to tackle the subject. I would also like to thank the various anonymous academic referees who have provided many detailed reports on the manuscript. In particular, I would like to thank Kate Haines at Palgrave Macmillan for the energy and enthusiasm she has given to this project from beginning to end. It has been an absolute pleasure to work with her on this project.

F. McD.

Chronology

21 April	Jewish ritual slaughtering of animals banned
22 April	Jews forbidden to work in German hospitals
25 April	Law against the Overcrowding of German Schools and Institutes of Higher Learning. Limit to numbers of Jews allowed in schools to be fixed at 5% with an immediate ceiling of 1.5%.
26 April	Gestapo created
10 May	The burning of books by 'undesirable authors' on Franz Josef Platz, Unter den Linden, Berlin. Works of Jewish authors, left-wing and progressive writers consigned to the flames. The poet and German democrat Heinrich Heine (1797–1856) had once remarked that burning books would lead to the burning of people. Goebbels declared 'The age of extreme Jewish intellectualism has now ended.'
14 July	Law on the Revocation of Naturalisation and Annulment of German Citizenship. Foreign, 'undesirable' German Jews naturalised in the Weimar period stripped of German Citizenship: Eastern European Jews automatically classed as 'undesirables'.
20 July	Concordat signed between the Vatican and the Third Reich
14 July	Law against the Establishment of Political Parties. All parties banned. The confirmation of the NSDAP (National Socialist German Workers' Party – the Nazi Party) one-party State.
14 July	The Law for the Prevention of Offspring with Hereditary Diseases. Forced sterilisation of the mentally and physically disabled, who were called 'life unworthy of life'.
28 September	Government institutions banned from employing 'non-Aryans' or their spouses
29 September	Reich-Entailed Farm Law: Jews banned from owning land. Only farmers who were proved to have no Jewish blood since 1800 could inherit land.
4 October	'Editors' Law' incorporates the 'Aryan paragraph' banning Jews from Journalism

1934

20 April	Heinrich Himmler declared Reich Inspector of Gestapo
24 April	Establishment of the 'People's Court' to try treason cases. Under Roland Freisler it was to become notorious for its vicious judgements (especially the sentencing of the July 1944 plotters).
1 May	Julius Streicher's anti-Semitic newspaper *Der Stürmer* re-establishes the myth of Jewish ritual murder
30 June	'Night of the Long Knives': the murders of Röhm and the SA Leadership, and Hitler's other political opponents
13 July	Heinrich Himmler, Chief of the SS, assumes command of all concentration camps
20 July	SS deemed an independent organisation
2 August	Death of Hindenburg: Hitler combines Chancellorship and Presidency to become 'Führer' of the Third Reich

1935

16 March	Introduction of conscription and re-armament contrary to Peace of Versailles
31 May	'Non-Aryans' declared ineligible for military service
8 July	An 'Aryan Certificate' is required to become a student. Already required for army officers since May 1935; for soldiers from 25 July.
15 September	Nuremberg Laws proclaimed. Jews deprived of citizenship (Reich Citizenship Law) and forbidden to marry or have sexual relations with 'Aryan' Germans (the 'Law for the Protection of German Blood and Honour'). Jews forbidden to employ 'Aryan' female domestic servants under the age of 45. Jews could no longer call themselves 'German'. The Laws brought a range of local discriminatory laws: many small towns and villages had large public signs proclaiming 'Jews are not welcome here.'
18 October	Law to Protect the Genetic Health of the German *Volk*. Strengthened assault on 'life unworthy of life'.

14 November	Supplement to Nuremberg Laws defines Jewishness and the 'Part-Jew' (*Mischling*). A Jew was descended from at least three grandparents. Those having no Jewish grandparents were classed as Jewish if they were of the Jewish faith. '*Mischling* of the first degree' were those having two Jewish grandparents, one grandparent indicated *Mischling* of the second degree.

1936

7 March	Germany reoccupies the Rhineland
29 March	SS expanded to 3500 men
17 June	Heinrich Himmler declared *Reichsführer* and Chief of the German Police. Reinhard Heydrich appointed Head of Security Police.
12 July	Work starts on the building, using prison labour, of Sachsenhausen concentration camp, Orianienberg, just outside Berlin. By September the camp held 1000 prisoners.
1–16 August	The Berlin Olympic Games. Anti-Semitic actions and propaganda were significantly reduced given the international exposure of the Third Reich. Anti-Jewish slogans were removed from the streets.
25 October	Rome–Berlin Axis proclaimed
19 December	Thomas Mann's name deleted from the University of Bonn's roll of Honorary Doctorates

1937

14 March	Pius XI publishes the encyclical 'With Burning Concern' (*Mit brennender Sorge*) critical of Nazi treatment of the Roman Catholic church
19 July	Buchenwald concentration camp set up four miles outside Weimar
5 November	The Hossbach Conference, at which Hitler outlined plans for European war and domination
8 November	Opening by Goebbels of the 'Eternal Jew' exhibition in Munich

1938

12–13 March	Germany marches into Austria: the 'Anschluss' is formed. Nazi anti-Semitic legislation applied to Austria.
26 April	Personal property of Jews valued at over 5000 marks to be state-registered. Prelude to confiscation.
14 June	Jewish businesses required to be registered with the Ministry of Economics
6–15 July	Thirty-two countries attend the Evian Conference called to discuss the international response to the problem of Jewish refugees fleeing from Nazism. Most countries refuse to increase immigration quotas.
25 July	Jewish Doctors' licences revoked
August	Adolf Eichmann, later Chief of Section IVD4 of the RSHA (Reich Security Service dealing with 'Jewish Affairs'), sent to Vienna to set up the 'Central Agency for Jewish Emigration' to enforce the emigration of the 200,000 Austrian Jews
1 August	Jewish men and women forced to adopt the middle names 'Israel' and 'Sarah' respectively.
30 September	The Munich Pact signed by Britain, France and Germany. Czechoslovakia forced to cede border territories (Sudetenland) to Hitler.
1–10 October	Germany occupies the Sudetenland
5 October	German Jews' passports marked 'J' signifying they are Jewish
28 October	Expulsion of 17,000 Polish Jews from Germany
7 November	Assassination of Ernst vom Rath, a Secretary at the German Embassy in Paris, by Herschel Grynszpan in retaliation for his family's privations as Polish Jews suffering forced emigration
9–10 November	'Reichskristallnacht', 'Crystal Night' or the 'Night of Broken Glass'. Extensive attacks on Jews and their property throughout Germany; 7500 shops, offices and 101 synagogues set ablaze as the police looked on. Named after the huge amounts of broken glass left by the Nazi

	violence. The pogrom left nearly 100 Jews dead and 20,000 were sent to concentration camps. Göring insisted the Jews pay for the damage.
12 November	German Jews fined 1 billion marks for 'Crystal Night'. Göring chairs meeting to arrange for the 'Aryanisation' of all Jewish businesses.
15 November	German schools expel all Jewish children
3 December	Forcible 'Aryanisation' of all Jewish businesses

1939

24 January	Heydrich given commission by Göring to force all German Jews to emigrate
30 January	Hitler's Reichstag speech in which he prophesied the Final Solution': 'Today I will once more be a prophet. If Jewish financiers . . . should succeed in plunging the nations once more into a world war, then the result will be not the bolshevisation of the earth, but the annihilation of the Jewish race in Europe'.
21 February	Jews required to relinquish all silver and gold in their possession
15 March	German troops occupy Prague and the rest of Czechoslovakia in breach of the Munich Agreement. The Nazis set up the Protectorate of Bohemia and Moravia.
22 May	Hitler and Mussolini sign the 'Pact of Steel'
4 July	German Jews refused right to government employment
21 July	Adolf Eichmann appointed as Director of the Prague Office of Jewish Emigration
23 August	The signing of the Nazi–Soviet Pact (Molotov–Ribbentrop Pact). The partition of Poland and Eastern Europe is agreed, to follow the Nazi invasion of Poland.
1 September	The German invasion of Poland: the start of the Second World War. Operations of SS and SD in Poland begin.
1 September	German Jews subject to curfew after 8.00 p.m. (9.00 p.m. in summer)

3 September	Britain and France declare war on Germany
21 September	Heydrich meets *Einsatzgruppen* leaders to explain Hitler's decision to expel all Jews into non-German eastern territories
23 September	German Jews' possession of radios illegal
27 September	Fall of Warsaw. The construction of ghettos in Poland begins. Jews begin to be concentrated in vastly over-crowded, insanitary and diseased walled-off corners of Polish cities such as Warsaw, Kracow and Lodz. Warsaw ghetto holds 350,000 Jews (over 30% of Warsaw's population) in about 2.5% of the city.
October	The euthanasia programme (T4) starts in Germany. Led by Drs Karl Brand and Philipp Bouhler it probably killed 150,000 people. T4 saw the first use of poison gas at killing centres such as Hadamar and Sonnenstein. T4 personnel were an essential part of the extermination programmes developed later at death camps such as Auschwitz.
6 October	Adolf Eichmann meeting with Gestapo chief Heinrich Müller to discuss extended deportation of Jews to the east. This was the 'Lublin' or 'Nisko' Plan.
7 October	Himmler declared Reich Commissar for the Consolidation of German Nationhood
12 October	Hans Frank made Chief Civilian Officer (later Governour-General) of Occupied Poland
12 October	Viennese Jews deported
15 October	Adolf Eichmann reports that Nisko, near Lublin, will be the transit camp for the extensive deportation of all Jews from the Greater Reich to the east
26 October	Upper Silesia, Pomerania, West Prussia, Poznan and the City of Danzig incorporated into Nazi Germany. The rest of Nazi-occupied Poland formed into the German vassal state of the 'Generalgouvernement'.
12 November	All Jews in areas of Poland annexed by the Nazis forced into the 'Generalgouvernement'

23 November	Polish Jews forced to wear the yellow Star of David.
28 November	Nazis impose Jewish Councils (*Judenräte*) on Jewish communities in Poland.

1940

9 April–10 June	German invasion and occupation of Norway and Denmark
30 April	Lodz ghetto now incarcerates 160,000 Jews
10 May	Churchill becomes British Prime Minister
30 June	The sealing of the Lodz ghetto in Poland with about 160,000 Jews now imprisoned and cut off from the outside world
10 May	German invasion of the Low Countries and France
20 May	Auschwitz concentration camp (Auschwitz I) established by the SS near Kracow (Oswiecim) in German Upper Silesia, about 160 miles south-west of Warsaw
14 June	First transport (928 Polish Jews) arrives at Auschwitz concentration camp
22 June	The defeat and occupation of the Low Countries and France (with the exception of Vichy France, which became a Nazi French satellite)
15 August	The Madagascar Plan for the mass emigration of Europe's Jews outlined by Eichmann
22 October	Jews from the Saarland, Baden and Alsace-Lorraine deported
28 October	Italy invades Greece
15 November	Warsaw ghetto sealed off; 500,000 Jews imprisoned.
November	Hungary, Romania and Slovakia sign Tripartite Pact as Axis Powers.

1941

1 March	Auschwitz concentration camp extended following visit by Heinrich Himmler. By 1942, 8000 prisoners a day worked on expanding the camp.

3 March	Hitler informs Alfred Jodl, Wehrmacht Chief-of-Staff, that the coming war with the USSR will require that 'The Jewish–Bolshevik intelligentsia, hitherto the oppressor of the people, must be eliminated.'
6 June	The Army Command (OKH) sends the 'Commissar Order' to combat units on the Russian Front: all 'political commissars' are to be shot when captured. The Order was also used for the execution of Jews.
22 June	Operation Barbarossa: the German invasion of the Soviet Union. *Einsatzgruppen* operations begin.
2 July	Reinhard Heydrich's written order to higher SS and police leaders requiring the liquidation of 'radical elements' including prominent Jews in the occupied areas of Russia
20 July	Ghetto at Minsk established
31 July	Göring's written authorisation to prepare the 'total solution of the Jewish Question in the German sphere of Europe'
15 August	Kovno ghetto sealed off
1 September	German Euthanasia Campaign is halted after protest by Bishop Galen
3 September	Auschwitz sees the first gassing experiments with Zyklon B
6 September	Ghettos set up in Vilna, Lithuania
15 September	Jews in Germany required to wear a yellow Star of David in public
29–30 September	Shooting of 33,700 Jews by Nazi *Einsatzgruppen*, Police battalions and army units at the Babi-Yar ravine near Kiev in the Ukraine
14 October	Mass Jewish deportations from Germany to the east begin
October	Start of the building of Auschwitz II (Birkenau). Auschwitz I remained the main camp.
October–November	Planning of 'Operation Reinhard' designed to kill all Jews concentrated in the 'General Government' of Poland.

	Necessary death camps set up at Belzec, Sobibór and Treblinka.
28 October	The 'Great Action' at Kovno ghetto where 9200 Jews are shot at the IXth Fort
24 November	Theresienstadt concentration camp set up in the German Protectorate of Bohemia and Moravia, 35 miles from Prague. Thought of as a more humane 'model' camp, but the thousands of inmates were eventually gassed at Auschwitz.
26 November	Auschwitz II established
December	The General Plan for the East (*Generalplan Ost*) prepared: 31 million non-Germans to be removed to allow for German *Lebensraum*
1 December	Report by Jäger, leader of *Einsatzkommando 3* (EK3) of *Einsatzgruppe* A, that EK3 had killed 137,346 Jews since June 1941
5 December	Soviet counter-offensive before Moscow signals the failure of 'Operation Barbarossa'
7 December	Japanese attack on US naval base at Pearl Harbor
8 December	United States declares war on Japan
8 December	The gassing, using mobile gas vans, begins at Chełmno death camp in the Warthegau (Polish land annexed by Nazi Germany)
11 December	Germany and Italy declare war on the United States

1942

16 January	Start of the deportation of Jews from Lodz ghetto to Chełmno death camp
20 January	The Wannsee Meeting chaired by Heydrich to coordinate the 'Final Solution'
16 March	'Operation Reinhard' begins. Transports to death camps at Majdenek, Belzec, Sobibór and Treblinka begin. Over 2 million Jews would die. The first deportations were from Lublin to Belzec.

17 March	Gas chambers used at Belzec. From 17 March to December 1942, 600,000 Jews are murdered there.
24 March	Transports to Auschwitz from Slovakia begin
28 March	First French Jews arrive at Auschwitz
May	Gassing begins at Sobibór. By November 1943, 250,000 Jews would be killed.
4 May	First 'selections' for gassing at Auschwitz. First estimates were that 900,000 died at Auschwitz. A later estimate is 1.1 million; another, 4 million. It is impossible to be completely accurate because many Jews (*c.*870,000) were killed on arrival and the Nazis destroyed the evidence; 90% of deaths were Jewish.
29 May	Assassination of Reinhard Heydrich in Prague by Czech partisans
31 May	The I. G. Farben labour camp at Auschwitz opened, known as Auschwitz III, the Buna plant or Monowitz
2 June	BBC broadcast report, secretly brought out of Poland by the Jewish Bund, on the killing of 700,000 Jews at Chełmno
10 June	In Czechoslovakia the village of Lidice and its inhabitants are wiped out by the Nazis in retaliation for Heydrich's assassination. In Prague and Berlin over 1000 are condemned to death.
14 July	Deportation of Dutch Jews to Auschwitz begins
22 July	Mass deportation of Jews from the Warsaw ghetto to the Treblinka death camp starts; 300,000 died.
23 July	Gassing starts at Treblinka. Between July 1942 and November 1943, 750,000 Jews would be slaughtered.
28 July	Jewish Combat Resistance Organisation established in the Warsaw ghetto
August	By end of August, 75,000 French Jews have died, mainly at Auschwitz
4 August	Deportation of Belgian Jews to Auschwitz begins. It lasted until July 1944, killing 25,000 Jews.

8 August	Gerhart Riegner of the WJC (World Jewish Congress) sends the 'Riegner Telegram' to the US and British governments containing the evidence for the Final Solution. The US State regards the information as totally unbelievable.
13 September	The number of Dutch Jews sent to death camps reaches 100,000
15 October	SS massacre of Jews at Brest Litovsk
25 October	Mass deportation of Jews from Norway to Auschwitz starts
2 November	Massacre of 170,000 Jews in Bialystok in Poland
4 November	British inflict defeat on German Afrika Korps at El Alamein
17 November	Allied Communiqué condemns mass murder of European Jews and promises retribution. House of Commons observes a minute's silence.
19 November	Russian offensive before Stalingrad. The beginning of the long German retreat from Russia.

1943

18–22 January	Deportation of 5000 Jews from Warsaw ghetto to Treblinka death camp. Action provoked armed resistance by Jewish Fighting Organisation (the ZOB).
31 January	Field-Marshal von Paulus surrenders the German Sixth Army to the Russians at Stalingrad. A military disaster for the Nazis that portended the German loss of the Second World War.
14 March	Kracow ghetto liquidated
15 March	Start of deportation of Jews from Greece to Auschwitz. By 18 August, 50,000 had been gassed.
19 April	Bermuda Conference: Britain and America fail to realise plan to rescue European Jews
19 April–16 May	Warsaw Ghetto uprising. Jewish fighters resist liquidation of the ghetto. The German Commander, Brigadeführer Stroop, used nearly 3000 heavily armed

troops per day to crush under 500 Jewish Fighting Organisation (ZOB) fighters and a few hundred other Jews. The ghetto was levelled and the vast majority of resistance fighters killed or captured. The first major mass revolt against the Nazis in Europe. Nazi tactics explained in the 'Stroop Report'.

June	SS exhumation of corpses in death camps to ensure their destruction as evidence of Nazi mass murder
21 June	Lvov ghetto liquidated. Himmler orders liquidation of all ghettos in the Baltic states and Byelorussia. All Jews to be sent to the death camps.
28 June	Four crematoria built at Auschwitz
1 July	All legal protection of Jews in Germany finally abolished under the Reich Citizenship Act
5 July	Failure of the German attack on the Russian Front at the Kursk salient: the greatest tank battle in history. Huge German losses bring overall defeat closer.
2 August	Mass rebellion and breakout of Jews in Treblinka; 300 escape but most caught and killed by SS, police and army units. Survivors forced to destroy the camp: they were then shot.
16 August	Bialystok ghetto liquidated. Jewish revolt fails.
23 September	Vilna ghetto liquidated: 4000 Jews sent to Sobibór and 3700 to labour camps in Estonia
14 October	Revolt and breakout at Sobibór by Jews and Russian POWs: 300 escaped; about 100 were captured and executed. SS close the camp and destroy it.
16 October	Nazi occupation of Northern Italy; beginning of deportation of Italian Jews to Auschwitz.
21 October	Minsk ghetto liquidated: 2000 Jews killed
3–4 November	'Operation Harvest Festival'. SS and police battalions murder the prisoners in labour camps in Lublin and surrounding area; 42,000 Jews killed at Trawniki (the camp-guard training establishment at Lublin), Poniatowa (a labour camp near Lublin) and Majdanek.

1944

22 January	President Roosevelt establishes the WRB (War Refugee Board) to help rescue victims of Nazism
19 March	Germany occupies Hungary. Eichmann sent to organise deportation of Jews.
May	Allied debate about the feasibility of bombing Auschwitz and its railway network
15 May	Start of deportation of 430,000 Hungarian Jews to Auschwitz; 50% gassed on arrival.
6 June	D-Day: the Allied invasion of Normandy
22 June	Great Soviet offensive in Byelorussia.
20 July	Failure of the 'July Plot' (or Stauffenberg Plot) to kill Hitler with a bomb at his Rastenburg Headquarters in East Prussia
22 July	SS evacuate Majdanek death camp survivors to the west before the advancing Russians
23 July	Majdanek liberated by Soviet forces before Germans could destroy evidence of mass murder. Germans enforce the evacuation of Dachau and Bergen-Belsen.
6–30 August	The last Jews (70,000) deported to Auschwitz from Lodz. Chair of the *Judenrat*, Rumkowski, included in the last batch murdered.
28/29 August–27 October	SS, Police and military units deport 10,000 Slovak Jews to Auschwitz
7 October	Jewish Sonderkommando revolt at Auschwitz. Crematorium IV blown up; 250 Jews die in battle with SS and police guards; 200 Jews captured and shot.
30 October	Last deportation from Theresienstadt to Auschwitz; 18,000 Jews from the camp killed in October.
2 October	Raoul Wallenberg, a Swedish diplomat, saves the lives of 4000 Jews in Budapest by giving away Swedish visas. SS and Arrow Cross (Hungarian Fascists) embark on 6-day mass murder rampage against Jews.
28 November	Last gassings at Auschwitz. Himmler orders destruction of the gas chambers.

1945

17 January	SS units evacuate Auschwitz and start the 'death marches', driving surviving prisoners westwards before the Russian advance
27 January	Soviet troops liberate Auschwitz camp complex; 8000 prisoners are left.
11 April	US Army liberates Buchenwald concentration camp outside Weimar; 20,000 survivors are found.
15 April	British Army liberates Bergen-Belsen concentration camp, Hanover, and has to bury 23,000 dead left in the open by the Nazis. BBC filming of the devastation of human life sends shock waves around the world.
25 April	American and Soviet forces meet at Torgau on the River Elbe.
29 April	US Army liberates Dachau concentration camp outside Munich; 32,000 survivors are in the camp.
30 April	Hitler's suicide in the bunker in Berlin
2 May	Surrender of German forces in Berlin to the Soviet armies.
1– 5 May	Death marches of concentration camp survivors continue. Thousands are killed as they are driven away from advancing Allied forces.
5 May	US forces liberate Mauthausen concentration camp, near Linz in Upper Austria; 36,318 entries had been recorded meticulously in its 'execution book'. The camp contained 17,000 survivors.
7 May	Surrender of German forces in western Europe
8 May	VE Day
9 May	German surrender in the East
20 November	Beginning of the Nuremberg Trials (IMT or International Military Tribunal) of Nazi war criminals

Introduction

The term 'Holocaust' is now commonly used to describe the attempt by the Nazi regime to exterminate all of Europe's Jews between 1933 and 1945.[1] Under Adolf Hitler's rule, approximately six million Jews were murdered. Although there are whole libraries full of detailed studies and articles examining just about every conceivable aspect of the Holocaust, we still do not know the exact date when the German government decided to murder the Jews, how that decision was made or who made it. Some historians have recently suggested that the Soviet labour camps of Stalin's communist regime are on a par with or even worse than Nazi genocide during the Second World War. But it is emphasised in this study that the government-directed and bureaucratically organised attempt by the Nazi regime to annihilate all Jews in Europe still makes the Holocaust the most far-reaching act of genocide so far attempted.

Adolf Hitler, who came to power in Germany on 30 January 1933 as the leader of the virulently anti-Semitic and nationalistic Nazi Party, had made numerous references to 'removing' Jews from German society. Hitler also made chilling remarks about the fate of the Jews. In January 1939, in a speech to the members of the German Parliament, he predicted that if the Jews 'provoked' another World War, he would ensure they would be 'annihilated' by the end of such a conflagration. Nazi propaganda frequently claimed that Jews were evil and had corrupted German politics and brought about military defeat, communist revolution, economic collapse and national disunity. The Nazi newspaper *Der Stürmer* [The Attacker] featured at the bottom of the front page of each edition the slogan: 'The Jews are our misfortune'. Yet before the war, the Nazi regime persecuted Jews using a series of laws. It excluded Jews from jobs in the civil service, universities and schools, and in law, science and medicine. The Nuremberg Laws, enacted on 15 September 1935, turned Jews into second-class citizens and laid the legal basis for their removal from German political, social and economic life. Jews were encouraged to emigrate. Approximately 65 per cent of Jews left Germany between 1933 and 1939. But emigration proved increasingly difficult during the late 1930s. There was little progress made towards the establishment of a Jewish state in Palestine during the inter-war years. It was the hate-filled Jewish riots of the evening of 9–10 November 1938 known as *Kristallnacht* (dubbed the 'Night of Broken Glass') that represented the most terrifying example of open violence in Germany against the Jews before war broke out in September 1939.

There remain major differences of opinion among historians – as we shall see in further detail in Chapter 6 – concerning Hitler's exact role in the 'Final Solution'. It is now generally agreed by historians that there was no 'Hitler master plan' or 'blueprint' for the systematic murder of the Jews before 1941. The Final Solution was not simply the acting out of Hitler's anti-Semitic ravings in *Mein Kampf*. Many historians believe that unforeseen events – especially those occurring after the Second World War began – provoked the decision to murder the Jews. Some think that Hitler must have taken the key decision at some point and might even have given an 'order' to kill the Jews in writing, or more likely verbally. But no exact date has ever been agreed among historians. Many others – within this multi-faceted debate – believe that the available evidence suggests the major initiative came from middle-ranking subordinates who were interpreting Hitler's desire for Germany and Europe to be made 'free of Jews', and that they implemented this policy 'from below' and in an increasingly radical manner once the war broke out in 1939 and especially after the invasion of the Soviet Union in June 1941. Ulrich Herbert, reviewing recent German writing on the Holocaust, has suggested that many German historians are increasingly suggesting that Hitler should be discounted as the leading figure in the move towards the physical exter-mination of the Jews, and view the Holocaust as something that was largely undertaken by local SS personnel in eastern Europe, supported by German military and civil authorities.[2]

Most historians agree that the outbreak of the Second World War opened up a new phase of open Nazi persecution of the Jews. After the Nazi occupa-tion of Poland, which began in September 1939, Jews were imprisoned in sealed ghettos thus isolating them from the rest of society. The ghettos in occupied Poland lacked the necessary food, water and sanitary facilities to prevent disease, starvation and death. As the Nazis occupied most of main-land Europe between 1939 and 1941, leading German officials began to discuss how the regime would deal with the 'Jewish Question' alongside other discussions of how other minority groups would be treated in Hitler's 'New Order' in Europe.

The invasion of the Soviet Union in June 1941 opens up the most murder-ous phase of Nazi genocide against the Jews. Behind the invading German army came four SS action groups (the 'Einsatzgruppen'), composed of men whose sole initial order was to track down and kill communists, Jewish offi-cials and other radical elements. With assistance from German police units,

SS combat troops, local collaborators and the army, the Einsatzgruppen increasingly murdered hundreds of thousands of Jews in the Soviet Union. They started with just Jewish men, but by August 1941 the Einsatzgruppen were killing Jewish women and children.

Before the murderous Russian campaign had begun, the favoured 'solution' for the Jewish problem within the Nazi regime was enforced 'emigration' and between 1939 and 1941 Nazi officials debated two plans. One was to move Jews to German-occupied Poland in preparation for a later movement 'east' and the creation of a 'Jewish reservation'. In the summer of 1940, a new scheme – suggested by the German Foreign Office – suggested the transportation of Jews to the French-ruled island of Madagascar. But without naval superiority, such a plan was not feasible and was soon abandoned. By the spring of 1941, Poland was desperately overcrowded with Jews and other displaced minorities. This influx of populations was causing problems for German officials 'on the spot'. In October 1941, Hitler made the situation even worse by agreeing to Jews being deported from inside Germany. The first trainloads went to the Lodz ghetto, but the next transports, from November 1941, went to Warsaw and then to Minsk and Riga in the region of the killing squads.

In July 1941, Reinhard Heydrich, a leading figure in the SS, was asked by Hermann Göring, Hitler's deputy, to draw up an overall plan to coordinate the 'Final Solution of the Jewish Question'. A great deal of circumstantial evidence – but no actual written document – indicates that sometime between June and December 1941, Hitler gave Heinrich Himmler, the SS leader, most probably a verbal order to make arrangements to murder all the Jews of Europe. On 20 January 1942, a number of leading senior officials in the German government met at a villa in the affluent Berlin suburb of Wannsee, under the chairmanship of Heydrich, to discuss procedures for the capture and transportation of all Jews in Europe. Those Jews who were fit enough to work would be used as slave labour and those who were unfit for work and all small children would be put to death immediately. But even the importance of Wannsee has been recently disputed. It is now seen by many historians as part of an evolutionary process in the mass murder of the Jews rather than a crucial turning point.

By the spring of 1942, the Nazi regime had established six major killing centres devoted to the task of killing Jews in a systematic manner: Auschwitz-Birkenau, Belzec, Chełmno, Majdanek, Sobibór and Treblinka. Instead of shooting, gas vans were used and makeshift gas chambers were created. At first these were just converted shower facilities, with carbon monoxide piped in from roaring diesel engines. The more highly developed gas chambers, most notably at Auschwitz-Birkenau, used pellets of prussic acid (Zyklon B) which vaporised into lethal fumes, and bodies were disposed of in adjacent crematoria. These 'extermination' camps were located in Poland and most were situated near to railway lines. The first opened at Chełmno in December 1941 but the major killing operations in the camps did not occur until the summer of 1942, and continued until 1944. The Nazi extermination camps – as will be explained in more full and graphic detail in Chapter 4 – were factories of slave labour and death. The smell of burning corpses drifting in white smoke out of the huge gas chambers at Auschwitz-Birkenau became all too familiar to the slave labourers in the camp. Approximately 1.9 million Jews were killed in the summer of 1942 at just three camps: Belzec, Sobibór and Treblinka, under 'Aktion Reinhard', named in honour of Reinhard Heydrich who was assassinated by Czech partisans in May 1942 in Prague. The most infamous camp of all was Auschwitz-Birkenau, at which between 1 million and 1.6 million Jews perished. In the last year of Nazi rule, the death camps were hastily dismantled as the Germans marched hundreds of thousands of starving and sick prisoners towards Germany so they could be used as slave labour. Around 250,000 Jews died on these horrible 'death marches'.

At first, historians fixed the guilt for the Holocaust on Hitler and a limited number of 'SS sadists and officials' who ran the camps and carried out the killings. It is clear only a few at the very centre of power knew everything: Hitler, Himmler, Eichmann, Göring, Heydrich, Kaltenbrunner and some leading officials in the SS–SD security policy and the RSHA (the Reich Security Office). Himmler, the SS chief, was the best informed of all. He told an audience of senior officials in October 1943 at Poznan in Poland that the Holocaust was 'an unwritten and never-to-be-written page of glory in our history'. But it is now equally clear that a wide variety of 'ordinary' German officials, soldiers, policeman, SS officials, doctors, civilians, railway workers and office workers were involved in the implementation of the 'Final Solution'. Private companies put in rival bids to procure the order to design and build the camps and the crematoria. Private companies manufactured the deadly Zyklon B, recycled the skin, the hair, the gold, and the possessions of the dead for profit. At the subsequent war trials, the directors of these companies claimed they were unaware of the lethal uses of Zyklon B even though they were supplying enormous quantities to the extermination camps. There is still a raging debate about how much the average German actually knew. It was once claimed that most citizens did not know anything at all. But recent oral testimony suggests that many Germans had detailed knowledge about the murder of the Jews. Most Germans had been subjected to anti-Semitic Nazi propaganda at schools, in the workplace and in the mass media for years. Most Germans were not immune from these prevailing and powerful prejudices. Many knew that Jews were being placed in ghettos in Poland. They knew Jews were being indiscriminately killed in mass shootings in the Soviet Union. Even if many people did not know the exact details of what was happening in the extermination camps in Poland, there were widespread rumours abounding. Robert Gellately, who conducted a wide-scale study of the German media during the war, suggested there was 'substantial consent and active participation' by large numbers of 'ordinary Germans' in all aspects of the Holocaust.[3] It cannot be claimed that the entire German population was in agreement with the killing of millions of Jews. But the German government found many people willing to follow orders and to undertake acts of murder. The German people were not exceptionally murderous but they followed the orders of a regime that most certainly was. The moral collapse of so many members of the German middle class who primarily carried out the Holocaust has not yet been adequately explained and it still requires further investigation.

There has already been an enormous amount of research devoted to explaining why so many people participated in the implementation of the 'Final Solution'. Perhaps surprisingly, it is psychologists who have provided the most revealing insights. The killers who carried out the Holocaust show the vast possibilities of human behaviour. The Nazi regime organised, promoted and legitimised anti-Semitism. The Nazis turned Jews into dehumanised non-persons. It was during the conditions of an international war that the Nazi regime became a thorough-going murderous community. Genocide by the Nazi regime directed against the Jews became incorporated within the goals of the Second World War. By making the murder of the Jews a key war aim, Hitler not only legitimised the Holocaust but he provided the perpetrators with a licence to kill and a clear motive for their actions. The Nazi regime said to its mid-level and lower-level functionaries that any murder they committed would not be punished. There are very few documents showing any Nazi official expressing much compassion for the victims.

However, it must be appreciated that it was not just the German Nazis or 'ordinary Germans' who carried out the killings. There were many collaborators from many nations throughout Europe. The French Vichy regime helped to round up 75,000 stateless or 'non-French' Jews for deportation to the death camps but resisted deporting French-born Jews. The Romanian pro-Nazi Antonescu regime was itself responsible for the extermination of 280,000 Jews. In 1944, the Hungarian police assisted the SS in sending over 400,000 Jews to the death camps. The Croatian pro-Nazi regime carried out its own brutal programme of genocide. This resulted in the killing of hundreds of thousands of Serbs and the murder of 20,000 Jews and 26,000

Gypsies. In Nazi-occupied Greece, approximately 90% of the Jews who lived there were murdered. In Slovakia, the pro-Nazi Tiso regime deported 70,000 Jews to Nazi killing centres. In Holland, the Nazi regime deported 107,000 Jews to the death camps with the active help of the civilian Dutch police force, but many people in the Netherlands found hiding places, for as many as 40,000 Jews. In Belgium, the local people gave information to the German authorities that ensured Jews were rounded up and transported to the death camps. In Norway, less than 1000 Jews were sent to the extermination camps. In Denmark, Bulgaria and Finland, the local authorities were also able to save most of the Jews. In Italy, Mussolini sent fewer than 8000 Italian Jews to the death camps. In the German-occupied territories of the Soviet Union and the Baltic states, however, there was extensive and often enthusiastic collaboration in the Holocaust, especially in Latvia, Lithuania and Estonia and most notably in the Ukraine. One of the most controversial aspects of the Holocaust revolves around the fate of the largest Jewish community to suffer under Nazi rule: Jews in Poland. There are many historians who have suggested that it is no concidence that the 'Final Solution' primarily took place in Poland. Many historians have suggested that pre-war Poland was exceptionally anti-Semitic and that many Poles were not inclined to help Jews hiding from the Nazis. Others have suggested the extent of Polish 'collaboration' has been exaggerated and have stressed the enormous hazards Poles faced if they helped Jews.

An even more controversial aspect of the 'Final Solution', fully addressed in this study, is the many Jewish accomplices. The Nazis encouraged Jews to spy on other Jews. In the ghettos, Jews were used as leaders and they led Jewish councils to organise, to list and eventually to collaborate in the deportation of Jews to the extermination camps. Often these 'prominent' Jews had full knowledge of the fate of the deportees. Many hoped to be spared by the Nazis or sheltered under the classic survivors' dictum: 'someone had to do it'. In the camps, the Nazis often used strong Jewish inmates to undertake the most unsavoury aspects of the disposal of bodies. In most cases, individual Jews felt they were acting in the best interests of their fellow Jews. In practice, Jewish collaboration actually helped the smooth flow of the 'Final Solution'.

Between 1942 and 1944, the extermination camps worked at a furious rate to kill many millions of Jews, who were transported to them by rail from every country under Nazi rule. By the spring of 1944, up to 7000 people a day were being gassed at Auschwitz-Birkenau alone. During 1943, the Jewish ghettos in Poland were brutally liquidated and their inhabitants dispatched to the extermination camps. The liquidation of the Warsaw ghetto provoked a major Jewish uprising, which began in January 1943 and continued until

April when it was finally suppressed by superior German armed forces. In May 1943, there was a further Jewish uprising at Treblinka and there were other instances of Jewish resistance at Sobibór, Auschwitz and in the Jewish ghettos in Vilnius and Bialystok. It is important to note that very few Jews were shipped from the occupied areas of the Soviet Union to the extermination camps. This was because of the mass killings of Jews by the Einsatzgruppen, which started in June 1941 and continued until the Germans were driven out of Soviet territory at the end of 1943. The shipment of Jews on the German railways continued even after the increasingly dire German military situation. The pace of the extermination reduced somewhat in the early months of 1944 as the Polish ghettos were emptied. The last major deportation to the death camps came in March 1944 when Hitler ordered the military occupation of Hungary. Approximately 400,000 Hungarian Jews were transported to their deaths in this last major act of the Holocaust. The decision to murder Hungarian Jews provoked some debate within the Nazi elite. Himmler felt the Hungarian Jews should be used as a bargaining chip for a favourable peace settlement with Britain and the USA but Hitler disagreed.

By the summer of 1944, the Final Solution was being drastically scaled down as the Soviet Red Army advanced towards Poland at a rapid pace. On 25 November 1944, the last thirteen prisoners were killed in Auschwitz, but there is no record as to whether they were gassed or killed by other means. With Germany now being attacked by the Western Allies in western Europe and the Red Army in the east, enormous efforts were undertaken by the Nazi regime to conceal what had happened to Jews during the 'Final Solution'. The gas chambers were hastily dismantled and the crematoria blown up. Some camps were completely destroyed. Many mass graves were dug up and the corpses were swiftly cremated. Many Polish farmers were drafted in at gunpoint to plant crops on the sites of camps. In October 1944, Himmler, who wanted to negotiate a separate peace deal with the Western Allies, without Hitler's consent, ordered the SS to end the 'Final Solution'. But Himmler's 'order' was generally ignored by many committed local SS commanders, who continued to kill Jews and ordered them to walk on 'death marches' from the camps to Germany until the very end of the war. It is estimated that approximately 200,000 Jews died in these forced marches. The first major death camp to be liberated by the Red Army was Majdanek on 23 July 1944. Auschwitz was liberated on 27 January 1945 but only 7000 inmates still remained there. Most of the camps liberated by the British and American troops in 1945 and displayed on newsreels, such as Dachau and Bergen-Belsen, were concentration camps and had not played a major role in the 'Final Solution' of the Jewish Question.

The Holocaust has left an enormous legacy for the subsequent history of the world. The sheer scale of the killing ensured the leading figures in the Nazi regime were offered no peace settlement but were instead put on trial at Nuremberg for their horrific 'war crimes'. One of the major questions at the trial was: How and why did the Nazi regime kill the Jews? None of the Nazis were tried for 'genocide' as no crime of that description existed at that juncture. The prosecution at the Nuremberg trials tried to prove that the Nazi regime had breached existing international laws and treaties such as the Versailles settlement, the Geneva Convention and the Munich agreement. Between 1945 and 1949, 5025 Nazi criminals were convicted in war trials. Many thousands were also sentenced by the Soviet Union and in eastern bloc countries for war crimes. Many of those who had collaborated with the Nazis in many of the Nazi-occupied nations of Europe were also executed. In actual fact, the feeble scope of the war trials allowed far too many Nazi perpetrators to escape justice. It was left to spirited private Nazi hunters such as Simon Wiesenthal to keep up the pressure on governments to continue to find and prosecute Nazi perpetrators and their willing collaborators

After the Holocaust, the drive to establish an independent Jewish state was supported by millions of Jews. Many Zionists argued that if a Jewish state had existed before the Second World War then the Holocaust might have been prevented. It was Palestine that became the desired choice for 350,000 Jewish refugees, and although most local Arab groups opposed the establishment of a Jewish state, in 1948 the independent and democratic state of Israel was established. In 1953, the Israeli state offered 'memorial citizenship' to all Jews killed in the Holocaust. Israel soon became the spiritual home of Holocaust remembrance. The Israeli government strives to keep alive the memory of the destruction of the Jews of Europe, but a recent study by Idith Zertal has suggested that contemporary Israeli identity is a great deal more nuanced than has been the case with previous generations and is not as singularly focused on the Holocaust as it was in the recent past.

The Holocaust has also had a profound impact on popular culture. It is seen not just as a key event in Jewish history but as a key part of the history of the world. So-called 'Holocaust mania' is particularly strong in the USA. It has recently been suggested that American popular culture has turned the Holocaust into a money-making industry in which the real Holocaust and the voice of the survivors have been replaced by a Hollywood-directed fiction-alised Holocaust with clichéd heroes and villains. Hardly a month goes by nowadays without a new US book, film or TV documentary about the Holocaust. Many films on the Holocaust, such as *The Diary of Anne Frank*, *Sophie's Choice*, *Schindler's List* and *The Pianist*, were major box-office hits. In addition, there are many museums and memorial sites dedicated to the Holocaust all over the world, most notably, the Anne Frank Museum in

Amsterdam, the Yad Vashem Holocaust Museum in Jerusalem, the Jewish Museum in Berlin and the elaborate US Holocaust Museum in Washington.

This important new study does not seek to examine every single event in the horrific history of Nazi genocide throughout Europe but instead attempts to explain why the German government arranged to murder the Jews, and examines the two places where the vast majority of Europe's Jews perished: the Soviet Union and the death camps in Poland. It analyses the key decisions which led to the execution of 'The Final Solution' and explores Adolf Hitler's role in some detail. It offers an original and detailed examination of the grim reality of life and death in the extermination camps, explores the impact of the Holocaust on popular culture since 1945, and will examine the scholarly controversies surrounding the Holocaust among historians. During a period when the prevailing trend within the existing Holocaust historiography is to relativise the Jewish experience within the broader umbrella term of 'genocide' and to suggest that Hitler's 'war against the Jews' was by no means the worst example of mass murder in the annals of recorded history, this study concludes that the attempt to murder all the Jews in Europe remains THE most singular and harrowing example of genocide.

Part I

The Road to the Final Solution

1
Hitler and 'the Jewish Question' before the Second World War

Few historians can agree about any aspect of the Holocaust. But what every historian can agree on is that Adolf Hitler held a dominant position within the Nazi Party and the governance of Nazi Germany. Any full and meaningful understanding of the Holocaust must begin with an assessment of Hitler's views and policies on the Jewish Question before the Second World War. This approach may seem to corroborate the intentionalist view that Hitler's views on the Jews displayed a remarkable consistency, and to reduce the 'Final Solution' to just another aspect of Hitler's 'master plan' to dominate Europe and destroy the Jewish race. In reality the alternative functionalist position, which suggests that Hitler never planned the destruction of the Jews in advance, can be equally invigorated by examining evidence culled from his early life and political career. Indeed, when Hitler's views on the Jewish Question are examined in detail it can be seen that there was no 'straight road' to Auschwitz. It was a much more complicated long and winding route. The so-called 'essential continuity' of Hitler's views on the Jewish Question so beloved of intentionalist historians is immediately compromised by an examination of his early life.

In the small Austrian town of Linz where he lived as a teenager Hitler described himself as a 'weak-kneed cosmopolitan' with no 'strong views' on the 'Jewish Question'. August Kubizek, his closest friend at this time, recalls that a virulent hatred of Jews was not a central obsession of the future rabble-rousing anti-Semite. Hitler had expressed heartfelt gratitude and respect towards Dr Bloch, a Jewish family doctor, who had looked after his mother while she endured terminal breast cancer. When Hitler moved to the cosmopolitan Austrian capital of Vienna in 1907 he came into contact with Jews of many nationalities for the very first time. Some historians have suggested that it was Hitler's personal encounter with Jews in Vienna that brought the whole question of anti-Semitism to the forefront of his thoughts. In *Mein Kampf*, Hitler claimed that his personal contact with Jews on the streets of Vienna led him to take more notice of their 'alien' physical appearance. Hitler was soon avidly reading the anti-Semitic attitudes expressed in Austrian nationalist newspapers, political pamphlets and periodicals. It would seem – from this scant evidence – that there was a basic continuity between this initial hatred of Jews in Vienna and his later burning desire to 'remove' them from German society when in power. But Hitler's time in Vienna is a very mysterious period. The real depth of his anti-Semitic thinking at this time is extremely difficult to fully establish, given the fragmentary nature of the evidence. It has recently come to light that Hitler, the young artist, always sold his drawings and paintings to Jewish dealers because he regarded them as by far the most trustworthy. He had many Jewish friends at the lodging house where he lived for several years. He regularly attended congenial musical evenings at the home of a local Jewish family. It seems Hitler's anti-Semitic views were by no means radical or exceptional in the context of Vienna during the time when he resided there. The views Hitler expressed in *Mein Kampf* on the 'Jewish danger' were more self-serving rhetoric, which attempted to reveal a future vision of the 'Jewish danger' as seen by Hitler during his Vienna period, when in reality his overall behaviour in the Austrian capital does not indicate he had already developed an unchangeable view of the Jews that led all the way to Auschwitz.

Even Hitler's period in the German army during the First World War does not appear to have brought forth any dramatic hardening of his alleged extreme anti-Semitic views. His fellow soldiers described him as a humourless, isolated, but patriotic soldier who was fully behind the German war effort. He was affectionately nicknamed 'Uncle Dolf' as he seemed more serious, much older (he was in his mid-20s) and less fun loving than most of his fellow comrades. No one remembers him talking about his views on 'the Jews' at all in the trenches. The one sure fact about his time as a soldier in the trenches we do know is that he was recommended for the award of an Iron Cross 1st Class by a Jewish officer. Only during the latter stages of the First World War did Hitler start to believe in the popular 'stab in the back' myth. This suggested the German war effort was being severely undermined by 'Jewish socialists' and 'war profiteers' on the home front. While on leave in Munich and Berlin, Hitler noticed that 'most of the people in offices and banks were Jewish', and after reading about most of the socialist agitators who opposed the war he also concluded they were Jewish too.

In November 1918, Hitler was not prepared for the German defeat. By his own admission, the news of the armistice which ended the First World War brought him anger, a flood of tears (the first he had shed since his mother's

death) and a bitter longing for revenge against Germany's internal and exter-
nal enemies. During his time at Pasewalk sanatorium, recovering from a
mustard gas attack, the link Hitler made between the military defeat and the
undermining of the German war effort at home by a 'stab in the back' grouping of what he called 'Jews and Communists' has been seen by some historians as an important factor in the remarkably strong and radical anti-Semitic
stance he adopted after 1918. Rudolph Binion, in a psycho-history on the
Nazi dictator, argues that Hitler's 'mission to remove Germany's Jewish
cancer' actually derived from an hallucination Hitler had while at Pasewalk
in which he equated the death of his mother, attended by her Jewish doctor,
with Germany's defeat in the war. He allegedly awoke from this dream determined to kill the Jews and avenge the German defeat in war.[1]

   After 1918, a violent hatred of the Jews does occupy a dominant place in
Hitler's political outlook and thinking. The defeat – according to Hitler – was
due to the Jews who had weakened German patriotism and incited Marxist
revolution at a vital stage of the conflict. On his return to Munich, early in
1919, his growing interest in the 'Jewish Question' was augmented by
attending an army-sponsored short course at Munich University. He made a
great impression on his tutors and it was his passionate anti-Semitic opin-
ions during the seminar discussions which were remembered. Many of his
army superiors in Munich were also greatly impressed by his anti-Semitic
and anti-communist political stance. Captain Karl Mayr, who at the time was
in charge of a clandestine Reichswehr counter-intelligence project, which
aimed to spy on left-wing fringe groups and encourage German workers to
abandon support for socialism, quickly recruited Hitler to this project. Mayr
initially asked Hitler to brief one of his army colleagues, Adolf Gemlich, on
the 'Jewish Question'. In a letter to Gemlich dated 16 September 1919, Hitler
offers his first lengthy recorded opinion on the 'Jewish Question'. He begins
by describing anti-Semitism 'as a political movement', which 'cannot be
defined by emotional impulses but only by recognition of facts'. The 'Jews
were a race', wrote Hitler, not a 'religious association', who maintained their
racial unity and racial purity by owing their primary allegiance to their own
'race', not any country in which they lived. To Hitler, Jews were like 'a racial
tuberculosis', and a critical opponent of national unity. They sought to
manipulate public opinion towards cosmopolitan and international ideologies through their control of the press. According to Hitler, Jews were quite
happy to promote racial inter-marriage, but they themselves only married
people of their own 'race'. For all these reasons, Jews had to be 'removed'
from society, not in violent 'pogroms', but as part of a rational and unemotional programme of anti-Semitic legislation en route to what he called 'the
final objective': the 'removal' (*Entfernung*) of Jews from Germany through a

programme of emigration. Hitler claimed that only a government of 'national vitality' would be capable of achieving this ultimate goal.[2] At the time it was written, this was a very routine letter, but in the context of the enormity of the physical annihilation of the Jews, it has been viewed by many intentionalist historians, most notably Lucy Dawidowicz, John Toland and Sebastian Haffner, as deeply significant. A major aspect of the intentionalist approach is to reveal evidence from Hitler's writings and speeches to illustrate their influence on his later actions towards the Jewish Question as German leader. The letter to Gemlich is certainly evidence that shows how quickly anti-Semitism had come to dominate Hitler's thinking at the end of the First World War. It is also possible to interpret Hitler's 'final' aim of the 'removal' of the Jews from German society, mentioned in this letter, as containing the possibility of violence and even genocide. But the letter is open to an alternative interpretation as Hitler explicitly rules out violent 'pogroms' against the Jews in the same letter and he clearly emphasises that the removal of the civil liberties of Jews by legislation followed by emigration abroad are the policies he favours to deal with the 'Jewish Question'.

Even so, during the early 1920s anti-Semitism was at the very core of Hitler's political ideology. Most of Hitler's earliest rabble-rousing speeches in the beer halls of Munich are full of bile and hatred towards Jews. On 13 November 1919, in his first major public speech, Hitler said: 'We will carry on the struggle [against the Jews] until the last Jew is removed from the German Reich.'[3] In a speech in Salzburg on 7 August 1920, Hitler said that 'the poisoning of our people' would not end 'unless the cause [the Jews] are removed from our presence'. But in similar speeches during this period Hitler stressed that he did not want to create a 'pogrom mood' against 'the Jews'. He mainly wanted his nationalistic audience to grasp the 'evil' aims of Jewish internationalism on German society and to see that the 'expulsion' of Jews from Germany would be the most 'thorough' solution to the Jewish Question.

Hitler was further influenced in the radicalising of his anti-Semitic views during the early 1920s by Dietrich Eckart, a poet and journalist with a serious alcohol problem. Under the influence of Eckart, Hitler's speeches added new anti-Semitic phrases. Hitler increasingly called the Jews a 'parasite race' and portrayed Jewishness as a sort of 'disease', disrupting any possibility of racial purification within Germany. Eckart wrote many of the anti-Semitic pamphlets, in which these phrases frequently occur. Hitler claimed he drew great inspiration in the development of his own anti-Semitic thinking from Eckart's best known anti-Semitic tract called *That is the Jew*, which Eckart handed to him at the end of one of the first Nazi Party meetings he attended.

The two books Hitler penned during the 1920s: *Mein Kampf* (1924) and the *Secret Book* (1928), offer a detailed outline of his views on the Jewish

Question at this juncture. They outline how his radical anti-Semitism was an integral part of his drive to 'purify' the German race in preparation for his primary foreign-policy goal of making Germany the most dominant power in Europe through the acquisition of living space (*Lebensraum*) during a war of conquest in eastern Europe, against the 'Jewish–Bolshevik' Soviet Union. *Mein Kampf*, which has a very ramshackle structure, is in part selective auto-biography, part ideological tract and part blueprint for future political action. At the very epicentre of Hitler's often contradictory and confused ideas is a single theory which postulates that history is not, as Marx suggested, a class struggle but instead a struggle for existence between the strong and pure races over the weak and mixed ones. The principle of 'natural selection' suggested stronger races would impose their strength and will on weaker races. In *Mein Kampf*, Hitler divided the world into three hierarchical racial groups in which only the purity of blood determined the historical pecking order. At the top were 'Aryans', who were defined as those who created cultures; below them were 'the bearers of culture', defined as those who cannot create cultures of their own but who can copy them from Aryans; and at the bottom, 'the inferior peoples', who cannot create or copy cultures but can only destroy them. The primary goal for Hitler was to reconstruct the purity of the 'Aryan' German race, which would involve a far-reaching programme of racial purification that would take many decades to achieve. To rescue the Germans from years of the so-called 'pollution of decadence' was a central aim of Hitler's world vision. The racist state he imagined would isolate and sterilise the 'incurables', the 'alcoholics', prostitutes and the 'mentally and physically disabled' and would subject them to sterilisation, thus ending their ability to procreate. Hitler said the 'preservation of the nation is more important than the preservation of these unfortunates'. The aim was to create a society built on the principles of eugenics.[4]

But Hitler placed two enemies at the top of his hit list in his drive for racial purity: Marxists – a political enemy – and Jews – his key racial enemies. A passionate and violent hatred of Marxism runs through every chapter of *Mein Kampf*. Hitler wanted to 'eliminate' Marxism within German society. He constantly used words such as 'extermination' or 'exterminating' when speaking of what he wanted to do about Marxism in Germany. At his infamous trial for treason – following the bungled Nazi attempt to gain power in Bavaria, known as the Munich Beer Hall Putsch (1923), Hitler told the indulgent right-wing judge that he wanted to be remembered as 'the breaker of Marxism'. But whenever Hitler mentioned Marxists he always implied they were either 'Jews' or were 'controlled by Jews'. He often said Marxism was just a convenient internationalist ideology which was used by Jews to promote the political wing of the 'world conspiracy'. This far-fetched conspiracy theory was supposedly outlined in *The Protocols of the Elders of Zion*, a faked document which originated from the Russian Tsarist government, which was itself fighting a growing communist threat. It outlines a very ambitious Zionist plan for world domination and was circulated widely among nationalist groups in Germany before 1914. Jewish organisations frequently pointed out that this was a fabricated document. But Hitler believed it was authentic. 'If, with the help of the Marxist creed, the Jew is victorious over the other peoples of the world', writes Hitler in *Mein Kampf*, 'his crown will be the funeral wreath of humanity.'[5] By 'removing' Jews from German society and waging a bitter ideological war against 'Bolshevism' in Germany, Hitler believed that he was 'fighting for the work of the Lord' and 'acting with the will of the Almighty creator'.[6]

For Hitler, 'the Jew' was a universal scapegoat responsible for all the things he felt undermined the racial purity and racial unity of the German people. The Jews, defined as a 'stateless race', sought to exploit every nation in which they lived and hoped to promote cosmopolitan ideas that would lead to their domination of a stateless world. The language Hitler uses in *Mein Kampf* against Jews is filled with derogatory and hate-filled anti-Semitic rhetoric. Hitler blamed 'the Jews' for the German military defeat of 1918, the German revolution, the growth of socialism, economic problems, cultural degeneration and much else. He describes the Jews variously in *Mein Kampf* as 'a maggot on a rotting corpse', 'not human', a 'germ carrier of the worst sort', mankind's 'germ of disunion', the 'spider that slowly sucks the people's blood', or as 'vermin', 'bacilli' and 'parasites'. Behind every 'anti-patriotic force' there lurked for Hitler 'the Jew', with 'satanic joy on his face' as he 'replaced democracy by the more virulent 'dictatorship of the proletariat'. He claimed Jews were seeking financial control over the stock market, contaminating art, literature and the theatre, and using the press to spread lies about patriotic nationalists. Even the long-cherished Jewish demand for a Palestinian homeland was denounced by Hitler as a means for Jews to establish a central organisation to promote what he called their 'international world swindle'. These highly prejudiced views provided Hitler and the Nazi Party with an explanation for the political chaos in post-war Germany. The Jews also occupy a central place in Hitler's foreign-policy aims. The Soviet Union was, according to Hitler, 'Jew-dominated' and communism had destroyed the old ruling classes and was Germany's major enemy in a future war. France was Germany's chief 'hate-filled enemy' in western Europe with a ruling elite that was supposedly 'tied up with the Jews' and had to be dealt with also in any future European war. Hitler held out some hope for better relations with Britain and Italy as he felt there was less Jewish domination over the political elites within these two nations. The battle to gain British friendship, however, would depend on whether the patriotic British could overcome the powerful Jewish influence in that nation. In Hitler's fanatical mind, the struggle against the Jews was a defensive one as he believed that unless Jewish domination was ended, Germany could not survive as a nation and would inevitably be gobbled up by the so-called 'Jewish–Bolshevik monster' and the 'Jewish world conspiracy'.

It can hardly be denied that in *Mein Kampf* and the *Secret Book* anti-Semitism occupied a central place in Hitler's ideology and aroused considerable feelings of hatred within him. Whenever he spoke of the German defeat in 1918, Jews were at the forefront of his thoughts. The Jew was the barrier to racial purity within Germany and a key enemy of Hitler's desire for a new world order. Hitler does use the words 'removal' and 'elimination' when describing how he will deal with Jews within Germany if he gained power. Yet there is no mention in either book of a desire to remove the Jews from Germany by killing them in a systematic fashion as occurred during the Holocaust. Hitler's attitude to the Jews encompassed a homicidal element, but there is no evidence of an extermination plan. He proposed only to combat the Jews by legal means within Germany. The slogan 'Jews out' was used frequently in Nazi electioneering propaganda during the 1920s. In Hitler's *Secret Book*, written in 1928 but not published in his lifetime, Hitler concedes at one point that the removal of the Jews could only be 'achieved by the sword' and that such a procedure was likely to be 'bloody'. But these words occur in the context of a passage that is discussing the need for Germany to gain 'living space' in eastern Europe by eliminating the 'Bolshevik Soviet Union' in a future war. Hitler also mentions in the *Secret Book* that not killing Jews who stabbed Germany in the back 'with poison gas' during the latter stages of the First World War was a major error. It seems the Jews Hitler was referring to in this context were Jewish 'Marxist leaders' and not the entire Jewish population.

Before 1933, anti-Semitism was quite clearly a central aspect of Hitler's world-view. But beyond a pledge – outlined in the Nazi Party programme – to remove Jewish civil rights, weaken their economic power and encourage them to emigrate abroad, there is little evidence to suggest that Hitler's ultimate policy objective was to exterminate Jews through a programme of physical extermination as happened during the Second World War. In fact, between 1930 and 1933, when the Nazi Party rose from relative obscurity to become the most popular political party in Germany, the strident anti-Semitic stance Hitler had adopted in his speeches in the 1920s was toned down quite markedly. This is not to suggest Hitler had altered his own strongly held radical anti-Semitic views, but to emphasise that Hitler spoke less of the 'Jewish danger' for tactical and political reasons. He knew the majority of the German electorate were not radical anti-Semites. Even the economic danger posed by 'international Jewry' was also downplayed in Hitler's speeches in the period before he came to office. At this time, Hitler was courting Germany's ruling elite and business leaders and so it was the 'Red Menace' and the power of the trade unions that were highlighted in Nazi electioneering propaganda.

On coming to power in January 1933, Hitler had no clear set of policy measures to deal with the Jews. A close examination of the various studies and plans produced by the Nazi Party before assuming office reveals that only a set of minimum legalistic goals had been agreed, most notably, the 'exclusion' or 'expulsion' of Jews from public office, a ban on marriages between Jews and Germans and the relegation of Jews to the position of second-class citizens. The only piece of evidence of a clear policy plan to deal with the 'Jewish Question' under Nazi rule is the 'Draft Law for the Regulation of the Status of Jews'. This was prepared in July 1933 not by the Nazi Party, but by the non-Nazi and conservative German Ministry of Foreign Affairs. This policy document actually proposes most of the laws that Hitler's regime enacted against the Jews between 1933 and 1939. Its very existence shows how far the desire to introduce legal discriminatory measures against Jews had penetrated inside the higher ranks of President Hindenburg's 'conservative' civil service.

In 1933, there were only 525,000 Jews living in Germany, representing just 0.76% of the population. A great majority of them lived in the large urban cities. The largest number resided in Berlin. But many Jews had a career profile very different from the great majority of the population. A mere 3% of Jews worked within the agriculture sector of the economy and a high proportion worked in the finance, banking and service sectors. Many were salaried employees in offices and retail outlets and 20% were self-employed. Jews also worked as teachers, lecturers, doctors, lawyers and dentists. The poorest Jews tended to be refugees from eastern Europe (with 70% of these coming from Poland) and they mostly lived in the working-class areas of major cities.

A number of established pressure groups represented Jewish interests in Germany, including: the Central Association of German Citizens of the Jewish Faith, the National League of Jewish Front Line Veterans, the League of National-German Jews and the German Vanguard. Most of these groups were patriotically German in outlook. One important sign of the gradual weakening of strict religious observance among German Jews was the rapid growth of intermarriage. In 1927, 25% of Jewish men and 16% of Jewish women were marrying non-Jews and most of the children of these marriages were being raised as Christians. In large cities the marriage of a Jew to a

Christian was becoming increasingly common. The members of the League of National-German Jews downplayed their 'Jewishness' after Hitler came to power and stressed their German heritage. In September 1933, the Reich Representation of German Jews was established, and allowed to operate by the Nazi regime as an independent organisation in an attempt to create a united voice representing all Jewish interests. This organisation was an umbrella federation group of all the major Jewish organisations which aimed to protect Jews from unauthorised violations of their civil rights.

Most German Jewish leaders feared Hitler's well known anti-Semitic views, but believed the coalition he headed – in which the Nazis were still in a minority – would not pursue policies of open persecution. Nor did many Jews predict how swiftly Hitler would break free of his coalition partners and create an all-powerful dictatorship. Hitler's increasing ruthlessness on the Jewish Question may now seem quite obvious with the benefit of hindsight. It did not seem that way to many German Jews at the time. The only major Zionist pressure group, the German Zionist Federation, tended to be out on a limb within the mainstream Jewish community as it urged most Jews to emigrate as quickly as possible. It also voiced concerns about the increasing isolation and ostracism of Jews within Nazi society. Jews left Germany in large numbers. Between 1933 and 1939, 240,000 German Jews emigrated. In Austria, approximately 100,000 Jews also left in 1938 and 1939.

From the first day of Nazi rule, there were spontaneous, random violent attacks on Jews in many parts of Germany. Many Jews married to Germans were led through the streets in humiliating parades in front of baying mobs. Jews were frequently assaulted by Nazi thugs in 1933 in violent street attacks and 45 Jews were killed during that year alone. On 10 March 1933, Hitler announced that he was opposed to 'individual actions' against Jews. This open call for restraint by Hitler was due to political considerations. The newly appointed German Chancellor, often seen at this time in a neatly pressed pin-striped suit, did not want to antagonise the conservative members of his 'national coalition' and especially the more powerful President Hindenburg, who could count on the support of the army.

Even so, Hitler gave his full support to one of the very first acts of open discrimination against the Jews. This was a national boycott of Jewish shops, goods and professionals which took place on 1 April 1933. According to Joseph Goebbels' diary, Hitler had summoned him to Berchtesgaden, his Bavarian mountain retreat, at the end of March 1933 and had told him of the importance of the Jewish boycott for dealing with 'slanderous attacks from abroad'.[7] The boycott was organised by a hard-line Nazi committee chaired by Julius Streicher, one of the most rabid anti-Semites within the Nazi Party. It was designed as a means of testing the water with the German public and his wavering coalition partners as to how far and how quickly the Nazis could proceed with radical anti-Jewish measures. However, after successful lobbying by ageing President Hindenburg and Konstantin von Neurath, the German Foreign Minister, and negative foreign media coverage, Hitler decided they would not go as far as he wanted and so he called off the boycott after just a single day. Most Germans had not supported it anyway. Many Jews sensibly decided to avoid trouble and just closed their shops for the day. In some areas, most notably, Frankfurt, Munich and Kiel, some SA men operated intimidating bully-boy picket lines outside the few Jewish shops that dared to stay open. Many shops were vandalised in sporadic acts of violence and hooliganism. Some very brave Jewish shop owners defiantly stood outside their shops, dressed in their First World War army uniforms, displaying their war medals. The high-profile April boycott of 1933 made Hitler realise that a radical programme of Jewish persecution on the streets of Germany was not popular and simply encouraged negative publicity of the Nazi regime abroad. It also antagonised Hindenburg and leading figures within the army, on whom the survival of his regime depended. Hitler knew that his Jewish policy at this stage had to conform to the existing national and international circumstances and so he adopted a moderate and sensible course of action in dealing with 'the Jewish question'.

Between 1933 and 1937, Hitler's regime opted to deal with the Jewish Question by means of orderly acts of government legislation, produced mostly by non-Nazi German civil servants. With the introduction of these laws, Hitler was able to gradually and peacefully erode the legal status of German Jews, to diminish their position in society and to transform them from 'citizens' into 'aliens' without any recourse to violence. As Walter Buch, a high-ranking judge, put it: 'National Socialism has recognised the Jew as not a human being. He is nothing but an agent of decomposition.'[8] The traditional German conservative right wing supported the legal restrictions on Jews with little comment as they fitted in with their own desire for an orderly authoritarian society. In April 1933, the 'Law for the Restoration of the Professional Civil Service' was the first of what eventually numbered 400 Nazi laws discriminating against Jews. Those Jews in the civil service and in other related jobs were categorised as 'non-Aryans' and stripped of a number of civil rights, including exclusion from a university education and from employment in the judiciary, the civil service, the media, farming and the health service. Professionals such as doctors, vets, dentists, teachers, lawyers and accountants were also deprived of employment. The 'Law against the Overcrowding of German Schools' restricted Jewish pupils in schools to a maximum of 5 per cent in any school. The number of Jewish students at any university was also limited to 5 per cent. Many school heads and university admissions tutors used this legislation to exclude all Jews straightaway as the measures emphasised that 'Aryans' were to be given priority in the allocation of all school and university places. On 20 May 1933, German doctors insisted no Jew should be allowed to undertake medical care of German citizens. In the autumn of 1933, further acts of anti-Jewish legislation excluded Jews from jobs in the theatre and from all parts of the media.

This first wave of anti-Jewish legislation prompted much vocal lobbying from prominent Jews. President Hindenburg, supported by leading conservative figures within the civil service, persuaded Hitler to allow Jewish civil servants and certain professionals who had served in the German army during the First World War to keep their jobs for the time being. The tension between traditional state organisations and the radical anti-Semitic elements in the Nazi Party is evident in the implementation of many of the anti-Jewish measures before 1939. Hitler, keen to appear moderate to his coalition colleagues, told his Cabinet that a proposal to bar Jewish doctors from practice was 'not necessary for the moment' and so he initially exempted Jewish doctors from the 'Aryan' clause. But many Nazi officials in the localities just ignored Hitler's wishes and banned Jewish doctors from health service employment anyway. Within the traditionally conservative and upper middle-class legal profession 47 per cent of Jewish judges and 30 per cent of Jewish lawyers continued to practise even though they clearly failed the criteria laid down in the 'Aryan' clause of the legislation. Nazi anti-Jewish legislation defined a 'non-Aryan' as a person who had one 'non-Aryan' parent or grandparent. The 'Aryan clause' progressively weakened the Jewish middle-class educated elite and led to large numbers of qualified Jews losing their jobs. Many wealthy and professionally qualified Jews opted to emigrate. To the USA went the brilliant scientist Albert Einstein, the noted film director Fritz Lang, the popular actor Peter Lorre and the singer Marlene Dietrich. But poorer Jews could not leave so easily. Nazi anti-Jewish legislation hit many lower middle-class and working-class members of the Jewish community very hard. Many postmen, rail workers, bank clerks and even refuse collectors and street cleaners lost their jobs and did not have enough money to emigrate.

From mid-1933 to the spring of 1935 there was no major new anti-Semitic legislation enacted by the Nazi regime. This apparent moderating of the anti-Semitic stance of the government greatly alarmed many of the rank and file. Goebbels denounced the failure of the Nazi regime to forbid marriages between Germans and Jews. The Nazi Party itself was calling for Jewish businesses to be identified by a Star of David. In the spring and summer of 1935, the party rank and file took part in a fresh wave of anti-Semitic violence in many German cities. They organised anti-Jewish demonstrations, which were often designed to prevent marriages between Jews and Christians. Hitler feared that the widespread reporting of localised instances of Jewish persecution in the foreign press might lead to a boycott of the 1936 Olympic Games, an event the Nazi regime wanted to use as a propaganda showcase for 'the New Germany'. In August 1935, a statement was issued by Rudolf Hess, with Hitler's approval, which called for a halt to 'individual actions' against Jews.

But the 'pressure from below' for further action on 'the Jewish Question' during the summer of 1935 finally persuaded Hitler that some further legislative action was required. The outcome was the introduction of the Nuremberg Laws on 15 September 1935. These laws were decided and drafted only a few days before they were announced. They lacked clarity and a clear set of definitional rules to carry them out. Two of the key demands of the Nazi activists in the summer protests had been for marriages and sexual relations between Jews and non-Jews to be forbidden and for the introduction of a special inferior citizenship for Jews. Both these demands were included in the legislation. Under the Nuremberg Laws, no full-blooded Jew – meaning a person with two Jewish sets of parents and grandparents – could be legally classed as a German citizen. Full citizenship was reserved for 'pure-blooded' Germans and marriages between Jews and Germans were prohibited. Jews of mixed parentage (*Mischlinge*) were given what was termed 'citizenship in the state' but not full Reich citizenship. Hitler pronounced that these 'half-caste' Germans would be allowed to assimilate with the rest of German society over the next few generations. This decision did not please Party activists who wanted so-called 'half Jews' to be defined as 'full Jews'. The full Jews were advised to emigrate. But the legal distinctions within the Nuremberg Laws – especially as they related to mixed-blood Jews – proved extremely complicated for the courts to decide upon. The legal problems related to the partners and children within mixed marriages between a German and a Jew proved equally complicated. The events of 1935 had illustrated the strength of rank-and-file opinion within the Nazi Party in favour of more radical action on the Jewish Question and had stressed that they would act if the German government became luke-warm on the idea.

Hitler – not wishing to align himself publicly with grass-roots opinion – presented the Nuremberg Laws as the foundation for 'peaceful coexistence' between Germans and Jews. He urged party members to 'avoid all individual actions against Jews'.[9] Hitler believed the Nuremberg Laws would encourage more Jews to emigrate abroad. It was really a sort of 'get out now' type of legislation. Jews who remained were now aliens and progressively de-humanised in the eyes of the state and the population. The introduction of the Nuremberg Laws led all the German Jewish leaders to accept that their efforts to prevent Jews being excluded from every aspect of German economic, social and cultural life had completely failed. They urged the younger generation of Jews to leave Germany straightaway. The older members of the Jewish community hoped they would now be left alone even if in progressively impoverished circumstances.

In the late 1930s Hitler was preoccupied by his chief foreign-policy aims, but he still took a keen interest in anti-Jewish policy. He constantly stressed to those within the party advocating more radical measures on the Jewish question that practical and tactical realities had to be taken into account.[10] Even Joseph Goebbels, one of the most radical anti-Semites within the Nazi elite, mentions anti-Semitic policy much less in his diary between 1935 and 1937. In the spring of 1937, Hitler decided not to enact a special document on Reich citizenship designed to clarify the muddled definition which had been outlined in the Nuremberg Laws. He also opposed further economic discrimination against the Jews. On 29 November 1937, Goebbels had a long conversation with Hitler about the 'Jewish Question' in the course of which the Nazi leader said, 'The Jews must disappear from Germany, yes out of Europe. That will take some time still, but it will happen and must happen.'[11] At the beginning of 1938, Hitler informed officials in the German Foreign Office that he was still in favour of encouraging Jews to emigrate.

The union with Austria (the Anschluss) in March 1938 gave a fresh impetus to anti-Jewish activity. It was in Austria – as would happen in other occupied territories – that much harsher policies against the Jews would be enacted. The peaceful Nazi take had been accompanied by general rejoicing among the Austrian population. On 26 March 1938, Göring announced there would be a vigorous policy of 'Aryanisation' enacted throughout Austria. Jews were swiftly deprived of civil rights, goods and property. They suffered countless public beatings and humiliations in front of jeering anti-Semitic crowds. Acts of violence and looting took place against Jewish shops and businesses in increasing numbers. The application of strict rules on 'Ayrianisation' produced a wave of Jewish emigration. It was in Austria that experts in the security service (SD) established a centralised emigration office, led by Adolf Eichmann, that ensured that when Jews left they did so with a visa but no material possessions.

The large number of Jews leaving Hitler's rule in Germany and Austria became a key topic of international debate in the aftermath of the Anschluss. Many German and Austrian Jews who wanted to leave found it increasingly difficult to find countries willing to take them in. Franklin D. Roosevelt, the US President, proposed an international conference to facilitate Jewish emigration from Germany and Austria and to try to work out an international solution to the growing number of Jewish refugees. In the summer of 1938, delegates from 32 countries, including the USA, Britain, France, Canada and Australia, met at the French resort of Evian to discuss the refugee problem. Ribbentrop, the German Foreign Minister, threatened to retaliate if the conference turned into a forum for anti-Nazi propaganda. The words 'Jew' and 'Germany' were studiously avoided throughout the proceedings of the conference. The US delegate was Myron C. Taylor, a little known business-man but a close friend of Roosevelt. The French delegate claimed France had reached 'saturation point' and could not admit further refugees. This view was repeated by almost every other delegate at the gathering. Only the tiny Dominican Republic agreed to take additional Jewish refugees. The only concrete proposal agreed at the Evian Conference was to establish an International Committee on Refugees (ICR), which would 'approach govern-ments' willing to offer refuge and try and persuade Germany to cooperate in establishing 'conditions of orderly emigration'. But the ICR had no real authority or funds. In the end, the conference at Evian, which happens to be the word 'NAIVE' spelt backwards, achieved next to nothing. It showed that the major democratic nations were not willing to do anything to help Jews escape from the anti-Semitic Nazi regime. The Nazi Propaganda Ministry commented that it was 'astounding' that the same foreign countries that had criticised Germany over its treatment of Jews for many years were so unwill-ing to open their doors to them. Chaim Weizmann, President of the World Zionist Organisation, commented in the *Manchester Guardian*, of Evian: 'The world seemed to be divided into two parts: those places where the Jews could not live and those where they could not enter.'

The night of 9–10 November 1938 was a night of brutal and destructive anti-Jewish violence, arson and vandalism (known as *Kristallnacht* – 'Night of Broken Glass'). One Nazi government report suggested 177 synagogues and 844 shops and department stores had been destroyed. The estimated numbers of Jews killed was 91. The Nazi government suggested *Kristallnacht* was a spontaneous response of the German people to the murder of a German diplomat in Paris by a Polish Jew named Herschel Grynszpan. It was the most brutal anti-Jewish pogrom seen on the streets of Nazi Germany since Hitler came to power. Many historians have viewed *Kristallnacht* as a hastily organised act of revenge by Joseph Goebbels and leading anti-Semitic activists in the Nazi Party in which Hitler played only a minor role. The finger of blame has also been pointed at Heydrich and Himmler's radical SS.

Goebbels gave an inflammatory speech in Munich stating that the assas-sination of the German diplomat in Paris would be met by a 'reign of terror' and he promised spontaneous demonstrations against the Jews throughout

Germany. In his diary, Goebbels reveals that he discussed his plan for anti-Jewish demonstrations with Hitler, who was also in Munich to honour the Munich Beer Hall Putsch of 1923. Hitler told Goebbels, 'allow the demonstrations to continue. Pull back the police. The Jews shall for once come to feel the anger of the people.' Yet there is no fully convincing evidence showing Goebbels orchestrating the violence and destruction on that night. There was later talk – at the war trials – of 'mysterious strangers' arriving in many German towns during the evening of 9 November 1938 urging local Nazis to attack Jewish property and synagogues. But no eyewitness was able to confirm whether these were Nazi Party officials or belonged to government security forces.

The next day, Hitler was surprised at the extent of the destruction and was extremely annoyed about the negative foreign press reporting of the open violence against the Jews. In a teletyped message from Hitler's office, Himmler ordered the German police to protect Jews from further violence. This led to the arrest over the next weeks of 30,000 Jews, who were taken into what was described as 'protective custody'. Certainly Goebbels' Munich speech had inflamed a situation which quickly got out of hand during the night. According to Karl Schleunes, the pogrom was 'the product of the lack of co-ordination which marked Nazi planning on Jewish policy and the result of a last-ditch effort by the radicals to wrest control over this policy'.[12]

One major consequence of *Kristallnacht* was that Hitler did not want Goebbels taking a leading role on Jewish affairs anymore. Henceforth, Göring and Himmler, who were very critical of the consequences of the open violence displayed on *Kristallnacht*, became much more trusted by Hitler to deal with Jewish policy. On 12 November 1938, Göring was given control over 'anti-Jewish' policy. Hitler wanted future measures against the Jews to be coordinated in a more centralised manner and he especially wished to avoid further open displays of public violence. After *Kristallnacht*, a number of anti-Jewish measures aimed at ending Jewish influence within the economy were introduced. In the autumn of 1937 there had been a series of measures designed to limit Jewish influence in the economy, but these were only partially implemented. The only concrete measure had come in April 1938 when Jews were obliged to declare all their assets. The November 1938 measures went much further. All Jews owning businesses had to give them up in return for a miserably small amount of compensation. It was also decided that insurance companies would have to honour policies held by Jews who suffered on *Kristallnacht*, but no Jew would receive an insurance payment as a result of the damage as this was confiscated by the state. A further punitive tax of 1000 million marks was imposed upon the Jewish community. Jews were also prohibited from taking any further part in the economic life of the Third Reich. A dedicated Centre for Jewish Emigration was established to encourage all Jews to leave Germany.

In the social field, further laws meant Jews were no longer allowed to use sleeping and dining cars on trains and could not bathe in public baths. Heydrich, a leading figure in the SS, suggested that all Jews should wear an identifying badge on their clothing. Hitler rejected this proposal as he felt it might provoke a fresh wave of anti-Jewish violence and more unwanted international condemnation. In December 1938, Hitler declared his strong opposition to a radical anti-Semitic proposal, put forward by Goebbels and Heydrich, for the creation of Jewish ghettos in Germany. Instead, by way of a compromise, he agreed to the creation of 'Jews only' apartment blocks and this measure came into force in April 1939.

After *Kristallnacht*, Hitler gave strong support to Jewish emigration plans and his response to foreign governments who attacked his anti-Semitic stance was to say 'Take the Jews'. In November 1938, he told Pirow, the South African Minister of Defence, that 'some day, the Jews will disappear from Europe'.[13] On 5 January 1939, he informed Beck, the Polish Foreign Minister, he favoured settling all European Jews in a distant land, mentioning Madagascar as a possible destination. On 30 January 1939, in a much-quoted speech in the Reichstag, Hitler said his two biggest enemies were 'Jewry and Bolshevism'. He promised that if the Jews provoked a world war, the only result would be 'the annihilation of the Jewish race in Europe'. This open, violent threat of physical extermination for 'the Jews' was probably an unguarded expression of his real underlying views concerning them. But this mortal threat to the Jews was only operative in the event of a world war. During this speech, Hitler had indicated that a 'world war' meant US involvement as part of an anti-Nazi coalition.

Ever since the end of the First World War, Hitler's thinking had been dominated by the idea of 'removing' Jews from Germany. No one can doubt that anti-Semitism was at the core of his political ideology, but unlike in the arena of foreign policy, where he took all the major decisions, on the Jewish Question Hitler allowed policy to be devolved to three groups. One important faction was the government elite, which was still dominated by traditional conservatives interested in ensuring a legal framework to all the anti-Jewish measures enacted by the German government. The Nazi Party represented a second group and proposed far more radical measures. Before 1939, many of the anti-Jewish laws were a compromise between Nazi radicalism and traditional German conservatism. The third and increasingly most powerful and influential grouping was the SS–SD police network led by Heinrich Himmler. After the blood purge of Hitler's storm troopers (SA) in June 1934, the SS gradually assumed control over the entire security apparatus of the Third

Reich during the 1930s. The SS had control over Nazi concentration camps and along with the Security Service (SD) was gradually coming to dominate the traditional internal security police (the Gestapo). After Kristallnacht, Himmler began to take an increasingly prominent role in proposing radical measures to deal with the Jewish Question, and developed a close relationship with Hitler on such matters.

On coming to power, Hitler had moved, step by step and within a legal framework, on the Jewish Question. It is probably worth adding that the most radical measures on the Jewish Question were mostly advocated by the party rank and file. Between 1933 and 1937, Hitler certainly encouraged Jewish emigration and frequently used government legislation to withdraw civil rights from Jews, which progressively lowered their social, economic and legal standing as he had promised in his speeches during the early 1920s. At the same time, Hitler was always prepared to make tactical concessions and even to postpone anti-Jewish measures for a number of reasons, including, at various times, the need to avoid adverse publicity for the Nazi regime overseas, or because his foreign-policy aims took greater priority. From 1937 to 1939, there was more open persecution of Jews in German society, exemplified by the *Kristallnacht* pogrom and legally by the removal of economic rights and the vocal encouragement of emigration. Hitler's rhetoric on the Jews grew ever more menacing as the Second World War drew nearer and there is little evidence to suggest that Hitler did not approve of most of the measures suggested by radicals.

By the late 1930s something even more crucial was happening in regard to anti-Jewish policy. Himmler's radical SS and police network was developing independence from both the Nazi Party and the traditional conservative bureaucracy. It was this SS–SD group that would lead Nazi anti-Semitic policy from this point onward. By 1939, Hitler realised that the aim of removing all Jews from Germany by emigration would not be achieved. In the event of war, Hitler's essential commitment to radicalise the persecution of the Jews who lived under Nazi rule remained very powerful, even though it would be difficult to suggest convincingly that such radicalism would inevitably and so quickly lead to the physical extermination of the Jews of Europe.

2
War, Resettlement and Ghettoisation in Poland, 1939–41

On 1 September 1939, the German armed forces launched an unprovoked military attack against Poland. Two days later, Hitler's regime was at war with Britain and France. Hitler had always wanted Britain as an ally in any future war. But the full economic and diplomatic resources of the British Empire were now ranged against his ambitious plan for European hegemony. The Soviet Union, his most hated ideological enemy, was now his diplomatic partner as a result of the last-ditch signing of the Nazi–Soviet Pact on 24 August 1939. Japan, his Axis ally in the Far East, was already embroiled in a bloody war against China. The Italian government led by Mussolini decided to remain neutral.

The initial period of the German occupation of Poland between 1939 and 1941 is sandwiched between the more heavily researched 1930s, which extreme intentionalists have viewed as a crucial period on the 'straight road to Auschwitz', and invasion of the Soviet Union in 1941. Some historians have recently attached greater importance to the various resettlement plans operating in Poland between 1939 and 1941. The Nazi occupation of Poland allowed two key Nazi organisations: the SS (*Schutzstaffel*) led by Heinrich Himmler, and its security wing, the SD (*Sicherheitsdienst*) controlled by Reinhard Heydrich, to expand the party's already growing influence over security and racial policies inside Nazi Germany into the newly occupied nations of Europe. The SS had been established in the 1920s as a personal security guard unit for Adolf Hitler. Under the leadership of Heinrich Himmler, supported by his loyal deputy Reinhard Heydrich, the SS became one of the most powerful organisations in Nazi Germany. It played a crucially important role in the Holocaust. The SS Einsatzgruppen murdered millions in mass shootings in the countries occupied by Germany during the Second World War. The SS was responsible for creating and staffing the concentration camps and ran all the extermination camps. At the Nuremberg war trials, the SS was declared a criminal organisation which was deemed chiefly responsible for the implementation of mass genocide by the Nazi regime. Before the war, the SS was the chief controller of the police and security services in Germany. In September 1939 the power of the SS and SD was further enhanced by the creation of the Reich Security Office (*Reichssicherheitshauptamt* – RSHA), which controlled the Gestapo (*Geheime Staatspolizei*), the Secret State (Political) Police, the 'Order Police' (*Ordungspolizei*) and the 'Criminal Police' (*Kriminalpolizei-Kripo*).

Adolf Hitler promised in two key speeches to his generals in the summer of 1939 that there would be an 'elimination' of all the forces of resistance to German rule in Poland and he looked to the SS to 'purify' the living space (*Lebensraum*) so that it would be suitable for Germans to occupy it.[1] The Sipo-SD (the state political and criminal investigation security agencies) took the leading role in this process by creating the *Einsatzgruppen* (Operational Groups). These were killing squads that were deployed to the rear of the advancing *Wehrmacht* troops during the invasion of Poland. The orders given to these units were to kill the 'enemies of National Socialism'. They murdered the Polish army high command, the political elite and what was loosely described as the 'intelligentsia', including artists, poets, civil servants and many middle-class professionals. The Sipo-SD had the reputation of being tightly disciplined, well organised and committed to the Nazi cause. The activities of the security services in Poland changed their nature. Though legally responsible for upholding the law, they were now being allowed to work outside it. Some former career detectives did not take kindly to the idea that 'the party was the state'. Such individuals were usually the older detectives who had started their careers in the democratic Weimar period. The younger middle-class professionals who had joined since 1933 were more committed, or proved more willing to blindly accept an ideological approach to policing. Heydrich maintained a tight control over recruitment to Sipo-SD. It was a very distinct advantage to be a Protestant. Many Catholics in the security services were targeted for demotion or they had their posts downgraded through constant reorganisation drives. Catholics in the SS-controlled security services were generally regarded as having a 'suspect loyalty' towards National Socialism. They are often described in SD documents as 'non-believers' (meaning non-believers in Nazism). The SD had already been rigorously purged before 1939. Many of the poorly educated, though fanatically committed, rowdy Nazi elements associated with the SA ('the Stormtroopers') were purged. This group was labelled by younger leaders of the SD as 'the old guard' and they were generally viewed as 'sub-standard' both physically and racially. Himmler increasingly set strict hereditary requirements for entry to the SS. All recruits needed to supply documented evidence of blood lines dating all the way back to 1750. This move mostly favoured the affluent and university-educated members of the middle class rather working-class or even lower middle-class recruits.

The policy of *Lebensraum* was quickly set in motion after the defeat of Poland. Nazi anti-Jewish policy became one aspect of a vast demographic movement of populations which aimed to racially restructure Nazi-occupied Europe. On 29 September 1939, Hitler decided the western part of Poland would be completely 'Germanised' and become part of what was called the 'Greater German Reich'. The non-Germans living there would have their homes and possessions confiscated and would be 'resettled' eastwards. The central part of Poland would become a Polish area. At the outset this was called a 'rump Polish state' and the eastern area of this was designated as a 'foreign-language territory'. It was to become a vast transit area for Poles, Jews, Gypsies and others deemed by the Nazis as 'undesirable'. Poles were so designated, providing primarily a pool of unskilled slave labourers, and so the idea of creating a self-governing Polish–Nazi puppet-state was quickly dropped. For the moment, Jews and other minority groups resided in: (a) the incorporated Polish territories (population 9.2 million), divided into (i) Danzig-West Prussia, which was administered as a separate Gau by Albert Forster, and (ii) Warthegau ('Reichsgau Wartheland'), including East Prussia and Posen, ruled by Arthur Greiser who felt it was his duty to 'carry out the Führer's will'; and (b) the *Generalgouvernement* (population 11 million) administered by Hans Frank, which included the major Polish province of Lublin and two other major cities, Warsaw and Krakow. Albert Forster, the Nazi ruler in Danzig-West Prussia, took a less than fanatical approach to the classification of the myriad races placed under his control and Himmler's policy of 'Germanisation' was never fully implemented. Any Pole who declared 'German blood' usually had this claim accepted by Forster's regime with few questions asked and thus escaped deportation to the Generalgouvernement. In contrast, Greiser, the Gauleiter of the Warthegau, was a much more fanatical Nazi who carried out the policy of Germanisation with enthusiastic relish, and he also took a vigorous approach to implementing harsh anti-Jewish policies. Greiser was frequently criticising Forster's so-called 'lenient treatment' of his Polish and Jewish residents when speaking to his Nazi superiors. Hans Frank, who was nominated as the governor of the *Generalgouvernement*, was another very committed disciple of Hitler. He wanted to build a large personal empire in the region. But Frank's dream of creating a satellite empire never came to pass. The *Generalgouvernement* became the epicentre of the 'Final Solution' and the site of all the major extermination camps. Frank was an emperor of murder.

On 1 October 1939 Hitler escalated his 'racial war' within Germany by signing a deeply significant order which allowed German doctors to sanction the killing of German children and adults under the 'Aktion T4 programme'. The jurisdiction of the order was backdated to 1 September 1939, the day of the invasion of Poland. The 'euthanasia programme' was not directed at Jews at all. It focused on the 'mercy killing' of the mentally ill, and the physically and mentally disabled. But the modern concept of 'euthanasia', which is often defined as the merciful ending of the life of a terminally ill person or a patient suffering from serious injuries to the functioning of the brain, with the consent of the patient or close relatives, was very different from the T4 programme. The decision to terminate a so-called 'worthless life' under T4 was outright genocide. It was medical experts who decided the fate of each patient, based on the Nazi idea of whether the life being considered for death was 'useful' to the 'National community'. Before the war began, the Nazis had already operated an extensive 'Eugenics' programme within the German health service. One important aspect of this was the sterilisation of 'racially unfit' persons. Hitler had made it clear what he thought of those he termed 'these defectives'. In 1935, he promised to 'take up the issue of euthanasia and enforce it' in the event of the outbreak of war. He believed that during wartime there would be less national and international opposition to such a programme. In the summer of 1939, Hitler gave Dr Leonardo Conti, the minister responsible for health at the Ministry of the Interior, the authority to organise a euthanasia programme. But when Philipp Bouhler, head of the Führer's Chancellery (KdF), heard of this, he persuaded the Nazi leader to allow his department to oversee the efficient running of the whole operation. Bouhler appointed Victor Brack, his deputy, to create and direct the T4 killing operation. It was administered from a large Berlin villa, with the address: Tiergartenstrasse 4. The location was used to conceal the role played by the Kdf in the whole secretive operation. The very fact Hitler ordered this programme is clear evidence of his willingness to sanction programmes of genocide once the war was underway.

The T4 programme is very important in any discussion of 'the road to Auschwitz'. It contained many of the methods of killing, and many of the key participants in the later implementation of the Holocaust in the extermination camps. It operated in very strict secrecy at a number of civilian German mental hospitals (Brandenburg, Hadamar, Sonnenstein, Hartheim, Grafenek and Bernburg) and was carried out by 'ordinary' Nazi bureaucrats and 'ordinary' doctors and nurses. A list of the proposed victims was drawn up which included the mentally handicapped, the schizophrenic and the psychotic, epileptics, the criminally insane, and the physically handicapped. After trying out lethal injections, which proved too slow for killing large numbers of people, the doctors chose gassing as their favoured murder weapon. The patients were selected for euthanasia by the T4 doctors, who then transferred them to the mental hospitals chosen as the killing centres. Shower rooms in the hospitals were often converted into gas chambers, and mobile gas vans were also used. The gas chambers used in the T4 programme used pure carbon monoxide piped into shower rooms. The first suggestion that gas should be used for mass killing came from Albert Widmann, a chemist working for Kripo (criminal police) who had carried out the first experiments using it to kill mental patients in Brandenburg in January 1940. This 'experiment' in killing was organised by Christian Wirth, another member of the security services.

The authorities created elaborate administrative measures to cover up the killings. The relatives of the deceased patients were informed their loved ones had been 'transferred' to another mental hospital for further examination. But they were not told where they had gone. After the killings, relatives were sent false death certificates by post which contained bogus causes of death. The inquests were often timed on dates before the letters had even arrived at the addresses of the relatives of the deceased. Senior members of the German medical profession such as Gerhard Wagner, the 'Führer' of the National Socialist Physicians League, justified the killing operation by using Nazi eugenicist and social Darwinist arguments about the 'cleansing of the race', which they backed up with what they claimed was 'scientific evidence'.

The testimony of many of the T4 nurses at their post-war trial, which took place in Munich in 1965, offers a valuable insight into the way in which the bulk of the German population in ordinary public-service occupations could view state-organised murder as an accepted part of their everyday life. They repeated the mantra of many Nazi functionaries at war trials: they were merely 'following orders from their superiors'. In fact, this was completely untrue. Many documents from the T4 programme show that it was perfectly possible for nurses and doctors to refuse to participate in the programme as long as they agreed to keep silent about it. Those nurses and doctors who did take part supported a fundamental Nazi belief in the aims of the 'mercy killing' programme as 'rational' and 'humane'. As one nurse put it:

My attitude to euthanasia was, should I become incurably ill I would consider it as a release if a physician . . . would give me a dose releasing me from everything. . . . Dr Mootz explained to me once that there was no need for reservation, should the situation arise he would cover up for me. From this statement I concluded that there had to be a legality for euthanasia. For me there were justified and unjustified cases of euthanasia. . . . Where I didn't regard the killing as necessary or appropriate [and] when I did participate in those killings against my inner attitude and conviction, this happened because I was used to . . . [obeying] . . . the orders of the physicians. I was brought up and instructed to do so. As a nurse or orderly you don't have the level of education of a physician and thus one can't evaluate if the order of the physician is right. The permanent process of obeying the order of a physician becomes second nature to the extent that one's own thinking is switched off. . . . The attitude of people to life and death depends on the situation. . . . I was aware of the fact that a person was being killed but I didn't see it as murder but as a release.[2]

Many of the doctors who had participated in T4 claimed they viewed those they selected for killing as 'animals in human form' whose lives were 'unworthy to be lived'.[3] About 70,000 adults and 6000 children were killed in the euthanasia programmes that operated under Nazi rule during the first two years of the Second World War. It has often been assumed that the 'mercy killings' ended with Hitler's 'stop-order' of August 1941 as public knowledge of the killings leaked out within German society. This led to the Catholic Bishop Graf von Galen's outspoken sermon denouncing the euthanasia programme in 1941. Yet in spite of such public protests, the killing went on. The major change was that the euthanasia operation moved out of 'ordinary hospitals' and into the concentration camps, where the sick and those incapable of work were killed. The mentally ill and handicapped patients were murdered at the newly created killing centres in the eastern occupied territories.

Hannah Arendt has suggested that the Nazi functionaries involved in killing programmes such as T4 were unthinking bureaucrats, who merely carried out orders, without any passionate ideological involvement. They simply internalised the discourse of murder and found it unexceptional. Arendt referred to this as the 'banality of evil' and she wrote of these 'desk-bound functionaries' as just cogs in the murder machine.[4] But this view does not fully explain the mind-set of all those who participated in the T4 euthanasia programme. Most were willing killers and deeply involved in what they were doing. They were proud of their achievements and they agreed with the Nazi policies of racial purification that justified them. In August 1941, the ten-thousandth person killed at Hadamar was commemo-rated with a boisterous party during which the T4 staff congratulated each other and then ghoulishly stood and watched as the naked body of a dead man was nonchalantly tossed onto the flames amid cheering normally asso-ciated with a sporting event.[5] Members of the T4 programme also boasted to the Nazi elite that each death of a 'useless life' had saved the state large sums of money in health care and social welfare costs. The whole programme was justified on both racial and pragmatic economic grounds. The T4 programme also showed it was possible to organise mass murder in a secretive, planned and organised manner. It is important to stress that many of the leading figures in the T4 programme played an important part in the extermination camps which carried out systematic killing in the 'Final Solution', as will be explained in more detail in Chapter 4.

If Hitler was clear about what he wanted to do with those 'unworthy of life' in Germany at the very outset of the war, the same was not true about Nazi policy towards the Jews. The German defeat of Poland added three million Jews to the 'Greater German Reich'. The Nazi authorities had no clear plans of what to do with them. They were simply identified with a Jewish insignia of either a yellow star or a white armband with a blue Star of David emblazoned upon it. Hitler's ultimate decision-making powers over the final fate of the Jews was made clear by Himmler on 14 September 1939 when he told leading members of the SS that it was Hitler alone who would sanction any proposals to deal with the Jews and other minorities.

In the autumn of 1939, the task of 'Germanising' Poland took the highest priority among the resettlement and emigration programmes of the Nazi regime. Himmler was put in charge of the 'Reich Commissariat for the Strengthening of Germandom' (RKFDV). This was the body specially created to coordinate the vast task of German ethnic resettlement. A territory could only be 'Germamised' by the expulsion of its inhabitants. Heydrich's Reich Security Office (RSHA) was given the task of handling all 'expulsions' eastwards.[6] In September 1939, Hitler approved the expulsion of Jews from Upper Silesia into the Russian zone, something that had been agreed under the secret terms of the Nazi–Soviet Pact. At the same time, Adolf Eichmann, who was in command of Jewish affairs at the RSHA, wanted to deport large numbers of Jews to the Generalgouvernement from Bohemia and Moravia, Austria and Germany. Eichmann was very ambitious, cold and detached. He was the epitome of the 'desk killer'. In 1938, Eichmann had established the 'Reich Central Emigration Bureau' in Vienna and had expelled 150,000 of Vienna's Jews in just two years.

After the swift defeat of the Polish armed forces, Himmler was more interested in his own policy of 'Germanising' West Prussia and the Warthegau than in supporting the deportation of large numbers of Jews to the Generalgouvernement. In fact, the desire to solve the 'Jewish Question' and the policy of the 'Germanisation' of occupied Poland were often competing rather than harmonious goals during the early stages of the occupation of Poland. In December 1939, Heydrich produced a document entitled 'Final

Solution of the Jewish Problem in Germany'. This promoted the idea that the Jews should be placed in some sort of 'self-administered' Jewish reservation and then, at a later date, moved to the 'east'. It was also suggested that Jews might be used as human hostages as a bargaining chip in some future settlement with the Western powers at the end of the war. The 'final goal' for the Jews was not specified in this document but it seems the idea of a 'reservation' somewhere in the east was the policy envisaged at this stage, and not extermination. In January 1940, Eichmann was once again pressing for massive deportations of Jews to Poland. But his plan was resisted by Frank, who was supported by Himmler and Göring.

Between September 1939 and June 1941, Nazi leaders considered a number of alternative policies to deal with the 'Jewish Question'. The need to find a 'solution' to this question intensified as the German empire expanded across the continent of Europe. Before 1939, the Nazi leadership had predicted that war would bring greater opportunities for Jewish persecution. What was happening during the winter of 1939–40 was the arrival in railway freight cars of thousands of Jews, Poles, Gypsies and other displaced minorities in the increasingly overcrowded Generalgouvernement. The dehumanising chaos in occupied Poland made it easier to contemplate 'more humane' means of ending what the Nazis viewed as 'worthless lives'.

In January 1939, Göring, who was nominally the government minister in charge of the Jewish Question, had signed the order which required Heydrich to solve the Jewish issue 'by emigration and evacuation'. On 21 September 1939, Heydrich issued some further instructions, clearly in agreement with Göring's earlier order, to the Einsatzgruppen in Poland concerning the 'Jewish Question', in which he stated there was a 'final goal' of Jewish policy and 'stages towards the achievement of this final goal'. At this time, the 'final goal' was not defined, but 'the first preliminary stage' in the achievement of that goal was: the concentration and isolation of Jews in the large cities.

Before the war, as we have already seen, the key elements of Nazi policy towards the Jews were the curtailment of civil and economic rights, social ostracism and emigration. After the war started, emigration to a sovereign state outside of German control was no longer feasible. Hence, the chief means of dealing with the 'Jewish Question' became 'resettlement' to Poland in preparation for the creation of some sort of 'Jewish reservation'. These 'resettlement' plans were not, however, exclusively designed for Jews, but included many groups, most notably, Poles, Gypsies, habitual criminals, 'asocials' and 'undesirables' and other so-called 'inferior' nationalities. The first major resettlement scheme was called the 'Nisko Plan' or in other documents, 'Nisko action'. Nisko was a swampy, wooded area in north-east Poland, near to Lublin. The intention was to settle Jews from Germany and other occupied lands there (principally from Bohemia and Moravia – former Czechoslovakia; and Jews from Austria and Poland) and then establish it as a cordoned-off and autonomous 'Jewish reservation'. This scheme was the brainchild of the ever-ambitious Eichmann. The first task was to resettle Jews still residing in the Greater German Reich, to the proposed Jewish reservation. At this stage, German Jews in the Old Reich were excluded from the scheme. It was proposed that the first Jewish 'able bodied' deportees would build a large 'transit camp', with their own funds, located near to the railway station. The first trainloads of Austrian Jews who arrived at Nisko suffered serious maltreatment on the journey and were either shot on arrival or were scattered into the adjoining Soviet territory to fend for themselves without any agricultural tools or equipment. Not surprisingly, the 'Nisko Plan' was soon quietly abandoned.

In spite of this initial setback, a second and more organised scheme ('the Lublin Plan'), designed to make the district of Lublin in the south-eastern part of the Generalgouvernement a 'Jewish zone', was attempted. The Nazi regime had rather prematurely announced in September 1939 that a 'Jewish state' would be established in Lublin. During the early months of 1940, Lublin was designated as a 'collecting area' for all Jews within the Generalgouvernement – especially for those Jews from the Greater German Reich. The implementation of Nazi 'resettlement' plans to and from Lublin was organised by Odilo Globocnik, an Austrian-born SS chief. He was called 'the man with the iron hand', which gives an indication of his well-established reputation for ruthlessness. In January 1940, 78,000 Jews had been transported to the Lublin region. In the following month, 30,000 'ethnic Germans' were also settled in the Warthegau as part of Himmler's 'Home to the Reich policy' and thousands of Poles from that area were also being evicted from their homes and sent to Lublin.

The deported Jews in Lublin were put in empty barracks, old warehouses, or else just left to fend for themselves in open fields, surrounded by barbed wire and armed German guards. Globocnik saw his task as creating large transit camps for the Poles, Jews and many other minorities. He also had the economically pragmatic idea of using Jews as slave labour in large concentration camps. This plan was soon put into operation. Jews and Polish slave labour built the first camps in the summer of 1940. By early 1941 there were 51 separate labour camps operating in the Lublin area even though the 'deportation of Jews' from outside Poland was halted in March 1940, after Hans Frank had bombarded Berlin with memoranda from his capital in Krakow raising objections to the 'dumping of Jews' in his territory. He claimed the arrival of millions of Jews into the region would simply destroy the already overstretched infrastructure of the Generalgouvernement. But the deportations continued without the consent of Frank. The whole Lublin episode shows that a determined Nazi 'man on the spot' was capable of operating his own vicious policy towards the Jews, which was actually very different from the 'order' given to him by his SS superiors and the authorities in Berlin. Globocnik just ignored the anti-Semitic thinking behind the Lublin plan, which had clearly implied the creation of a singular Jewish self-governing 'reservation', and he pushed ahead with his own plan of creating a vast series of slave-labour concentration camps in which Jews, resettled Poles and other deported minority groups were used for economic gain and to support the war effort. It is probably worth adding that Globocnik was a leading figure in the conversion of some of his slave-labour camps into extermination centres for the Jews. He also played a pivotal role in setting up the 'Operation Reinhard' extermination camps, which accelerated the killing of Jews in 1942 through the use of gas chambers. On 12 March 1940, Hitler announced that the creation of a Jewish reservation around Lublin was not a solution to the Jewish Question as Jews in the area were too crowded together to create a viable community.

A third 'resettlement scheme' for the Jews (the Madagascar Plan) suggested by the German Foreign Office also came under serious considera-tion within the Nazi elite between 1940 and 1941. Debate still rages about how serious this scheme really was. The aim was to move four million European Jews to the small island of Madagascar, located in the Indian Ocean off the east coast of Africa. It had been a French colony since 1896, with a native population of 3.8 million and a mostly French settler population of 36,000. During the 1930s the French and Polish governments had discussed projects to use the island as a colony for Jewish settlers. Hitler appears to have been very attracted by this scheme. At a very rare Nazi Cabinet meeting in November 1938, Hitler told his colleagues that he would ask the Western powers if they were willing to solve the Jewish Question by 'creating a Jewish territory in Madagascar'. After the German defeat of France in June 1940, the German Foreign Office took a keen interest in the idea. Franz Rademacher, an ambitious official in the German Foreign Office, suggested using Madagascar as a 'Jewish reservation'. The scheme would also allow the Nazi regime to use the Jews as human hostages or as a useful diplomatic bargaining chip in any future peace settlement. The project ruled out the creation of a Jewish state in Palestine, which had been a central demand of Jewish pressure groups in the years leading to the Second World War. The fate of the Jews in Madagascar was clear enough. As the island was not large enough to sustain even a projected Jewish population of 4 million a slow attritional death for the Jews was the most likely long-term outcome. It is hardly surprising to learn that Hitler found the idea of isolating Jews on an island, starving and humiliating them, very attractive. But the costs and the difficulties of implementing the project at a time when the German Navy was vastly inferior to the Royal Navy were not seriously considered. What is more, the Madagascar project provoked great in-fighting between the Foreign Office, not thought of as an out-and-out Nazi organisation, and the SS, which wanted overall control in solving the 'Jewish Question'. The highest authorities within the Nazi regime took the Madagascar Plan very seriously. Philipp Bouhler was even touted within Nazi circles as an ideal candidate as a Nazi Governor of the island. The SS gained Hitler's assurance that if the Madagascar Plan went ahead, they would be in charge of it. The Madagascar Plan was not really feasible and was quietly shelved during the early months of 1942 even though Hitler went on calling it a 'good idea' until the end of that year.

At the time the Madagascar Plan was being seriously discussed, the vast territorial expansion of the Nazi empire in Europe was increasing and the prospect of a pan-European solution to the 'Jewish Question' was becoming a real possibility. Himmler was now able to outbid all the other competitors in gaining the Führer's agreement that the SS should lead the drive to find a 'Final Solution' to the Jewish Question. Himmler firmly believed that solution should take place in eastern Europe. Himmler had already gained Hitler's blessing for Jews to be isolated in ghettos in Poland. This was an idea Hitler had talked about for many years, but he refused to implement it in Germany before 1939. As early as 1935, Hitler had promised that the Jews would again be concentrated in ghettos: '[The Jews] will be enclosed in a ghetto, in an area where they can behave according to their nature, where the German people may observe them as one observes wild animals.'[7] But confining Jews in ghettos did not originate with Hitler's regime. In many other countries, Jews had been forced to live in designated – usually poor – areas. Nazi ghettos differed in that they acted as a mere holding area before a decision was made about their eventual fate.

The ghetto system allowed Jews to be easily identified and quarantined by the Nazis as if they were a dangerous infection. The Jews had long been thought of in Nazi anti-Semitic discourse as disease-carriers, harbourers of dangerous (Bolshevik) ideas, blood-sucking capitalists, demonically powerful as controllers of world finance and sources of parasitism, poverty and cultural decay. The ghetto system was an important phase in Nazi social engineering for the Jews in the areas they occupied in central and eastern Europe. The Jewish community was to be stigmatised, placed in complete isolation and progressively wasted in run-down urban areas, incapable of supporting the great numbers concentrated in them.

The administration of the ghettos was placed by the Nazis in the hands of

Jewish-led councils known as *Judenräte*. These were composed of Jewish elders, rabbis and other leading figures within the Jewish community. They were responsible for most of the functions usually associated with a local government council in a major city, including policing, fire protection, post, food distribution, housing and sanitation. The *Judenräte* raised funds to create hospitals, soup kitchens and orphanages. These councils gave some sense of autonomy to Jews in the sealed ghettos but they had no independent authority to represent the needs of the Jewish community. They were simply there to ensure Nazi policy was carried out. Any time the Nazi regime wanted to procure slave labour or deport Jews to concentration camps and later death camps, these Jewish councils became witting and unwitting collaborators in the fate of their own people.

The conditions in the two major ghettos in Warsaw and Lodz at least give some indication of how the ghetto system operated in Nazi-occupied Poland. The Warsaw ghetto was planned as early as 21 September 1939. It was not effectively sealed until 16 November 1940. In Lodz, the ghetto was ordered in December 1939 but not opened until 1 May 1940. The Warsaw ghetto – set up on 16 October 1940 by Hans Frank – was the largest established by the Nazi regime and was in existence for three years. It was not sealed by a brick wall until 16 November 1940. The population of 380,000 was crammed like sardines into an area measuring just 2.4 per cent the size of Warsaw. Jews were brought to the ghetto from smaller towns and cities. To say life in the Warsaw ghetto was truly appalling would not do full justice to the depressing quality of life that existed for Jews who were forced to live there. Broken-down and unsanitary lodging houses accommodated several families under the same roof. The plumbing could not cope and human waste was often thrown into the back yards with only accumulating rubbish and vermin as company. Everyone was ill-fed and poorly clothed. In winter the ghetto dwellers suffered from the terrible debilitating effects of frostbite. Jews died in their thousands of starvation, disease, neglect and the complete lack of protection against the weather. In spite of this horrendous deprivation, the *Judenräte* helped to organise the allocation of the limited food rations as best they could. One of the most important cultural activities carried out in the ghetto was the establishment of a secret archive of life there, by the historian Emanuel Ringelblum, which was buried underground in a time capsule and discovered after the war. Some German officials wanted famine to take its course, but this view was not accepted and so Jews worked for the Nazis and for private companies in return for food.

The leader of the twenty-four-member *Judenrat* in the Warsaw ghetto was Adam Czerniakow who was born in 1880. He had worked previously as an engineer and a schoolteacher before becoming a leading figure in the local politics of the Polish capital. Czerniakow really did want to protect the Jews from Nazi violence, but he also had to meet the increasing labour demands of the Nazi government of the ghetto (the *Gettoverwaltung*) and work closely with the Nazi Liaison Office (*Transferstelle*). This entailed paying huge sums extorted from ghetto residents to the SS; ensuring thousands of Jews met the demands for labour battalions; and organising the ghetto economy to convince the Germans it was a valuable contributor to the German war effort. He had the grim task of reporting on the death toll in the ghetto and trying to persuade the Germans to increase the meagre starvation-level rations. Lastly, and perhaps most painfully of all, he was ordered to ensure that deportations 'to the camps' were efficiently filled on time. Eventually the attempt to mediate between the Jews and the Nazis proved too taxing a psychological burden for Czerniakow's troubled mind. After he was informed on 23 July 1942 that all Warsaw Jews were to be 'deported east', he went to his office and swallowed a cyanide capsule. He left a brief suicide note that contained the lines, 'I can no longer bear all this. My act will prove to everyone what the right thing to do is.'

The mass deportations from the Warsaw ghetto to the Treblinka extermination camp continued from July to September 1942. It was the Jewish ghetto police force, later supported by German police battalions, who deported 300,000 during this period. Only 60,000 remained in the ghetto, either working in German factories in the ghetto, or in hiding. In January 1943, a brave group of ghetto resistance fighters using smuggled weapons fired on German troops who were rounding up more Jews for deportation to the death camp at Treblinka. After a few days of bitter fighting, the German forces were forced to retreat. The Jewish resistance fighters believed that the January revolt in the Warsaw ghetto showed the Germans would back down in the face of force. On 19 April 1943, the Warsaw ghetto uprising began, after 2000 German troops, strengthened by an SS Panzer division, attempted to deport the remaining Jews living there to Treblinka. A mere 750 armed Jewish resistance fighters bravely resisted the German forces for twenty-seven days. The Warsaw ghetto was finally razed to the ground by German forces on 16 May 1943 by German troops led by Jürgen Stroop, whose reports, which contains a detailed photograph album, have survived. The Jews are dismissed as 'the dregs of humanity' and in one of his last reports, on the 16 May 1943, Stroop wrote, 'The Jewish Quarter of Warsaw is no more.'

The Lodz ghetto was the second largest Jewish ghetto in Poland. It was originally intended as a transit camp. It soon became a major industrial centre with a high productivity level and remained operative until August 1944 when its remaining inhabitants were moved to Auschwitz for extermination. When the German army occupied Lodz in September 1939, a population of 672,000 people lived there and one-third was Jewish, making it the second largest Jewish community in Europe, after Warsaw. The city was placed in the Warthegau region of the Greater German Reich and was renamed Litzmannstadt, after a German General who had been killed trying to capture the city in the First World War. The original plan was to 'Germanise' the city and then deport all the Jews and most of the Poles to the overcrowded Generalgouvernement. But for the next few months Jews were subjected to beatings and random killing on the streets. On 10 December 1939, the local Nazi governor Friedrich Uebelhoer announced a plan to set up a ghetto for the 230,000 Jews in Lodz. It was decided to locate it in an area of only 4.3 square kilometres in the Batuny suburb near the old city of Lodz. On 8 February 1940, the order to establish the ghetto was publicly announced. On 1 May 1940 the area became a sealed ghetto. Most Jews actually welcomed the establishment of the ghetto as it stopped non-Jews entering and inflicting violence on them.

To maintain order in the Lodz ghetto, the Nazi authorities set up a Jewish council led by Mordechai Chaim Rumkowski, who was the 62-year-old, 'Elder of the Jews'. Rumkowski – with his distinctive long grey hair – firmly believed the ghetto could become an autonomous sealed city. He replaced German currency with a ghetto currency bearing his own image on notes and coins. His image was also on stamps sold in the local ghetto post office. He became known mockingly in the ghetto as 'King Chaim'. He ran Lodz ghetto as a dictator. The Jewish Police (*Jüdischer Ordnungsdienst*) he established were particularly hated as the willing enforcers of Nazi persecution. The decision of the Jewish police force in Lodz to participate in murderous German actions against Jews within the ghetto aroused fierce condemnation. Rumkowski felt the best way for Jews to survive was for the ghetto to become a thriving industrial centre at the service of the Nazi war machine. By 1943, 95 per cent of the Jewish population were employed as slave labour, working twelve-hour shifts in factories and workshops, producing electrical equipment, metalwork, army uniforms and much else. The high productivity in the Lodz ghetto was the main reason the ghetto survived. But conditions were harsh in the extreme, and food was always in short supply. Approximately 44,000 people died of malnourishment in the Lodz ghetto.

In the autumn of 1941, 20,000 Jews from other German-occupied areas were transferred to the already overcrowded Lodz ghetto. The new arrivals were extremely shocked by the starving emaciated people they encountered. In addition, 5000 Gypsies were transported to Lodz in October 1941 and housed in a separate area of the ghetto. On 10 December 1941 came more bad news. The Germans wanted 20,000 Jews to be deported to the newly established extermination camp at Chełmno but Rumkowski managed to get the Nazis to send all the Gypsies to Chełmno instead and 10,000 Jews. In the first four months of 1942, 34,073 Jews were transported to the death camp at Chełmno from the Lodz ghetto. In September 1942, the Nazis ordered Rumkowski to send all the old, the sick and the very young children to Chełmno. Rumkowski claimed he was in an impossible situation. He felt only by meeting German demands could any Jews hope to survive at all. Up to the last days of the Lodz ghetto, Rumkowski was exhorting Jews to come forward for the transports which he knew were taking them to their deaths. On 10 June 1944, Himmler ordered the liquidation of the Lodz ghetto. Albert Speer, the Armaments Minister, opposed the move as he felt the ghetto was still useful for the German war effort but the liquidation was carried out anyway. One of Rumkowski's last proclamations was on 17 August 1944, at which time he was still encouraging Jews to go to the death camps: 'It is for your own good, and the good of your families, to appear of your own free will. You will spare yourself much unpleasantness.' Rumkowski was not repaid by the Nazis for his loyal collaboration with them. On 28 August 1944, he and his family were killed in a gas chamber in Auschwitz. On 19 January 1945 when Soviet forces liberated the Lodz ghetto a mere 877 Jews out of an original figure of 230,000 were left alive.

A key feature of debates surrounding the ghetto system is the role of the *Judenräte* as key collaborators with the Nazis in the implementation of anti-Semitic policy. Many critics feel that the Jewish elders betrayed their people in their hour of need. They worked their people to death and they delivered the victims for the Nazi executioners to transport to the extermination camps. Many employed a fanatical police force in the ghettos, thus weakening the possibilities for resistance. Hannah Arendt has argued that if the *Judenräte* had not existed more Jews would have survived. Hilberg condemned the *Judenräte* for their naivety and inability to plan ahead, their failure to make contingency plans and face the realities of German viciousness and their murderous routines. But it is just too simplistic to dismiss the activities of the *Judenräte* as that of willing collaborators with the Nazis. Of those appointed to *Judenräte*, only 12 per cent survived the war, which is an extremely low figure when compared with Nazi collaborators in other places throughout Europe. Service on *Judenräte* was a very dangerous occupation. The forces arraigned against Jewish communities made any kind of organised opposition exceptionally difficult. In the early stages of the setting up of the ghettos there was no clear indication that the inhabitants of the ghettos would be systematically exterminated. The overwhelming firepower of German forces and their well known ruthlessness proved very decisive in limiting resistance and in ruthlessly suppressing it whenever it occurred. A full understanding of ghetto life must also accept that it was exceptionally debilitating and frightening. Death and its explicit threat was a constant factor in the midst of starvation, disease and Nazi brutality. What the ghettos did was to provide an incredible deterioration of the living conditions of Jews, and the conditions within them persuaded Nazi 'men on the spot' in Poland to realise sealed ghettos were not 'the Final Solution' and to impress this argument on the authorities in Berlin. The arguments raged in Poland among Nazi functionaries between the 'productionists', who believed the Jews could be utilised as slave labour, and the 'attritionists', who believed starvation and hard labour would ensure Jews were killed off in ever increasing numbers. In the end, a compromise was possible between both of these officials. Jews who were not capable of work were simply surplus to requirements and the rest could be used as slave labour. In January 1941, Himmler suggested that a mass sterilisation of Jews might be the long-term solution.

By the spring of 1941, what was clear was that none of the emigration schemes discussed by the Nazi regime amounted to a 'Final Solution of the Jewish Question'. Everything that had happened in Poland up until this point was a temporary or an interim solution to the Jewish Question. There was little discussion of a pan-European solution at all. In May 1940, Himmler had described the 'physical extermination' of all Jews as 'impossible' and 'contrary to the German nature'. Hitler was still supporting the idea of deporting European Jews to Madagascar more than any other policy. In most other Nazi documents in this period it is clear 'deportation' and 'emigration' are viewed more as a 'Final Solution', not 'extermination', which is never mentioned. Given the weight of evidence, it can be said with some confidence that it is unlikely there was any plan to exterminate the Jews of Europe in place before, at the very earliest, the spring of 1941.

The only agreed outcome to all these various plan and schemes operating in Poland was a vague agreement that Jews would eventually be 'evacuated to the east'. According to Heydrich, the 'final goal' or the 'ultimate solution' remained 'vague' or 'could not be set down here in all their details'.[8] During the period 1939 to 1941, in occupied Poland, there had been – as we have seen – numerous conflicts and compromises over the implementation of various resettlement schemes. Peter Longerich has recently suggested that the consequences of crowding millions of Jews and other minorities into Poland between 1939 and 1941 were always going to prove disastrous and lead to ever more extreme and most probably genocidal solutions. He suggests it was the conflicts and the twists and turns of policy during the occupation of Poland from 1939 onwards that led the gradual evolution of the policy in a genocidal direction.[9] The only viable area for a Jewish 'territorial solution' being discussed seriously by the Nazi functionaries carrying out Jewish policy in the spring of 1941 was to establish a 'Jewish reservation' in 'the east', located on the territory of the Soviet Union. The crucial event – the 'key turning point' or the 'quantum leap' – which most historians view as acting as a radicalising influence on the 'Jewish Question' was the events before and during 'Operation Barbarossa'. It was during the early period of the Soviet campaign that the territorial solution was completely abandoned in favour of a radical 'Final Solution' based on the mass murder of all of Europe's Jews.

3

From Operation Barbarossa to the Wannsee Conference, 1941–2

In the months leading up to the German invasion of the Soviet Union (code-named 'Operation Barbarossa'), which began on 22 June 1941, detailed preparations were being put in place by Adolf Hitler's regime to destroy the first major communist state in Europe. In March 1941 Hitler appointed the anti-Semitic fanatic Alfred Rosenberg to lead the Political Bureau on Eastern Affairs. Rosenberg spelled out the key aims of Nazi policy towards the Soviet Union. The central objective was the 'complete destruction' of the 'Judeo-Bolshevik' administration. A major subsidiary aim was a 'comprehensive settlement' of the Jewish Question. Jews in the Soviet Union would be ruthlessly exploited as forced labour and confined to ghettos in preparation for their later deportation to a designated 'Jewish zone' further 'east'.

On 30 March 1941, Hitler spelled out to his leading Generals how vastly different the Russian campaign was going to be from what had already happened in western Europe and Poland. The coming conflict in Russia was a struggle not just between armies on a field of battle but of two conflicting 'world-views'. One of the main tasks of the unprovoked invasion of the Soviet Union was the 'utter destruction' and 'extermination' of 'Bolshevik commissars and the Communist intelligentsia'. On 28 April 1941, the Commander-in-Chief of the German armed forces issued a profoundly important order to leading military figures. It accepted that the *Einsatzgruppen* would carry out 'special tasks outside the ambit of the military forces' and would be entitled to take 'executive decisions' regarding the 'civilian population'.[1] In line with these plans, the leading Generals in the Wehrmacht had made no contingency plan for feeding the predicted hundreds of thousands of Soviet prisoners of war.

There were also many meetings before the attack on the Soviet Union at which genocidal plans were discussed. The fate of Soviet Jews cropped up frequently in these deliberations. Traudl Junge, Hitler's loyal private secretary, recalls seeing a worried looking Heinrich Himmler coming out of Hitler's office in the spring of 1941 declaring: 'My god, my god, what I am expected to do [for the Führer].' Himmler never gave any details of the instructions he had just received. Junge is convinced that this was the day when Hitler ordered the 'Final Solution'. But no written evidence of a 'Führer order' for the Europe-wide killing of Jews exists and such an order has not been found in the vast array of surviving documentation from officials involved in implementing the 'Final Solution'.

Rudolf Höss, the first camp commandant of Auschwitz, in testimony at the famous Nuremberg war trial in 1946 claimed there was a 'Hitler order' for the 'Final Solution'. In the summer of 1941, Höss claimed Himmler told him: 'The Führer has ordered that the Jewish Question be solved once and for all and we, the SS, are to implement that order,' and he also stressed that 'the large actions which are anticipated' required that Auschwitz be used as the key extermination centre for the murder of the Jews.[2] This testimony has been questioned by many historians. But the notes from the autobiography of Höss and the record of his pre-trial interrogation by the British legal team do indicate that the meeting with Himmler probably did take place, at the end of August 1941. So the testimony of Höss can be accepted but it cannot be corroborated. The list of surviving Nazis who testified at all the various war trials to the existence of a Hitler 'order' for the Holocaust dating sometime between the spring and early autumn of 1941 is fairly extensive. It seems doubtful, given the nature of Hitler's power within the Third Reich, that a decision to murder all of Europe's Jews could not have been carried out without Hitler's knowledge and approval. Whether it was ever committed to paper cannot be verified. A far more likely scenario, given what is known about Hitler's style of leadership, is that it was a secret verbal order which Himmler was communicating during the summer of 1941. The fact that Himmler visited so many key figures involved in Jewish policy between May and December 1941 indicates that the conveying of a verbal order from Hitler to make preparations for the implementation of the 'Final Solution' is a persuasive interpretation, but it is again not conclusive.

In the spring of 1941, Himmler and the SS hierarchy were preoccupied with planning 'a racial war of destruction' in the Soviet Union. At the centre of SS activities in preparation for 'Operation Barbarossa' were the *Einsatzgruppen* – the mobile killing units – who were to kill designated groups of people, as the German army swept through the Soviet Union. Of the 75 *Einsatz* commanders, carefully chosen by Himmler and Heydrich from a short-list supplied by RSHA Department 1, the vast majority were young and ambitious members of the SS. There were four *Einsatzgruppen* groups:

A – operating in the Baltic states, led by Colonel Dr Walther Stahlecker; B – venturing to White Russia, commanded by General Artur Nebe; C – journeying to North and Central Ukraine with General Dr Otto Rasch in charge; and D – which operated in South Ukraine, the Crimea and the Caucases, controlled by Otto Ohlendorf. These four units were further subdivided into much smaller units referred to as *Einsatzkommandos* and *Sonderkommandos*. These units drew recruits from German police detachments (Orpo and Sipo), the SD (the SS Intelligence service), the Reserve Police Battalions (known as the 'Order Police' – *Ordnungspolizei*) and the Waffen SS (the military wing of the SS). Himmler assigned three SS and police leaders (North, South and Central) to coordinate all joint police activities behind the advancing German military forces. The *Einsatzgruppen* mostly travelled on horseback with horse-drawn carriages, and included cooks, translators, radio operators and clerks. The total number of personnel attached to these genocidal units was between 600 and 1000. After the attack on the Soviet Union began, the *Einsatzgruppen*, often with the collaboration of army units, rounded up communist officials, members of the 'intelligentsia' and male Jews. Once their identities had been fully established, the prisoners were marched or taken in trucks to the edge of cities, towns and villages, where they were ordered to dig mass graves, strip naked and then stand on the edge of these pits, at which point they were mown down by rifle or machine-gun fire.

Himmler and Heydrich had several briefings and meetings with the commanders and some of the key personnel of the *Einsatzgruppen* before Barbarossa. The exact orders communicated to the commanders of the *Einsatzgruppen* at these meetings remain a matter of some dispute. There was a briefing of a large number of recruits which took place in the Border Police school in Pretzsch, north-east of Leipzig, in the last week of May 1941. This police school as well as similar places such as Trawniki were key centres of ideological indoctrination into the racial and anti-Semitic ideas and racial policies of the SS. This important meeting at Pretzsch was discussed extensively at the later *Einsatzgruppen* war trial (1947–8). It was chaired by Bruno Streckenbach, Chief of Department 1 of the RSHA, who acted as the spokesman for Himmler and Heydrich. Ohlendorf, the commander of *Einsatzgruppen* D, described what occurred, in his cross-examination at the Nuremberg trial. Many others – under oath – corroborated his testimony. Ohlendorf claimed that Streckenbach gave clear orders to the *Einsatzgruppen* commanders and recruits present at this meeting to liquidate 'Jews and Soviet political commissars' in the Soviet Union.[3] At the time of the *Einsatzgruppen* trial, Streckenbach was presumed to have been killed by the Red Army. It later transpired that he had been captured by the Red Army and had served a prison sentence in the Soviet Union before returning to West Germany alive and well in 1955. He soon denied he had ever communicated an order from Himmler to 'liquidate the Jews' in the Soviet Union at the meeting in Pretzsch. He claimed he had just outlined the famous 'commissar order' to kill Jews in the Communist Party and state posts, and not civilian Jews. Ohlendorf's evidence – and that of the other defendants at the *Einsatzgruppen* trial – has been somewhat discredited or just disregarded by some historians, who claim it was carefully concocted by the defence team in order to give a unified defence which argued they were all acting on pre-existing orders from their superiors and not taking local initiatives 'from below'.

A further meeting of the leaders of the commanders of the *Einsatzgruppen*, attended by Heydrich, was held on 17 June 1941. Dr Walter Blume, an *Einsatzgruppen* unit commander, also in testimony at Nuremberg, stressed that a 'Führer order' to murder 'all Jews' in the Soviet Union was openly discussed at this gathering. One of the Gestapo officials present asked Heydrich if they should shoot Jews in the Soviet Union and he replied 'Of course.' Many other *Einsatzgruppen* commanders – and many recruits – also claimed they attended another speech, shortly before the assault on the Soviet Union, given by Heydrich at Prince Albrecht Palace in Berlin in which he said 'Eastern Jewry was the intellectual reservoir of Bolshevism' and in the 'Führer's opinion' must be 'exterminated'.[4] Many Einsatzgruppen commanders could have clearly interpreted this speech as a green light to kill civilian Jews and viewed it as something different from the more narrowly defined 'commissar order'. In October 1941, Dr Walther Stahlecker claimed that a 'general order' to kill Jewish men, women and children had 'existed from the beginning' of the campaign. In January 1942, a leading *Einsatzgruppen* commander recorded that the main goal his own unit 'had in mind' from the very start of the Soviet campaign was a 'radical solution' to the Jewish problem by means of 'the execution of all Jews'.[5]

What is more generally known is that the German high command was issued with the now famous 'Guidelines for the Treatment of Political Commissars' (the so-called 'Commissar order') on 6 June 1941 by Heydrich. This gave clear instructions that all 'political commissars' must be 'finished immediately with a weapon' and that 'Jews in state and party positions' should also be executed.[6] In the Soviet Union killing Jews was a military objective. In meetings with their commanding officers, German soldiers were being urged by their officers to harden themselves in order to defeat the two 'hate-inspired' antagonists 'The Jews and the Bolsheviks'. Theodor Eicke, who had served as Camp commandant at the notorious Dachau concentration camp and was the General leading the SS 'Death's head' units, told his troops the war in the Soviet Union was a life-and-death struggle between National Socialism and Jewish-Bolshevism. It would demand the most ruthless and uncompromising conduct to ensure victory.[7]

From the very start of Barbarossa it is clear the instruction to limit the killing of Jews in 'party and state positions' was either ignored or being interpreted on the ground much more broadly. Himmler and Heydrich raised no objection to what was happening 'on the spot'. As early as 27 June 1941 – a mere five days after the start of the attack – a Wehrmacht soldier who had witnessed a mass execution of Jews by *Einsatzgruppen* C, was told the killings were being carried out as part of a 'Führer order'. This soldier felt that this mass execution of run-of-the-mill civilian Jews was something very different from the 'commissar order' he already knew about. The *Einsatzgruppen* commanders quickly widened their circle of victims way beyond the narrow and clearly defined lines of the commissar order. The first documented written 'order' to kill 'all Jewish males' aged 17 to 45 was given to local *Einsatzgruppen* units by the SS on 11 July 1941.[8] On 17 July 1941, Heydrich gave a set of further instructions which ordered that all Jews found in Russian Prisoner of War camps were to be killed 'straightway'.[9] The same day, Hitler told the Croatian Marshal Kvaternik, 'The Jews are the scourge of humanity, the Lithuanians as well as the Estonians are now taking bloody revenge on them.'[10]

There are also firm indications that a broader plan for a Europe-wide 'Final Solution' based on physical destruction was now being seriously contemplated within the Nazi elite. The mass murder of Jews in Russia was already clearly underway and the circle of victims was widening by the day. In Berlin, the planning for the extermination of all Jews in Europe was being put in place only weeks after the start of Barbarossa. An extremely important surviving document, signed by Hermann Göring, the 'number two' in the Nazi state, dated 31 July 1941, is regarded by some historians as a vital turning point in the move towards a 'Final Solution' of the Jewish Question on a Europe-wide scale. Great excitement greeted the presentation of this document at the Nuremberg trial. It provided documentary evidence that Göring was more closely involved in the 'Final Solution' than had been previously assumed during the earlier stages of the trial. In the document – which, Göring claimed, 'I just signed without a second look', he asked Heydrich to make 'all necessary organisational and technical preparations' and to devise 'an overall plan' after making preliminary 'organisational, substantive and financial measures' for a 'final solution of the Jewish Question'.[11] Though the Göring memo still mentions 'emigration and evacuation' as the chosen earlier 'solutions' it is apparent Heydrich is being commissioned by Göring to work out a wideranging plan for the systematic mass extermination of all European Jews.

By far the most extensive collection of surviving documents relevant to the systematic murder of the Jews by mass shooting are the written reports of the four *Einstatzgruppen* units in the Soviet Union. Between 23 June 1941 and 24 April 1942, 195 detailed operational event reports were sent to Heydrich's staff in Berlin, who circulated them to leading Nazi figures, including Adolf Hitler. Eleven 'Activity and Situation Reports', which summarised the events of the event reports, were also compiled by Heydrich's office. Copies of these were sent to the Nazi dictator. As Heinrich Müller, the head of the Gestapo, put it, 'The Führer is to be kept informed continually from here about the work of the Einsatzgruppen in the East.'

The *Einsatzgruppen* reports provide important and extensive evidence of the escalating murder of the Jews in the Soviet Union. These documents contain open admissions of the killing of Jews and sometimes use a camouflage language to cloud what is actually going on. Some record 'executions' and openly mention the 'extermination' of Jews. Others use the words 'special treatment' or 'deportation' when discussing the fate of Jews in the Soviet Union. There is an attempt in some reports to suggest that Jews are being killed in a 'reprisal' or because they are 'partisans' or because the 'local population wants them killed'. On many occasions the aim of making areas 'free of Jews' is openly admitted. On 1 July 1941, *Einsatzgruppen* B alludes to receiving 'order no 2' from Heydrich, which emphasises that 'cleansing activities have to extend first of all to the Bolsheviks and Jews'.[12] On July 6, *Einsatzgruppen* B, based in Lithuania, reports that in all of its major 'cleansing actions' in Garsden, Krottingham and Polangan, 'mainly Jews were liquidated'.[13] On 7 July, *Einsatzgruppen* C points out that 'according to orders', liquidation of 'government and party officials' and 'Jews' have taken place.[14] On 11 July, *Einsatzgruppen* A records that in the nineteen days since the attack on the Soviet Union began, 7800 Jews have already been murdered in pogroms, organised by Lithuanian Kommandos.[15] Many local nationalists in Latvia, Lithuania, Byelorussia and the Ukraine used the German attack as a starting point to take their own 'revenge' against Bolsheviks and Jews. On 16 July *Einsatzgruppen* A in Latvia notes that actions against the Jews are 'going on in an ever-increasing number'. In spite of the large numbers of Jews being killed in these locally initiated Jewish pogroms, *Einsatzgruppen* commanders reported that the numbers murdered were 'inadequate' in the context of their own more wide-ranging objectives.[16] What the *Einsatzgruppen* reports also indicate is that the members of the killing squads observed how closely identified many Soviet Jews were with the Bolshevik regime. These observations by the 'men on the spot' emphasise how closely linked in eastern Europe nationalism was to anti-Semitism and anti-communism.

At the Nuremberg trials, *Einsatzgruppen* commanders claimed that ordinary recruits showed some hesitation about killing women and children by mass shooting. Some rank-and-file soldiers and ordinary police recruits in the *Einsatzgruppen* apparently suffered similar qualms of conscience about the killings. This was often outwardly displayed by heavy drinking, which was encouraged by officers at social gatherings in the evenings. One policeman who took part in the mass killings claimed in later testimony at Nuremberg that he had attended a four-month training course at the Border Police school in Pretzsch but was not told that one of his key tasks in the Einsatzgruppen would be to execute Jews in mass shootings.[17]

All the evidence from the first weeks of the campaign suggests the number of male Jews killed was relatively small compared with the vast numbers that came later. The killing figures for *Einsatzkommando* 3, operating in the Ukraine, show 4239 Jews being murdered in July. In August this figure rises dramatically to 37,186. By September the death toll increases to 56,459, with 26,243 women and 15,112 children included in the total. The War Diary of Police Battalion 322, operating in the Soviet Union, shows that in early August they were killing only male Jews. In September they were killing women and by early October 1941 they are shooting men, women and children. Christopher Browning has suggested that the actual 'order' to exterminate 'all Jews' in the Soviet Union probably did not come before the invasion at all. It was probably issued some weeks after the invasion, with mid-July 1941 the most likely date.[18] Browning also suggests the decision was taken in a spirit of euphoria, with victory in the Soviet Union seemingly assured, but other historians, most notably Burrin and Aly, have suggested that 'unexpected set-backs' in the Soviet Union prompted the escalation in the killing of Jews.' Longerich views the Soviet campaign as part of the 'evolution' towards the Final Solution.

The term 'Final Solution of the Jewish Question' does not start to appear regularly in the *Einsatzgruppen* operational reports until mid-August 1941, and even then its meaning is unclear. From 15 August 1941, there is clearly a policy in place to make the Soviet Union *Juden Frei* (free of Jews). After this date, Jewish women and children are included in the killings and the age range is suddenly extended, from 16 to 65. The families of Soviet political 'commissars' were not included in the extended killing operations. In other words, the rapid escalation of the victims of the mass killing in the Soviet Union was being confined to Jews. There are indications that Himmler was communicating an 'escalation order' in August 1941 to *Einsatzgruppen* commanders and even to run-of-the-mill recruits. On 1 August 1941, Himmler informed the SS group accompanying the 2nd SS cavalry unit, which was preparing to clear the Pripet marches: 'All Jews must be shot.

Drive the female Jews into the swamp.' Ohlendorf claimed that in the 'late summer' of 1941, Himmler visited Nikolaiev, and 'assembled the leaders and men of the *Einsatzkommandos*, repeated to them the original order [from June] and pointed out that the leaders and men who were taking part in the liquidation [of the Jews] bore no personal responsibility for the execution of this order. The responsibility was his, alone, and the Führer's.'[19] This public presentation by Himmler of the policy to kill the Jews was designed to emphasise that only severe punishment of Hitler's key racial enemies, 'The Jews', would ensure Germany conquered the 'Jewish-Bolshevik' Soviet Union. This line of argument served to help the men cope with the increasingly taxing psychological burden being placed upon them by the Nazi regime. Himmler, who had recently witnessed these mass shootings in Minsk, appreciated their feelings but he justified the escalation of the killing of Jews as the best way to support Nazi racial-ideological principles.

The implications of the escalation of the mass murder in the Soviet Union was also being discussed in Berlin. On 19 August 1941, Goebbels recorded after a meeting with Hitler, 'The Führer is convinced his prophecy in the Reichstag is becoming a fact: that should the Jews succeed again in provoking a new war, this would end with their annihilation.'[20] At his infamous show-trial in Israel in 1961, Eichmann mentioned that he was 'ordered' to go and see Heydrich sometime 'in the later summer of 1941' (he remembered the leaves on the trees were changing to their autumnal colour) and he was informed that 'The Führer has ordered the physical extermination of the Jews.'[21]

From mid-August 1941, the indiscriminate killing of Jews in the Soviet Union escalated quite dramatically. By September 1941, the killing campaign shot up once more. Entire Jewish communities were being murdered in what were called by the SS 'large-scale actions'. Between June 1941 and January 1942, as many as 750,000 Jews were killed in the mass shootings in the Soviet Union. Out of 240,410 people murdered by *Einsatzgruppe* A alone in this period, a staggering 229,052 were Jews. One of the most ghastly massacres of Jews in the Soviet Union took place in the Ukraine, at Babi Yar, just outside Kiev, the Ukrainian capital. Between 29 and 30 September 1941, the *Einsatzgruppen* killed 33,771 Jews. This figure is actually higher than all the American soldiers killed on the Western Front during the Second World War. Jews were ordered, in posters displayed prominently on billboards throughout the city, to assemble at a designated point by 6 p.m. on 29 September. Such was the fear, among local Jews, of a Nazi 'order' that over 30,000 Jews turned up. They were then ordered to walk from there, with no indication of their subsequent fate, to a ravine, in groups of a hundred or so; they were forced to undress on arrival and were then killed by machine-gun fire. It took two days to complete this vast killing operation. The *Einsatzgruppen* report on the incident suggested a major Jewish pogrom in the area was requested by the local Ukrainian militia, who claimed: 'The local population was extremely infuriated against the Jews because of their preferential treatment under Soviet rule.'[22]

By the autumn of 1941, leading Generals in the Wehrmacht were fully aware of the monumental level of the killing of Jews in the Soviet campaign but responded in contradictory ways. On 12 September 1941, Wilhelm Keitel, a member of the German high command, sent to his officers a carefully worded 'order' entitled 'Jews in the Occupied Territories' which emphasised that, 'The struggle against Bolshevism demands ruthless and energetic action, and first of all against Jews as well as the main bearers of Bolshevism.'[23] On 24 September 1941, Gerd von Rundstedt, another member of the Wehrmacht high command, gave a stern warning to all army units in Ukraine not to watch, take photographs of, or participate in 'excesses by the Ukrainian population against Jews'. This warning was issued because the German high command was concerned that its soldiers participating, even as spectators of these mass shootings, could encourage a breakdown of army discipline.[24] The many surviving photographs of the mass shootings taken by Wehrmacht soldiers show that this order was largely ignored. By November 1941, Erich von Manstein, the commander of the 11th Army in the Soviet Union, a close confidante of Hitler, claimed in an order he issued to German soldiers that the German people were 'engaged in a holy battle with the Bolshevik system' and that as part of this crusade, the 'Judeo-Bolshevik system should be destroyed once and for all'. He tellingly ends his memo by stating, 'The soldier should understand the necessity of the punishment of Jewry – the carrier of the very spirit of the Bolshevik terror.'[25] During the same period, the *Einsatzgruppen* in the Ukraine reported on 2 November 1941 that there had now developed 'a complete understanding' between the killing squads and the German junior army officers 'on dealing with the Jewish question'.[26] In fact, recent studies have shown that Nazi anti-Semitic ideology had permeated the younger officer class by the time of the assault on the Soviet Union, and the work of Bartov has shown how closely implicated the German army was with the activities of the *Einsatzgruppen* in the Soviet Union. The brutal killing of Soviet civilians, using flame throwers, by the 'ordinary soldiers' of the Wehrmacht, and the brutal treatment of Soviet prisoners of war, was creating as much de-population as the activities of *Einsatzgruppen* and the death camps put together.

But there were some tensions between the military aims and supply needs of the Wehrmacht and the implementation of Nazi racial policy. The Reich commissioners in the Soviet Union and the Baltic states were seemingly more concerned with economic rather than anti-Semitic imperatives. Some Wehrmacht officers complained that the indiscriminate killing of Jews in the Soviet Union often meant many important skilled workers were being sacrificed for no sensible economic reason. Lohse, the Reich commissioner in the Baltic, fearing that the indiscriminate killing of Jews was removing vital skilled labour needed for the war effort, asked the Reich Ministry of the Eastern Territories in Berlin in November 1941 if any directive to 'liquidate all Jews in the east' actually existed. He pointed out that even if one did exist it should be 'harmonised with war production'. It took until 18 December 1941 before Lohse's question was finally deemed worthy of reply. Otto Bräutigam, the head of the political department, informed Lohse: 'The Jewish Question has probably been clarified by now through verbal discussions' and 'economic considerations are to be regarded as irrelevant in the settlement of the problem'.[27] This appears to indicate that the radicalisation of Jewish policy was being directed from 'above' during this period, but discordant views from below were the exception rather than the rule.

In the latter months of 1941, Soviet Jews were already being exterminated in a systematic fashion. The escalation of killing was, in Browning's phrase, 'a quantum leap'. It may have influenced the decision to expand the killing of Jews to the rest of Europe. In September 1941, Hitler finally agreed – after resisting for such a long time – to transport all of Germany's Jews to Lodz, Riga, Minsk and Kovno. On 30 November 1941, the first mass shooting of German Jews took place in Riga.[28] At the same time, the Nazi dictator sanctioned the deportation of all Jews within the German sphere of influence in western Europe to Poland. On 24 September 1941, Hitler told Goebbels he wanted Jews to be deported east 'step by step'.[29]

There are other indications, from September 1941, that a stage-by-stage movement towards the 'Final Solution' may have been taking place. *Einsatzgruppen* reports are just littered with comments about 'killing all Jews' and of wide-ranging massacres of Jews in all parts of the Soviet Union. In October 1941, construction work began on a camp at Belzec which was designated as a major killing centre for Jews. The first experiments with Zyklon B also took place during this period at Auschwitz. By November 1941, one *Einsatzgruppe* commander makes it clear he thinks he is already participating in the 'Final Solution of the Jewish Question' in the Soviet Union but he points out that mass shootings are not the best way to achieve this goal. When Hitler had met Haj Amin al Husseini, the leading Arab leader, known as 'The Grand Mufti of Jerusalem', on 2 November 1941, he told him the Nazis and the Arabs were 'natural friends' as both hated the Jews, and he assured him there would be 'no Jewish state or homeland established in Palestine at the conclusion of the war'.[30]

On 16 November 1941, Goebbels declared in an article in *Das Reich* that Jewry had to contend with 'a gradual annihilation process'.[31] At a press conference on 18 November 1941, Rosenberg stated that the 'Jewish Question' could only be solved by the 'biological extermination of all the Jews in Europe'. The same month, Heydrich gave approval to anti-Semitic attacks on synagogues in Paris. At the end of November 1941, Heydrich had seemingly devised an 'overall plan' concerning how the 'Final Solution' on a Europe-wide basis could be achieved. To this end, he asked Eichmann to set up an inter-ministerial meeting at a villa at Wannsee, involving the SS and numerous civil servants and ministries involved with the Jewish Question. The date of the meeting was set for 9 December 1941. In early December, the first extermination camp at Chełmno began its first killing operations.

Given all these developments, it seems clear that a general framework for the 'Final Solution' was either being put in place or evolving quite rapidly in the last months of 1941. After the Japanese attack on Pearl Harbor on 7 December 1941, the Wannsee conference was postponed on Hitler's explicit order. President Roosevelt soon made it clear that the defeat of Nazism in Europe would be the key US objective in the war. The 'global war' Hitler had frequently made reference to in speeches was now underway. In the latter half of 1941, Hitler's speeches and private utterances were littered with worried words about the possibility of a 'Jewish world conspiracy' and linked the USA with the Soviet Union. On 12 December 1941, Hitler said in a speech to local Party leaders that the Jews 'must pay with their lives' for the world war, and he made a direct reference to his Reichstag speech (delivered in the Reichstag in January 1939), in which he had threatened the Jews with 'annihilation' in the event of a global war. During the next few days, Hitler had a number of meetings with Nazi leaders directly involved in the Jewish Question. After one with Himmler, the SS leader notes that Hitler had told him the Jews 'were to be exterminated as partisans'. On 16 December 1941, Goebbels wrote in his diary, 'With respect to the Jewish Question, the Führer has decided to make a clean sweep. He prophesied to the Jews that if they again brought about a world war, they would see their annihilation in it. That wasn't just a catchword. The world war is here and the annihilation of the Jews must be a necessary consequence.'[32] The same day, Hans Frank told a meeting of senior officials in the Generalgouvernement, discussing the upcoming conference at Wannsee, 'Regarding the Jews – I will be quite open with you – they will have to be finished off one way or another. . . . I will only operate on the principle that they will disappear. . . . We must exterminate the Jews wherever we find them whenever it is possible to do so.' But Frank was equally aware that killing millions of Jews was by no means an easy task and would require 'large scale measures' as yet not fully worked out in detail.[33]

On 20 January 1942, leading officials involved in the 'Final Solution' finally met in a villa in the smart Berlin suburb of Wannsee, which overlooks a beautiful lake, much favoured by local holidaymakers, to map out a coherent and efficient programme of 'exterminating the Jews'. The plan to resettle Jews in the 'east' was deemed no longer feasible. Senior figures from the SS, the Generalgouvernement and the Ministry of the Interior, Rosenberg's Ministry for the Eastern Occupied Territories, and personnel from the Ministry of Justice, the Foreign Office and the Four Year Plan Office were in attendance. The minutes were taken by Eichmann, who had considerable experience of proposing and coordinating many previous Jewish deportation schemes.

Because the Holocaust was seen as exclusively an ideological, racial, political and security matter, the representatives of the armed forces were not even present. Heydrich made it clear that his RSHA would direct operations to fulfil the 'Final Solution' of the Jewish Question. The difficulties involved in removing millions of people from their homes and transporting them to Poland threw up massive organisational problems which would require the involvement of numerous authorities. According to Browning, there was nothing improvised about the purpose of the gathering. 'It was to organise the participation of the ministries in an already decided Jewish policy, not to debate that policy.'[34] Others have suggested the meeting was just one aspect of an evolving policy and have downgraded its importance as a 'crucial turning point'. The meeting does offer evidence of the wide range of Nazi government agencies that were to be deployed in organising the mass murder of the Jews. Heydrich was determined to stress his role as the overlord of the project and he sent a copy of the authorisation he had received from Göring in July 1941 to emphasise that the SS had complete control over the Jewish Question.

The minutes – often using camouflaged language – reveal the Europe-wide sweep of Nazi plans to kill the Jews. Heydrich told the meeting that the ultimate aim of the Final Solution was to exterminate all 11 million Jews in Europe. They included Jews from all of western Europe and eastern Europe except Estonia, which was already considered 'free of Jews'. The Nazis included 330,000 Jews from England, 865,000 from France, 342,000 from Romania, 742,000 from Hungary, with additional figures included for all the other countries of Europe including even the neutral countries of Switzerland, Spain and Portugal. The largest numbers noted were 5 million from Russia and 2.9 million from the Ukraine (the Germans regarded the Ukraine as a separate territory). Poland was listed as having 2.3 million Jews. There were also a further 446,484 Jews from 'White Russia' included in the list. The figures for Poland, the Soviet Union and the Ukraine had already taken account of those Jews who had already been killed and those who had perished in ghettos and camps. The combined planned total for Poland and the Soviet Union (including the Ukraine and White Russia) was a staggering 8.3 million. The 'Final Solution' is actually minuted by Eichmann at Wannsee – not as the physical extermination of Jews in extermination camps, but as meaning 'evacuating Jews to the east', which sounds very similar to the many earlier territorial solutions discussed and abandoned. Once again, camouflage language was used to disguise the fact that the true purpose was the murder of the Jews. But several passages remain which leave little doubt of the murderous intentions of the Nazis regarding the Jews. Those present at the meeting knew what the 'Final Solution' now meant. As Eichmann put it:

> In the course of the Final Solution, and under appropriate
> leadership, the Jews should be put to work in the east. In
> large single sex columns, Jews fit to work will work their way
> eastwards constructing roads. Doubtless the large majority will
> be eliminated by natural causes. Any final remnant that
> survives will no doubt consist of the most resistant elements. They
> will have to be dealt with appropriately, because otherwise, by
> natural selection they would form the germ cell of a new Jewish
> revival (see the experience of history).[35]

In 1961, Eichmann, under cross-examination at his trial in Israel, explained more fully and clearly how the euphemistic language used at Wannsee disguised direct references in the verbal discussions to the 'killing', 'elimination' and 'annihilation' of the Jews.[36]

By January 1942 – and given what was already happening in the Soviet Union and in Poland – the term 'put to work in the east' and 'resettlement' now meant physical extermination. All Jews in Europe under Nazi control were now designated for exterminaton. Those Jews who were fit enough would be worked to death through strenuous slave labour, termed 'destruction through labour' (*Vernichtung der Arbeit*), and those 'unfit' and small children would be exterminated straightaway. Hence, the 'Final Solution' as it operated in the extermination camps in Poland was to combine slave labour with extermination in a secret operation. The major killing operations in the Europe-wide 'Final Solution' were an enlargement of the mass killing of Jews that was already underway in the Soviet Union and were part of that process. On 30 January 1942, only ten days after the the Wannsee meeting, in a speech broadcast on radio throughout Germany, Hitler promised that his prophecy of the annihilation of the Jews, in the event of a global war, would now be fulfilled. He repeated this grim prophecy in further speeches on 24 February and 8 November 1942. After a meeting with Hitler in Berlin on 24 February 1942, Goebbels recorded in his diary that Hitler was determined to 'cleanse Europe of its Jews', and the Propaganda Minister believed that 'we must accelerate this process with cold brutality'.[37]

4
Life and Death in the Extermination Camps

All Nazi camps were death camps and millions of people of every race, colour and creed were starved, tortured and murdered in them. The mass murder of the Jews that was already in full swing in the Soviet Union from June 1941 was extended from 1942 onwards to constitute a clear attempt to kill all Jews in Europe under German occupation or influence. The six extermination camps which played the most important role in carrying out the policy of physical extermination of the Jews, outside the Soviet Union, were Chełmno, Belzec, Majdanek, Sobibór, Treblinka and the most infamous camp of all: Auschwitz-Birkenau. They were all located in the Generalgouvernement area of Poland. The murder of Jews in these extermination camps was accomplished through the authority of a group of German bureaucrats operating within a clear administrative structure. The vast majority of the leading figures who carried out the Holocaust in the extermination camps were middle-class, university educated academics, lawyers and doctors who were supported by high-ranking police and security personnel and a plethora of administrators who carried out the process at each level with cold and detached efficiency. The major focus of this chapter is to go in search of the insular world of the extermination camps that implemented 'the Final Solution of the Jewish Question'.

Chełmno (renamed Kulmhof) was established in December 1941 in a run-down castle located near a small village about fifty miles from the Polish city of Lodz. The camp consisted of a makeshift barracks, a storage warehouse for the plundered goods of the victims and a cremation and a burial site. The camp had been established because of pressure from a middle-ranking Nazi bureaucrat called Arthur Greiser, the Gauleiter of the Warthegau, who was more concerned about over-population in the Lodz ghetto rather than starting 'The Final Solution'. Greiser wanted to reduce the population in the ghetto by murdering 20,000 German Jews and 5000 Gypsies. Greiser was not 'taking orders from Hitler', in carrying out this major act of genocide. He had decided – on his own initiative – that these murders were necessary to lower the population of the Lodz ghetto. The Jews who were selected for gassing at Chełmno were not the 'fit' ones who were still capable of working but those defined as 'unfit for work'. The Gypsies were killed regardless of whether they were fit enough for work or not. Herbert Lange, who had pioneered the use of gas vans during the T4 euthanasia programme, was selected as the camp commandant to carry out the task of extermination at Chełmno. In December 1941, the Jews and Gypsies selected at Lodz arrived by train. They were then transferred to the camp in a convoy of lorries. On their arrival, events followed what was soon to become a predictable pattern. The prisoners were gathered in the castle courtyard, forced to hand over their valuables and told they would be transferred to a nearby 'work camp' after they had been disinfected and given a cold shower. Afterwards, they were all led up a ramp into large vans, which held fifty to seventy people. These 'gas vans', simply had the exhaust pipe of the vehicle connected to a specially converted, airtight, sealed compartment at the back of the van. Victor Brack, who had also been a key figure in the T4 programme, designed the gas van. It took approximately ten minutes before all those locked inside the van had died of the effects of carbon monoxide poisoning. It was then driven over two miles away to Rzuchzow forest, at which point a team of forty to fifty strong Jewish prisoners (known as the *Sonderkommando*) were waiting. They unloaded the tangled jumble of corpses and threw them into mass graves. By these means, approximately 145,000 were killed at the Chełmno death camp between December 1941 and March 1943. The killing of Jews at Chełmno increased pretty dramatically during the summer of 1942. Most of those killed were Jews from the Lodz ghetto but a significant number of Gypsies were also murdered at this camp. After March 1943, the Chełmno camp was demolished, but then it was suddenly reactivated between April and July 1944 in order to assist in the complete liquidation of the remaining Jews from the Lodz ghetto. After this, a unit of 1000 Sonderkommando labourers were ordered to remove all traces of the mass murder. There were actually very few survivors from the first phase of extermination at Chełmno. For this reason, it has become known as 'the forgotten camp' in discussions of the annihilation of the Jews. In January 1942, Yaakov Grojanowski managed to escape and he told the ghetto leadership in Warsaw about the horrors he had witnessed. This information was then circulated through the Polish underground and news even reached the British Foreign Office.

The Belzec, Sobibór and Treblinka extermination camps formed part of what was eventually termed 'Operation Reinhard'. This aimed to exterminate all Polish Jews who were 'unfit for work' in the Generalgouvernement area. This killing operation was named in memory of Reinhard Heydrich, the leading SS figure at the Wannsee Conference of January 1942, who was assassinated by Czech partisans, trained in the UK, as he travelled to work in an open-topped limousine in Prague in May 1942. Odilo Globocnik (known by the Nazis as 'Globus'), a leading SS figure, was originally given the task by Himmler of finding suitable locations for the three extermination camps back in the autumn of 1941. The major tasks given to Globocnik were to organise the planning and deportation of Jews to the camps, commission the construction of the extermination facilities, and secure the belongings and valuables of the dead and transfer them to the appropriate German authorities. According to a letter written by Globocnik, dated 27 October 1943, there were a total of 434 men involved in 'Operation Reinhard'. Most of these were middle-ranking Nazi bureaucrats and it has been estimated that approximately 126 had been previously involved in the T4 euthanasia programme.

The Belzec camp, located in the south-east of the Lublin district, began its existence as a forced-labour camp in April 1940. Construction work to convert it into an extermination camp started on 1 November 1941 under the direction of Richard Thomall. Belzec was just five hundred metres from a railway station. It occupied only 1220 square yards, was ringed by a barbed wire fence, with guard towers containing a machine-gun nest manned by Ukrainian guards, and was surrounded by a tree-lined perimeter. The Ukrainians were willing collaborators with the Nazi regime. Many had openly welcomed the German invasion of the Soviet Union and saw the Wehrmacht as a liberating force. The Ukrainians had a well established tradition of anti-Semitism and had participated in many of the mass killing of Jews already enacted in the Soviet Union. The camps set up during 'Operation Reinhard' required auxiliary forces to ensure they functioned effectively and Ukrainians willingly volunteered for this task. Many of the Ukrainians were given ideological training in Nazi anti-Semitic doctrine at Trawniki labour camp near Lublin, and the Ukrainian 'Trawnikis' were recruited by Globocnik.

Belzec was divided into two sections. One contained an administrative office, a barracks and storage for the goods of the victims. The other housed the extermination facilities and the burial pits. There were initially three gas chambers in the camp but they were extremely rudimentary. These were soon replaced by six new and much more reliable airtight chambers housed in a functional concrete building. Carbon monoxide gas was piped into them using a hose pipe from a large diesel engine. When the Jews arrived at the local railway station in cattle wagons they were told they were entering a 'transit camp' and that before they were allocated jobs they would be disinfected and given a shower. Men and women were divided into two separate lines. The children of both sexes were marched off immediately to a large hut. The Jews were brutally manhandled into the showers by guards. The systematic killing of Jews at the Belzec camps started on 17 March 1942 and ended in December 1942. The best estimate of the number of killings at this camp ranges between 500,000 and 600,000 people. The majority were Jews, mostly from the regions of Lublin, Galicia and Krakow. But as many as 100,000 Gypsies and thousands of Jews from France, Slovakia, Germany, Greece and Holland were also murdered at Belzec.

A group of Polish and Jewish slave labourers began work on the Sobibór extermination camp in March 1942. This was located in a thinly populated small village near the Chelm–Wlodawa railway line to the east of Lublin. It measured just 1300 by 2000 feet and was surrounded by triple barbed wire fences, with watchtowers guarded by a combination of Ukrainian and SS personnel. It was – like Belzec – divided into two parts, with one containing a barracks and storage for plundered goods and the other the gas chambers, the crematoria and a burial ground. At first there were three gas chambers but this was soon increased to six. The camp used carbon monoxide gas for killing. In April 1942, Franz Stangl, an SS officer with experience of killing from the T4 programme, was initially appointed as the first camp commandant. He was soon sent to command the Treblinka camp and Christian Wirth, a career police detective and able administrator, took charge at Sobibór. A group of 200 to 300 Jews were formed into a *Sonderkommando* at the camp, who did all the gruesome tasks associated with the killing such as removing corpses from gas chambers, pushing trolleys to the crematoria and throwing the dead bodies into the burial pits. From May 1942 until October 1943, approximately 250,000 Jews were murdered at Sobibór, including Jews from Lublin, Czechoslovakia, Germany, Austria, Slovakia, France and Holland. In July 1943, Himmler paid a visit to the camp and shortly afterwards he ordered it to be converted into a concentration camp. In October 1943, there was a major uprising at the camp. It was swiftly closed down and all the gas chambers destroyed.

Treblinka was located on a railway line, close to a tiny village of the same name situated in a remote forest in northern Poland about 120 kilometres from Warsaw. The camp was roughly the same size as Sobibór. The local station looked normal enough, with a ticket office, a clock and timetables displayed on notice boards. But the camp was surrounded by barded wire fencing and guarded watchtowers. The mass killing at Treblinka began in July 1942. Dr Irmfried Eberl, yet another eugenicist veteran of the T4 programme and an SS officer, was the first commandant but he proved extremely inefficient. The gas chamber he established did not work properly. He had no plan to dispose of the large number of corpses, which were left in piles in the open air. The stench soon made its way to the nearby village.

Christian Wirth, who had been given the task of coordinating 'Operation Reinhard', soon discovered the chaotic killing process at the camp. He drafted in the ever reliable Stangl to replace Eberl. Stangl quickly transformed Treblinka into the second most efficient Nazi factory of death, after Auschwitz. There were a total of thirteen large gas chambers in use at Treblinka. They used carbon monoxide gas from diesel engines, with a capacity to kill 2000 people at a time. Treblinka was viewed by the SS as a model extermination centre. It killed thousands of Jews every single day. Estimates of the number of people killed at the camp range between 800,000 and a staggering 1.3 million. The majority were Jews from the Warsaw ghetto but many thousands of other Jews were sent to the camp from Germany, Yugoslavia, Greece and Austria. It has now come to light, from a recently discovered teletyped message, that 813,000 Jews were killed at Treblinka in 1942 alone. A large number of Gypsies were also killed at this camp. In November 1943, the last group of Jewish slave labourers were ordered by the SS to dismantle the camp.

Majdanek, located close to nearby Lublin, was a forced-labour camp containing a combination of Poles, Soviet prisoners of war, and Jews. Unlike most of the other extermination camps – and most of the German concentration camps – the sign *Arbeit macht frei* ('Work sets you free') was not displayed over the entrance to the camp. There were a total of six commandants at the camp during its operation, most notably, Karl Otto Koch, who was actually tried by the Nazis for fraud, Max Koegel, who was executed by a British war crimes court in 1946, and Martin Weiss, who suffered a similar fate in an American court. There was no railway line serving this camp. Prisoners arrived via a shuttle service of trucks from the main railway station in Lublin. In September 1942, construction began on three gas chambers at the camp, which used carbon monoxide and also a limited amount of Zyklon B. The Soviet Red Army liberated Majdanek on 23 July 1944. Shortly afterwards, the authorities in the Soviet Union announced that 1.7 million people had been murdered there. But this figure was lowered at the Nuremberg Trial of Nazi war criminals to 1.5 million. One reason why the Soviets originally thought so many people had died at this camp was the grim discovery of 800,000 pairs of shoes in the camp warehouse. It was later proved by the Americans that Majdanek had acted as a processing centre for all the goods confiscated from prisoners in the 'Operation Reinhard' camps. As a result, the death figure at the camp has now been estimated at between 200,000 and 350,000, with the number of Jews at this camp being put at approximately 60,000.

The most infamous Nazi factory of death and the major centre for the killing of Jews in the Holocaust was Auschwitz-Birkenau, located near the small Polish town of Oswiecim, Galicia, in the south-east district of the Generalgouvernement. The original camp (Auschwitz) was a former Austrian barracks but became a concentration camp in the spring of 1940. In December of the same year a second camp (Birkenau) – a forced-labour camp – was opened. On 4 May 1940, Rudolf Höss, an SS officer who had worked at both the Dachau and Sachsenhausen concentration camps, was appointed as the camp commandant. He was to preside over a veritable empire of death and slave labour. Eventually Auschwitz-Birkenau covered eighteen square miles and operated during its existence five huge gas chambers with four additional gassing rooms. Höss claimed at the Nuremberg trial that he was ordered by Himmler in the autumn of 1941, acting on an order from Hitler, to establish extermination facilities at the camp to carry out 'The Final Solution of the Jewish Question'. The first group to be gassed using Zyklon B, a deadly hydrogen cyanide compound, licensed by I. G. Farben to subsidiary companies and originally used as an industrial pesticide, were Soviet prisoners of war on 3 September 1941 when 600 men were crowded into the cellar of Block 11. The windows and doors were sealed and Zyklon B was thrown into the cellar but it was found soon afterwards that some prisoners had survived, and so double the amount was used and the job completed. It was only at Auschwitz and Majdanek that Zyklon B was used extensively. But the camp only really became an efficient 'factory of death' during the spring of 1943.

The actual number of Jewish deaths at Auschwitz-Birkenau remains a subject of enormous historical controversy. The Polish Communist government originally estimated, shortly after the war, that 4.1 million people were killed at the camp, mostly by gassing. At the Nuremberg trials, Höss claimed 2.5 million Jews were killed at this camp. This figure was also discovered in a report on the killings, signed by Adolf Eichmann. Under severe cross-examination by the British and US lawyers at Nuremberg, Höss admitted that he did not really know the exact figure, as Himmler had forbidden him from compiling detailed systematic records. On the original monument at Auschwitz, erected by the Polish government, the figure of 4 million killed at the camp was inscribed, with the figure of 2.7 million Jews killed. Ever since, these figures have been quite dramatically revised downwards. In 1961, Hilberg put the figure at a much lower 1.1 million Jewish deaths but he stated this was a minimum figure. He said 1.6 million was the highest he thought possible. In 1991, Bauer estimated the total Jewish deaths at the camp complex at the much lower figure of 1.35 million. There were many thousands of others killed at Auschwitz, most notably, Gypsies, Soviet prisoners of war, forced-labourers from Poland and numerous other nationalities. The most recent inscription on the Auschwitz-Birkenau monument claims

1.5 million people were killed, with the majority being 'Jews from diverse European countries'.[1]

Given the monumental scale of mass murder in the extermination camps, much scholarly attention has been focused on the mentality of the human beings put in charge of this grisly task. The controlling authority in each camp was the SS commandant. He (and they were all male) was ultimately responsible for the official bureaucracy and the implementation of all aspects of the 'Final Solution' and the slave labour policies of the Third Reich. The SS commandant had overall control of policy, liaised with the Nazi central authorities and was in charge of camp organisation, development and staffing. In the Nazi camp system, the commandant was an all-powerful figure. Most of those who ran the camps were not low-ranking party activists but middle-ranking bureaucratic officials, many of whom were involved in the security forces, and a significant number had participated in the T4 programme.

Christian Wirth was 56 years old when he was appointed as camp commandant at Sobibór. He had joined the ordinary police force in 1910. During the First World War he was awarded the Iron Cross (1st and 2nd Class) and the Gold Military Cross for bravery. He had joined the Nazi Party in 1921 and was certainly a member of the 'old guard'. During the 1930s he became a leading criminal investigator in Kripo. He was known as a strict disciplinarian and a very capable administrator. These qualities soon came to the attention of Hitler. In 1939, he made it known to Wirth that he would soon be assigned 'special tasks for the Führer' during the war. Wirth worked in the Reich Chancellery and had played a leading role coordinating the administration of the T4 programme. It was Wirth who supervised the installation of gas chambers for T4. He devised the procedure to get victims into the gas chamber in the false belief they were taking a shower. When the decision was taken to accelerate the killing of Jews in 'Operation Reinhard', during the summer of 1942, Wirth – already camp commandant at Sobibór – was given overall responsibility for the whole operation. Wirth had already spoken of 'doing away with useless mouths' during the T4 programme. He ruled Sobibór with a fist of iron, often walking around the camp, with a pistol and a whip in his hand, bellowing and screaming out orders and spreading terror wherever he went. According to testimony at a later war trial from a close member of his staff: 'Wirth was a Jew hater on an unimaginable scale.' It was also claimed in testimony at the war trials that Wirth once tied a Jew to the back of his car and accelerated along a village street, dragging the Jew to his death.[2]

Franz Stangl was Austrian and he had worked at Sobibór before taking charge at Treblinka. He was also intimately involved in 'Operation Reinhard'.

Stangl was another life-long member of the police force and was promoted to the rank of detective in 1935. Before the Anschluss (the union between Germany and Austria in 1938), he was not even a member of the Nazi Party. He actually falsified his personal police employment file to show he had been a member before the Nazi take-over. But the evidence suggests Stangl was a very committed Nazi and he fervently supported Hitler's racial policy. In 1940, he was ordered by Himmler to take part in the T4 programme, following a recommendation from Wirth. This was a very important moment in Stangl's career, as this 'ordinary' policeman now become involved in state-sponsored murder. Stangl became known as a person who would carry out orders promptly and obey the instructions of his superiors without any comment. Stangl was the kind of likeable but essentially spineless individual who, by simply following orders quietly, can flourish within any bureaucratic organisation. Wirth liked him a great deal, which shows what a pliant character he was. Survivors from Sobibór and Treblinka described him in testimony at the war trials as being charming, courteous, softly spoken and very polite. Stangl, in conversation with Gitta Sereny in 1949, tried to rationalise his role in the extermination process and revealed his astonishing aloofness from the frightful atrocities he organised:

Sereny: 'But if you made this offer [to run Treblinka] to Globocnik, it means you actually volunteered your collaboration doesn't it?'

Stangl: 'All I was doing was to confirm to him that I would be carrying out this assignment as a police officer under his command.'

Sereny: 'But you and Michel [a colleague of Stangl's at Hartheim], months before, had acknowledged to yourselves that what was being committed here was a crime. How could you in all conscience, volunteer – to take any part in this crime?'

Stangl: 'It was a matter of survival. What I had to do while I continued my efforts to get out was to limit my own actions to what I – in my own conscience – could answer for. At police training school they taught us that the definition of a crime should meet four requirements: there has to be a subject, an object, an action and intent. If any of these four elements are missing, then we are not dealing with a punishable offence. . . . The only way I could live was by compartmentalizing my thinking. By doing this I could apply this to my own situation; if the "subject" was the government, the "object" the Jews, and the "action" the gassing, then I could tell myself that for me the fourth element, "intent" (he called it "free will") was missing.'[3]

The ability of Stangl to make a sharp distinction between the public acts of brutality that were carried out at Treblinka and his own personal responsibility for them may appear startling but this type of detachment when discussing the acts of mass murder they were ordered to carry out was fairly typical of many of the SS personnel who ran the death camps.

Rudolf Höss had been in the SS since the late 1920s and was a leading figure at the Dachau concentration camp during the 1930s. At the beginning, he was merely the commandant of a very small concentration camp in the small town of Auschwitz in Upper Silesia. The SS decided the camp had such good railway links that it could act as a major resettlement camp for Polish prisoners. After Höss became commandant, the Auschwitz complex grew and grew until it eventually covered eighteen square miles. It was at one and the same time a major industrial slave labour camp, which attracted investment from leading German industries such as I. G. Farben and Krupps, and a major killing centre with purpose-built crematoria with a capacity to kill 20,000 individuals a day. Höss believed the gas chambers at Auschwitz were an improvement on the mass shootings carried out by the *Einsatzgruppen* on the Eastern Front:

> I was always horrified of death by firing squads, especially when I
> thought of the huge numbers of women and children who would have to
> be killed. I had had enough of hostage executions, and the mass killings
> by firing squad ordered by Himmler and Heydrich. Now I was at ease. We
> were all saved from these bloodbaths, and the victims would be spared
> until the last moment.[4]

Höss felt the primary role of a camp commandant was to carry out the Nazi policy of extermination of the Jews and to ensure slave labour was used to aid the war effort. Individual concern for the victims was repressed or ignored. He could observe the trauma of the Jews and the other victims placed in his charge and he was able to describe in graphic detail the hysteria of individual men, women and children. But when he went home he never discussed his work with his wife or family at all. He played games with his children like any 'ordinary' parent and even wrote sentimental poems. In the office at Auschwitz-Birkenau, a similar sense of detachment prevailed. Clerical administrators ensured card indexes and files were kept up to date. They liaised with the SS Camp Inspectorate, ordered deliveries of the deadly 'Zyklon B' as if they were ordering milk, and instructed contractors to build the gas chambers and to carry out repairs to the crematoria as if they were calling an everyday workmen to their homes. Everyone seemed to have no moral responsibility for what was going on: all everyone needed to be told to comply was that 'It was the Führer's wish'.

What is much less well known is that the 'internal administration' of the camps was in the hands of an elite group of 'selected prisoners', generally known as *Prominenten* or 'prisoner-functionaries' (*Functionschäftlinge*). Their importance grew because the numbers of prisoners rose so dramatically during the war. The SS had to rely increasingly on prisoner-functionaries for the detailed 'internal' running of the camps. At the top of this 'internal' organisation was a prisoner called the 'Camp Elder' (*Lagerältester*). The SS chose this man very carefully as it was through this person that the efficient internal lines of communication in the camp would flow. Second in rank to the Camp Elder was the Camp Clerk who ran the *Schreibstube* – the office that kept the camp administration going, held prisoner records, details of roll call figures, prisoner death rates and transfer records, and organised food distributions. There was also a Labour Statistics Office (*Arbeitsstatistik*), also run by prisoners, which recorded the activities of the work kommandos and kept control of the work programmes. There were opportunities here to subvert the system and save lives. Prisoners could be detoured to work details that were not as arduous as working on hard-labour outdoor projects. The control of rations for prisoners allowed the prisoner-functionary to obtain extra supplies of food, which many used as currency for bribery and the creation of a client base in the camp. In such ways, elite prisoner-functionaries could draw power from their SS overlords and make themselves indispensable as a means of securing for themselves the most favourable means of surviving.

A key member of the *Prominenten* was the *Kapo*. These prisoners ran the work kommandos and inflicted the harshest of discipline on their fellow prisoners. They had the power of life and death over their charges. Most *Kapos* were just common criminals, some were murderers and most were extremely violent. Described as 'the aristocrats of the camps' by Otto Friedrich, they ensured that the 'internal organisation' of the camp ran smoothly and as brutally as the SS demanded.[5] One simple rule was that a 'green prisoner' (all criminals had a green badge on their prison uniform) could kill a 'red one' (a 'political' prisoner: usually a communist). In fact, *Kapos* could and very often did kill anyone they disliked. There were some Jewish prisoners who were *Kapos*. Primo Levi calls them a 'sad and notable human phenomenon' and 'monsters of insensitivity'.[6] At Treblinka, there was a group of Jews selected from the transports, called *Hofjuden* or 'Court Jews', who helped the SS carry out all the tasks associated with extermination. The Jewish *Kapos* at Treblinka were not loutish criminals but were chosen for their leadership qualities and their standing within the Jewish community. The *Kapos* were generally seduced by the privileges that membership of this elite offered. They were well clothed, had their own rooms, and ate and drank very well. In the women's camp at Auschwitz, the women *Kapos* beat and murdered the prisoners without restraint.

The inmates at Auschwitz also ran, with some SS surveillance, each uniformly similar barrack block, which housed up to a thousand people crammed into three-tier bunks. The 'Block Elder' (male: *Blockältester*; female: *Blockälteste*) ensured rigid discipline, assisted by a secretary and medical assistants. In the women's barracks, a 'Blockova', whose brutality equalled that of any of the male Block leaders took on this role. As well as Block discipline, their duties included the distribution of the meagre daily food rations. They also monitored hygiene and supplied clothes, blankets, shoes and other individual needs. One historian has described Block Elders as having the powers of 'military regimental commanders'.[7] Many used their power delegated from the SS to ensure that they enjoyed the privileges of power: good food, warm clothing and, in many cases, sexual favours. They helped some prisoners but usually acted in their own selfish interests. If they could establish a corps of corrupt helpers and sycophants, their personal empires could even resist SS interference.

Some prisoners could weaken formal controls by playing on the greed of SS officers. The looting of prisoners' belongings and the practice of farming out inmates to outside commercial enterprises, who paid for the slave labour, meant that Block Elders often had the power of life and death over those in their barracks and could be very useful for the SS as they siphoned off the valuables and income. There was great rivalry in the camps between the different sections of the delegated control structures. Where the camp 'internal' administration might be in the hands of the political 'reds', their enemies, the criminal 'greens', could establish an alternative power centre in the Blocks. Thus was the social stratification of the camp made more complex as the lines separating the controllers and the controlled became blurred.

At Auschwitz-Birkenau, the *Sonderkommando*, or 'Special Squads' of prisoners, disposed of the remains of the murdered. Thousands upon thousands of corpses had to be taken from gas chambers and then transported to the crematoria facilities. Those who carried out these tasks worked in an environment in which death and degradation became normal. Otto Friedrich's graphic eyewitness testimony of Auschwitz, aptly entitled *The Kingdom of Auschwitz*, reveals how the *Sonderkommando*, who were mostly strong, fit and tall Jews selected by the SS, worked in the crematoria. They had to pick up the bodies in the gas chambers with their bare hands, drag them across floors to the trolleys or wheeled carts, often carrying two or more corpses at a time, and then push them into the burning ovens. The crematoria at the extermination camps worked around the clock when large transports arrived. The first gassing took place in Block 11. The two houses then chosen as permanent gas chambers were dubbed the 'red' and 'white' houses because of the red brick of one and the whitewash on the other. The 'Little Red House' was known as Bunker 1 and the 'Little White House' as Bunker 2. According to Filip Müller, a surviving *Sonderkommando*, each of the six ovens in the older crematoria could only burn three corpses every twenty minutes, which meant a total of 54 bodies per hour. His eyewitness account contradicts official German figures which suggest a killing rate of 340 bodies in Crematorium I every 24 hours. Nevertheless, only four *Sonderkommando* were employed per oven and they were often overwhelmed by the number of bodies to be disposed of. Given the limited capacity of Crematorium I at Auschwitz-Birkenau, four new crematoria were built after July 1943. A fifth was planned but never built. All the 200 *Sonderkommando* personnel were then transferred to the new installations and eventually 900 people were involved. In the new killing blocks killing became a grim factory process. Crematoria II and III, for example, could burn 2500 corpses a day. Müller remembers seeing 500 corpses burn in one night and he also saw the aftermath of death in the gas chambers:

> As the doors opened, the top layer of corpses tumbled out like the contents of an overloaded truck when the tailboard is let down. They were the strongest ones who, in their mortal terror, had instinctively fought their way to the door; the one and only way out. . . . The corpses were hosed down. This served to neutralize any gas crystals still lying about, but mainly it was intended to clean the dead bodies. For almost all of them were wet with sweat and urine, filthy with blood and excrement, while the legs of many women were streaked with menstrual blood. . . . It was for this reason that the bottom layer of corpses always consisted of children as well as the old and the weak, whilst the tallest and the strongest lay on top, with middle-aged men and women in between. . . . The people in their heaps were intertwined, some lying in each other's arms, others holding each other's hands; groups of them were leaning against the walls, pressed against each other like columns of basalt.[8]

Many of the *Sonderkommando* were skilled stokers who ensured the ovens were always kept fully stocked with coal and heated to the very highest of temperatures. Additional duties included the collection of valuables from the unsuspecting victims. There was a *Sonderkommando* that had the duty of collecting the hair of the thousands who died every day. It was carefully washed and dried and then sent to Germany for use as wigs and insulation fabric. Other special squads removed gold teeth (to be melted down and turned into gold bars), false teeth, glasses, watches, money, gems, food, shoes and clothing. If much of this was required for the Reich, a considerable quantity found its way into the camp's 'black economy' and became a vital resource for the 'organising' of essential material for prisoners to obtain those extra pieces of bread or soup bowls upon which a life might hang.

Often the members of the *Sonderkommando* recognised the bodies of their own friends, wives, children and other relatives when they opened the doors of the gas chambers. Long-term survival was only possible if the SS could be convinced that the prisoner could carry out his orders robotically, efficiently and immediately. If not, a bullet would be the reward. Müller reports the cases of two *Sonderkommando* who were flung by the SS into the red-hot ovens alive, because they had tried to warn unsuspecting arrivals of their fate. As well as the gassing of victims, the SS executed many prisoners by other means. Killing with silenced carbines and revolvers was a frequent practice. Prisoners could be clubbed to death at any time. Elsewhere, injections with phenol were commonly given in the camp hospitals to stop the heart of those considered a drain on resources.

Those arriving at Auschwitz-Birkenau and at most of the other extermination camps came in sealed trains. Crowded into the locked cattle wagons, not fitted out for human beings, were men, women and children, transported from all over Europe. Over 100 people were placed in a single compartment usually used to transport eight horses or cattle. They were plunged into darkness without food or water. The old, the sick, the young and the weak were bewildered, terrorised and frightened. As the trains passed through stations on their way to the camps those jammed inside the trucks could hear the insults and jeers of onlookers on the platforms. So the fight for survival, the hysterical struggle for every inch of space, for every breath, began in the cattle trucks even before they reached the camps. Primo Levi has left eloquent testimony of his experience of the transport that took him form Italy to Auschwitz:

> We suffered from thirst and cold; at every stop we clamoured for water, or even a handful of snow, but we were rarely heard; the soldiers of the escort drove off anybody who tried to approach the convoy. Two young mothers nursing their children, groaned night and day, begging for water. Our state of nervous tension made the hunger, exhaustion and lack of sleep seem less of a torment. But the hours of darkness were nightmares without end.[9]

Upon arrival, everyone in the wagons was already suffering from terrible thirst in a carriage with floors full of human excrement and the wrenching stench of urine. Most at this stage were unaware of the purpose of the camps. There was a sense of bewilderment as the doors in the cattle wagons finally opened at the end of the journey into either daylight or darkness depending on when the train arrived. Elie Cohen observed the initial reaction of those arriving at the extermination camps and he shows how individuals quickly disintegrated, completely losing their understanding of who they were, or where they were, because what they were experiencing was outside the bounds of their perceptions of normality.[10] Dozens of survivors describe similar feelings. The Jews, all wearing the compulsory and easily recognisable yellow 'Star of David', were lined up in rows on the platform with men on one side and women with children on the other. Each Jew was then tattooed on the arm with a number. Meanwhile, strange, grey, emaciated creatures, 'wrecks', as one survivor calls them, wearing dirty, blue-striped uniforms, grabbed the entire luggage from the rail cars. New arrivals were by now mystified and frightened but still unaware of what would happen. The presence of German officers, barking out orders – always in German – appeared to bring a sense of order. The SS men on the platform, some of whom were doctors, held medical cases in their hands and inspected the ranks as they shuffled towards them. The SS separated people: one line to the left, one to the right. Left meant death straightaway in the gas chambers, right meant the dubious task of slave labour ('destruction through labour'). To the left went the old, the sick, the weak and young children. Mothers with babes in arms were torn from their children screaming in terror. But very few resisted. The few who did or became hysterical were clubbed with rifle buts or just shot on the spot. Some children stood on tiptoes in an attempt to convince selectors they were big and could work. Others had been advised to inflate their ages, by other inmates who opened the cattle trucks.

All the inmates who survived the initial selection process at Auschwitz were housed in barracks. These were forty metres long, and ten metres wide, containing a thousand inmates. With over 200 barracks it was to become not merely a slave town but a charnel city. New prisoners were initially mystified by the pall of white smoke that came billowing out of the large chimneys near the shower rooms, but they soon recognised the odour of burning corpses. The words 'life' and 'survival' in connection with the reality of being an inmate at one of the camps are somewhat misleading. Survival was not a matter of just hanging on until the end, having avoided the gas and arbitrary violence. Survival literature shows that prisoners measured survival on a very short-term basis, perhaps even from minute to minute. To imagine enduring beyond the immediate imperative of pure existence often seemed impossible. In fact, the subject of 'survival' has to be approached with extreme care. There are very few archival documents to verify the later testimony of survivors. The words of those who survived have to be taken at face value. We must appreciate that any of them might have a good reason to conceal many aspects of their own roles. A survivor of the death camps is not necessarily a reliable witness. It must be appreciated that some prisoners survived by collaboration in some way with the Nazis who ran the camps.

The testimony of survivors reveals that the daily routine in the camps was extremely gruelling. All the orders were given in German, often by signals and gestures. Those prisoners who failed to understand the signals or did not know any German were immediately beaten mercilessly. At Auschwitz a gong sounded the start of the day. In the barracks, the bunks were just three-tier wooden pallets with each space occupied by three or more prisoners often sharing a single blanket. After going to the toilet in the morning, followed by inadequate rations, the prisoners cleaned out the barracks. After this, prisoners were gathered in front of the barracks – in all weathers – for the daily roll call of names, which often went on for over an hour. Quite often, the endless calling out of names went on so long that even some of the strongest of prisoners swayed with fatigue in summer heat or shivered in the winter. This dreadful treatment was complemented by the ritual of 'off caps', which consisted of prisoners being forced to doff their caps and stand immaculately to attention. The SS estimated a slave labour prisoner could survive about three months at most under this regime. If anyone survived longer they were looked upon as 'thieves', 'criminals' and 'shirkers' and were watched very closely by SS guards.

Many of those who survived, for any length of time, at Auschwitz became known by fellow inmates as 'walking skeletons'. Primo Levi called them 'Null Achtzehns'. These tragic figures shambled around the camps, deranged by the merciless regime. Almost all of the survival literature makes references to these prisoners, who had completely abandoned themselves to their fate. Those who had any wish to survive tried to treat the SS staff with exaggerated respect at all times. As within any institution, exaggerated flattery could pay off. But it was even more important to try and blend in with the crowd; to carry out tasks without fuss or hesitation and take any punishment in silence. All signs of weakness had to be disguised. Some survivors felt that the only way to survive in the camps was to abandon all previously assumed concepts of civilised behaviour. Any self-regarding actions were permissible against fellow inmates: theft, violence, hoarding of food and the denial of assistance in any form. It was, believe it or not, imperative to look after shoes. They were absolutely vital to protect feet, and easily damaged by the harsh conditions. Injured feet meant the inability to work, which often meant immediate selection for the gas chambers. Another priceless asset was a spoon. It was also vital for a prisoner to get near to the front of the food queues in order to get the lion's share of the meagre scraps on offer. Primo Levi was able to quench his ever-raging thirst when he found, by chance, a forgotten water pipe that dripped; but he never mentioned his secret water supply to his fellow inmates. Similar examples of a selfish strategy for survival are to be found in the accounts of many other survivors. Helping a terminally ill prisoner was often no act of a kind selfless carer, but a well-known strategy for acquiring the victim's food, clothes and shoes.

In his work on Auschwitz, Levi divided the prisoner population in Auschwitz into two categories: 'the Drowned and the Saved'. Those with 'low numbers' tattooed on their arms were prisoners who had arrived during the early years of the camp's operation. Very few inmates of this type were still alive in 1944. Levi estimates the survival rates of the first inmates from 1940 at about 0.2 per cent. He observed something similar about this very small group of exceptional survivors: they were usually doctors, musicians, tailors, shoe-makers and those who had been given camp responsibilities by the SS. In some cases a young, good-looking homosexual could extract favours from their SS partners. Similarly, some beautiful women survived because they had caught the eye of an SS officer. Others Levi places in the 'Saved' category are those who ruthlessly exploited others in their own interests. One Auschwitz inmate Levi highlights is 'Henri', who stole and worked mercilessly to gain the sympathy of other inmates. Levi describes him as 'enclosed in armour, the enemy of all, inhumanly cunning'. But the majority, according to Levi, were the 'Drowned', who were worked to death, died from the innumerable epidemics that infected most camps, or were arbitrarily murdered by their guards. Luck also played a part. In Auschwitz, Sara Nomberg-Przytyk, was, miraculously, saved from selection literally right at the door of the 'shower' gas chamber by her friend Sonya Rozawska, a member of the *Prominenten*, those prisoners fortunate to have positions in the camp administration, upon whom the SS relied for the efficient running of the camp.

All the camps used public flogging as a regular method of punishment. Auschwitz established the solitary punishment cell, in which prisoners were left to simply die of thirst and starvation in a hole in which they could not lie down or take any sort of rest. Public hangings were used in all the camps to show what would happen if anyone flouted the rules. Executions in public were so frequent at Auschwitz that one killing site was called the 'Death Wall'. It is probably worth adding that many prisoners were killed for the most trivial of offences. Having dirty shoes meant laziness, shoes that were too clean meant a shirker: both cases could bring execution from a trigger-happy guard.

At Auschwitz, the prisoners were given three meals a day: breakfast, lunch and an evening meal. The nutritional value of these meals was extremely poor. The SS removed any food of any quality from the prisoners' diet. The SS often exchanged bread for the gold teeth prised by the *Sonderkommando* from the mouths of the corpses of the gassed. Supplies of food were also stolen by the prisoner-functionaries. For those exhausted prisoners awaiting meagre rations after a gruelling day in a work party there was the very dubious pleasure of a thin watery soup usually made out of potato peelings. A thin type of porridge was nearly always on the menu but it could have been left out in the open to decay before it was cooked.

Food became an obsession with most prisoners. They talked about lack of it, dreamed of imaginary feasts and often recalled huge meals they had consumed at past family celebrations. Cohen refers to this as 'Gastric Masturbation'. There is also evidence that hunger pangs were so great in Auschwitz they sometimes led to cannibalism. One prisoner, in a post-war interview, recalled his friend finding a severed hand, which was then eaten by five prisoners.[11] Other testimony also refers to the eating of human flesh. Borowski reports being told by another prisoner in Auschwitz that 'real hunger is when one man regards another man as something to eat'.[12]

Another equally constant craving was for water. At Auschwitz, no water was given to prisoners. At Birkenau, thirst was an ever-present problem, because prisoners there were only given a quarter of a pint of water per day. Levi writes of lying in his bunk at night, being nearly driven insane by an inescapable thirst that could not be quenched. When it rained prisoners opened their mouths as wide as possible as a means of getting some fluid into their bodies. During the heat of summer a prisoner would trade anything for water. Given such deprivation, all prisoners suffered the prolonged agony of progressive malnutrition.

Survival, in such tough conditions, depended on whether a prisoner could get additional rations. Human nature being what it is, this often meant stealing and bribing other prisoners who had access to food and water. Most of the camps had a 'black economy' which operated with the connivance of the SS guards. Food supplies for the SS staff – as well as those for the prisoners – were often siphoned off into private hands. Some of the SS officers at the camps ate and drank in the style of the Romans. The ability to 'organise' became a key aspect of a successful survival strategy. Goods had to be obtained in order to barter with other prisoners. The key was to know where the extra rations, clothes and shoes could be found. It is important to remember that for the prisoner, to 'organise' meant obtaining 'extras'. At

Auschwitz, one of the most important sources of 'organised' goods was the vast warehouse, nicknamed 'Canada', where all the valuables taken from the dead were stored. Levi describes the activities of the so-called 'professional merchants' who inhabited the camps. Some were Greek prisoners who worked together assiduously to acquire the bread and soup which acted, with cigarettes, as hard currency. Levi admired the ingenuity of the Greeks in Auschwitz, as their creation of a black market kept many Jews alive. All the 'merchants' had their favourite sources of supply. Those who worked in the kitchens were in the most favourable positions.

Bread was commonly traded for tobacco in the 'north-east market' of Auschwitz. Tobacco – as in most prisons – was a valuable currency. An inmate could exchange it with a civilian worker if contactable through the barbed wire fence and get more bread for it than had been paid on the camp black market. The extra bread received from the civilian would be eaten and the remainder used to purchase more tobacco in the hope of a repeat transaction. Of course, this was only possible if secure contact with the outside world was maintained. Factory work gangs had more opportunity than most to carry out such transactions. In Auschwitz, the vast Buna plant designed to make synthetic rubber was a rich source of stolen goods introduced into the camp to extend the range of 'currency'. Tools, wire, brooms, paint, light bulbs, soap, nails and anything else portable were carried away to be bartered on the black market. Survival, therefore, could be bought but only if a prisoner had access to, or a prominent role within, the black market.

There remains one further important factor to discuss in relation to these 'open market operations', namely, the role of the camp hospital at Auschwitz. It was in the hospital that the surveillance of the SS was at its weakest. To be admitted to hospital was a mixed blessing. One could avoid for a few precious days the rigours of slave labour. But a hospital patient could become a candidate for medical and drug experiments. It is well known that the nurses took the possessions of the dead and sold them on the black market. Of supreme value for prisoners was a feeding bowl and spoon. Without these essentials, the food rations so vital for survival could not be eaten. Primo Levi thought that the nursing staff made enormous profits selling the spoons of all who came into the hospital. Spoons were also made secretly by prisoners in the Buna factory at Auschwitz III (Monowitz) and sold to new inmates.

But the camp hospital was not a place any inmate wanted to stay too long. To become sick usually meant to be doomed. The SS doctors regularly sent prisoners admitted to the hospital immediately to the gas chambers. There were prisoner-doctors working in the hospitals, and some of the nurses were also inmates. Dr Jacques Pach at Auschwitz was in charge of a small hospital reserved for the Birkenau *Sonderkommandos*. Pach was a Polish Jew who had emigrated to France. In Paris, he had married an 'Aryan' woman but this did not prevent him being transported to Auschwitz. He was a gentle man who worked heroically and selflessly in the hospital to keep the prisoners alive. Inevitably, however, Dr Pach was 'selected' – as a Jew – for the gas chambers.

The hospitals were also the scenes of horrific medical experiments. At Auschwitz, the notorious Dr Mengele murdered twins and dwarfs amongst other inmates in pursuit of his racist research interests. Prisoners were injected with malaria to study the effects of the disease on human blood, and people were immersed in freezing water until they died, or their arteries were cut and doctors would measure the exact time between the making of the cut and their death. There were also drug and sterilisation experiments. All of this was done in the name of 'medical research' but humans replaced animals as the key raw material for experimentation.

It is most important to emphasise that the prisoner population was not simply an undifferentiated mass of 'Jewish' victims. Camp social hierarchies existed. Many different social and ethnic groups experienced contrasting treatment. German-speakers were far more likely to land jobs in the 'internal' camp organisation as 'privileged prisoners' and thus claim prerogatives that could save their lives. In general, those who could not speak German were at a particular disadvantage and were unable to function as prisoners as well as others. A group that was able to climb the social hierarchy was the Poles who spoke German and were able to establish themselves as an important element in the administration at Auschwitz, and as the camp grew so did their indispensability to the Germans.

The insignia all prisoners wore on their clothing reinforced the hierarchy of the camp. Prisoners wore coloured triangles sewn on their now familiar-looking blue and white striped uniform. These 'racial badges' were placed alongside the prisoner's identification number. Jewish prisoners wore the Yellow Star: this was a yellow base triangle with another inverted coloured triangle drawn above it and pointing down on it. The result was a 'Star of David'. A black inverted triangle indicated that the wearer was a 'Race Defiler' (*Rassenschande*), meaning those who had sex with an 'Aryan' woman.

Political prisoners wore red triangles. Many of these were communists and because the regime saw them as especially suspect they were often treated very badly. The insignia could also have a letter indicating the prisoner's country of origin: 'F' for Frankreich (France), for example. Further categorisation was shown by the addition of a bar across the top of the triangle, thus indicating that the prisoner needed to be kept under constant surveillance. A black dot under the triangle meant the wearer was to be singled out for particularly savage treatment. These prisoners would be the first to be sent to punishment squads. Prisoners thought likely to escape had a target drawn on their backs. Blue triangles were for foreign migrants and refugees of uncertain racial value and political reliability. Many were Spanish exiles who had fled to France from Franco's regime after the Spanish Civil War.

Green triangles signified a criminal. When the triangle pointed down, the offence was deemed of a less serious nature, such as theft or assault. A green triangle pointing upwards meant the convict had committed far more serious crimes such as murder, rape, and severe assault. Some had been in institutions for the criminally insane. Such prisoners were labelled as extremely dangerous and unpredictable but they became what Levi called the 'effective masters' of other prisoners.[13] These violent and bullying criminals came to dominate the 'internal' organisation of the camps. Mauve was the colour assigned to members of the religious groups that were opponents of the Nazi regime. Priests, pastors and clergymen of all faiths wore these triangles. Others in this category were 'Jehovah's Witnesses' and 'Conscientious Objectors'. A pink triangle denoted a homosexual. Gays were singled out by the camp authorities for severe punishment and were subjected to ridicule and violence from other inmates. A black triangle meant an 'asocial'. This was an extremely vague classification which enabled the Nazis to lump together all manner of individuals, including Gypsies, those defined as 'malingerers', or the 'feckless', prostitutes, vagrants and 'disrespectful' youths. The mentally ill had a badge which read *Blöd* ('stupid' or 'imbecile'). It meant that they suffered appallingly at the hands of anyone: fellow prisoners and the SS alike.

All ethnic groups faced lethal camp regimes but not all in the same way, nor were they all faced with immediate execution. Different nationalities and 'races' knew their specific rank in the camp social hierarchy. At the very bottom of the social pyramid were the Jews and Gypsies. As well as their 'racial classification' as *untermenschen* ('sub-human') they could also be marginalised as 'asocials' (i.e., feckless and parasitical), 'criminals' and 'political prisoners'. Clearly identified by the yellow triangles on their prison garb, Jews were often singled out for the most sadistic treatment of all.

The elite prisoner *Prominenten*, such as the Camp Elder, Block Elders and Kapos, constituted a class stationed between the formal SS elite and the mass of the prisoners. In effect they looked above to the SS for reward, security and authority and below to the mass of prisoners as objects of their limitless disciplinary powers. But in neither direction did they look with confidence. They could be shot or physically attacked by the SS for making en error or failing to carry out their tasks. Alternatively, they could be attacked by an angry camp inmate. They were generally regarded as 'traitors' and 'Nazi stooges'. There was thus a complex social order in the camps. The more the SS devolved power to the *Prominenten* and the greater the powers of the prisoner elite, the more obscured became the chain of command.

The elite *Prominenten* inhabited what Primo Levi has most effectively called the 'the Grey Zone', in which lines of authority were unclear. There were many acutely defined levels of power and status within the prisoner cohort. For those who were new to the camp world, any simple idea that the prisoners were a separate species controlled from outside by the SS and their auxiliaries was soon shattered. The new prisoner (*Zugang*) often found it extremely difficult to know who to look to for help and support in order to survive. There were countless boundaries and insignia dividing one prisoner from another. There were many prisoners collaborating in the running of the camps with the SS and they were all in positions of authority. The new prisoner was just as likely to be attacked by a fellow prisoner as by an SS guard. Thus was the 'Grey Zone' a place in which no one was safe and no one could count on another prisoner for help and support. The 'Grey Zone' was also the realm of the collaborator. The camp could not function without the help of the privileged inmates. In Levi's 'Grey Zone' it is difficult to distinguish who emerges from the camp system with clean hands or a clean conscience.

An often-neglected aspect life in the camps is the particular experience of women. Some historians, such Dalia Ofer and Lenore Weitzman, have argued that a gendered perspective to the Holocaust is very important because a deeper understanding of the unique experiences of women victims helps to break down any generalised discussion of Nazi bestiality and bring a more specific awareness of the appalling extent of the barbarity.[14] Upon arrival, women – like men – were stripped and their hair was shaved off. Many had to cope immediately with the loss of their children, their husbands or other close relatives. Some women found themselves quickly 'selected' to offer sexual 'services' to men in the camp brothel or they suffered rape and extensive sexual abuse.

And yet it must also be stressed that for women, life and death in the camps was greatly affected by who they were. Women with appropriate secretarial skills might secure a job in a camp office or become a *Blockova* or a translator. Women developed many different survival strategies.[15] The story of the Jewish girl Elli Friedmann and her mother in Auschwitz provides an uplifting example. In May 1944, Elli and her mother were sent to Auschwitz by the Hungarian military police after the ghetto in Nagymagyar was cleared. Elli went to quite extraordinary lengths to keep her sick mother alive. She gave her mother some of her food rations. She managed to persuade a guard to get her mother put in the prison hospital and when it seemed she was likely to be selected for the gas chambers she managed to get her released. Elli and her mother were selected to die in the gas chamber but were spared by another obliging guard as they neared the very doors of the gas chamber. In September 1944, they were deported to a labour camp in Augsburg and survived death again. In April 1944, they were deported again to Mühldorf, a sub-camp of the infamous Dachau concentration camp. On 30 April 1945, American troops found Elli with her mother. They assumed she was in her sixties – not a young girl of fourteen, whose incredible will to survive had been vital in her own and particularly her mother's survival.[16]

The camps constructed new forms of female identity and forced women to accommodate to them. Traditional mores about the place of women in society as mothers, 'carers' and 'the weaker sex' were completely obliterated. At Auschwitz, any babies that were born were immediately drowned in buckets of water. Women arriving on the selection ramps with their children, provided they were not seen as Jewish and had 'Aryan' characteristics such as blond hair and blue eyes, might manage to keep their children. The filth in which women lived in their barracks was overwhelming and this was made even worse by the inevitability of menstruation, which was turned into a public humiliation for many women during long roll calls. The women's quarters in Auschwitz were in an area dubbed 'Mexico', in the most neglected and run-down part of the camp.

The capacity for the abuse and defilement of women was limitless. *Kapos* and supervisors in the factories in which women were forced to work regarded women as sexual property. The Nazis forbade sex between Poles and Jews. Germans who pursued sexual relations with Jewish women could be accused of the serious crime of *Rassenschande* ('race defilement', i.e. the offence of sexual relations with an inferior 'race'). When a Jewish woman prisoner was found to have had sex with a German overseer, both would be punished. The man might receive a short imprisonment or be transferred to another factory or camp but the woman was usually flogged to death or executed. As the numbers of women prisoners increased, sexual liaisons, forced and consensual, did develop. Some women opted for lesbian relationships, in which many found genuine friendship and emotional support.

Women in the camps were forced into what the Nazis assumed were the traditional female spheres of work. Hence, women worked in offices, laundries, 'hospitals', bakeries and kitchens, and food depots. They also worked in 'Canada' warehouses sorting out the clothes and other possessions of the camp's victims. But they were not restricted to 'women's work'. At Auschwitz women were employed in agriculture, growing crops and breeding animals; many worked in forests clearing trees; some dug ditches. A great many more worked in factories and textile mills. Some camps had female 'penal work crews', which inflicted the severest of labour conditions.

It seems incredible that Nazi camps could promote 'sport and leisure' but the SS sometimes encouraged such activities. At Auschwitz, there was a camp orchestra that organised concerts at which SS officers would request favourite pieces of classical music. A string quartet made up of four attractive female prisoners often played outside the shower facilities. Prisoners were often forced by Nazi guards to sing songs as they marched to work, in a sort of macabre version of 'Whistle While you Work'. Leon Greenman remembers Sunday at Auschwitz as a day of 'entertainment', when an inmate called 'Samson' would bend iron bars and perform feats of strength in the camp square. On workdays, the guards used Samson to inflict punishment on prisoners.[17] 'Sport' could sometimes be designed to entertain the sadistic minds of some of the guards. Those chosen for 'recreation' would be forced to do extreme physical exercises for hours. Many of the inmates forced by the SS to do this were exhausted and emaciated individuals hardly capable of standing up.

The principal daily activity of those who survived the gas chambers on arrival was work. The Nazis called work at the camps 'destruction through labour' (*Vernichtung durch Arbeit*). At Auschwitz, prisoners built the camp and were employed through the various phases of its expansion. Many died carrying out these tasks for there was little regard for safety. Prisoners often carried 50kg bags of cement and were driven by their captors with sticks and whips as they unloaded and stacked these and other building materials. The Auschwitz-Birkenau State Museum reports that 10,000 Soviet prisoners died in the five months from October 1941, while building Birkenau (or Auschwitz-Birkenau II), the extermination camp. Other prisoners worked in a wide variety of industries such as farms, woodwork, chemical plants, iron works, and in aircraft and armaments factories. Some were employed in mines, 'lamp-black' factories (where the conditions in the sulphur-impregnated air were often lethal) and textile firms. Particularly demanding was work digging trenches, levelling ground, hauling railway sleepers and clearing bomb damage from rubble-strewn streets. In the factories, prisoners could be under the supervision of a civilian employee and there was the possibility of some support, perhaps even a scrap of bread or a piece of fruit. The worst conditions were in the outside work gangs where workers suffered during winter in freezing temperatures at the hands of their sadistic *Kapos*. Prisoners repairing railway rolling stock or digging tunnels could be held for days at a time at their place of work with the barest of rations. In all cases, the Jewish members of the work gangs were the more harshly treated.

Among the many myths about the extermination camps is that there was no resistance. But in many of them, most notably, Auschwitz, Treblinka, Sobibór and Chełmno, there were revolts in which prisoners used weapons and explosives. Although very few of the brave escapees survived these revolts they are remembered as the most courageous forms of resistance. However, there were other ways of resisting the Holocaust than outright rebellion. In the camps, prisoners began to devise opposition of a different sort, one that was indirect, invisible to the SS system and perhaps the more effective. Many prisoners were determined to collect information about the atrocities and to send the facts to the Allies. Jewish escapees were able to get information to the Jewish Council in Slovakia in 1944 and to bring the first confirmation of the fate of Hungarian Jewry killed in Auschwitz. Some prisoners stored diaries in tin cans and buried them in the ground. Many prisoners attempted to sabotage the industrial enterprises in which they were forced to work. Other forms of opposition included making contact with outside partisan organisations. In Auschwitz, a number of resistance groups merged to form 'Battle Group Auschwitz', led by German and Polish prisoners. Working to escape was another means of keeping hope alive. There were few escapes in the early years, but as the camps grew in size and the less secure satellite camps were built, the number of escapes rose. Escapes could be made from outside work parties or factory work groups. At Birkenau some Russian prisoners were able to bring down a watchtower and rush through the gaps created in the wire fences. They were not recaptured. But all too often the prisoners were captured and executed in front of the camp as an example to all.

What is not generally known is that women featured prominently in many camp revolts. Women were in the forefront of the revolt at Sobibór. They stole hand grenades, pistols, a rifle and a sub-machine gun from the SS quarters where they worked. In the ensuing breakout the majority of prisoners were tracked down and killed. But some of the women escaped to fight with partisan units against the Nazis until the end of the war. Women played a prominent role in a revolt of the *Sonderkommando* at Auschwitz in October 1944. At Auschwitz women engaged in acts of sabotage while working in armaments factories, such as stealing explosives, and others were involved in forty individual attempts to escape. One prisoner's exceptional courage needs recognition. Mala Zimetbaum escaped from Auschwitz in June 1944 and her two weeks' absence gave hope that she had succeeded. To the camp's despair, however, she was recaptured and presented at roll call for the inevitable hanging. But she bravely cheated the gallows by slashing her wrists with a concealed razor blade. It was a courageous act of defiance in the face of monstrous tyranny.

Part II

The Impact of the Holocaust since 1945

5

The Holocaust and Popular Culture

In 1945 newsreels showed harrowing images of starving prisoners in Nazi concentration camps to shocked cinema audiences. Hitler and Nazism were forever associated with brutality of a kind that seemed more extreme and unique than anything else in human history. But the presentation of mass murder enacted by the Nazi regime was not at first singularly focused on the Jews who had perished. It covered the many countless millions of victims scattered across the length and breadth of the European continent. As the years went by, the Jewish Holocaust began to overshadow the broader dimensions of Nazi genocide. Nowadays the Holocaust is viewed not merely as an important event in history, but as a global phenomenon encompassing novels, films and many museums. It seems, as the Jewish historian Yaffa Erlich put it: 'There is no business like Shoah business.'[1] No serious history of the murder of the Jews can simply concentrate on the events of the Holocaust; it must also consider the impact of the Holocaust – especially on modern global and largely westernised popular culture since 1945.

In the immediate post-war period, the Holocaust was, surprisingly, not a popular subject. Many of the survivors resided behind Stalin's 'Iron Curtain' in Soviet-dominated Eastern Europe. Many Jews who had understandably left Europe to live in Israel, the USA and elsewhere suffered from what has been described as 'survivor's guilt'. Most had no pressing desire to talk about their awful experiences. Even the term 'Holocaust' was not in widespread use before the late 1950s. The word 'Holocaust' is not mentioned at all in the first major scholarly work, written by Raul Hilberg and published in 1961.[2]

Before the 1960s the most well known single victim of the Holocaust was Anne Frank, a teenage Jewish girl. She was born in Germany in 1929, but brought up in the Netherlands from 1933 and later died in a Nazi concentration camp. Her story became known throughout the world because she kept a diary of her experiences under Nazi rule. *The Diary of Anne Frank* (published in 1947) was written while she was evading detection by the

Nazis with her parents in a secret apartment of her Amsterdam home. It offers no gory details of the vicious Nazi persecution of the Jews in the extermination camps and downplays her Jewishness. 'I hope one thing only,' she records in 1942, 'that this hatred of the Jews will be a passing thing.' In 1955, Anne Frank's heavily edited diary was adapted into a very successful play at New York's Court Theater on Broadway. In 1959, *The Diary of Anne Frank* became a successful Hollywood film, directed by George Stevens. But there are no scenes which show Anne as a prisoner in Auschwitz or Bergen-Belsen. At one point in the film she says, 'We're [the Jews] not the only people that have had to suffer' [under the Nazis]. The director of the film later claimed that he had not highlighted Anne's Jewishness in order to give the story a more universal appeal. The film ends with a 'feel-good' Hollywood statement from Anne: 'In spite of everything, I still believe that people are good at heart.' This classic Hollywood 'happy ending' is more comforting than alarming. Even so, the popularity of Anne Frank – as the archetypal symbol of the Holocaust – has grown within popular culture over the years. Every year over a million people visit a museum sited on Anne's hiding place in Amsterdam: Prinsengracht 263; but in 1960 when the house was first opened to the public it attracted a mere 9000 visitors. The universalistic Anne Frank of 1950s Hollywood has been replaced in the museum presentation in Holland today by a clear acknowledgement that she is the most famous Jewish victim of the Holocaust. Her Jewishness is now highlighted and so is her death in Bergen-Belsen concentration camp.

But it was the newly created state of Israel which brought the Jewish Holocaust to the centre of worldwide attention during the early 1960s when agents of the Israeli intelligence services dramatically captured Adolf Eichmann, one of the leading Nazi perpetrators, in May 1960. Eichmann's trial in 1961 was broadcast on radio and TV around the world. Before the high-profile Eichmann trial the Holocaust had played only a surprisingly marginal role in Israeli popular culture. By 1949, a total of 350,000 Holocaust survivors had settled in Israel. When a Holocaust Day was established in Israel in 1951 and a Holocaust Museum, known as Yad Vashem, opened in 1953, the emphasis was placed not on the misery of the Jewish experience in extermination camps, but on the heroism displayed by Jews during the Warsaw ghetto uprising. The Israeli Holocaust Day was placed on the anniversary of the Warsaw uprising, not the date when Auschwitz was liberated by the Red Army in January 1945. In fact, the Israeli government used the term *Shoah Vegurah* [destruction and heroism] to describe the Jewish experience in the Second World War rather than 'the Holocaust'.

What mass media coverage of the Eichmann trial did was to elevate the Holocaust into a unique Jewish experience. The testimony of Holocaust survivors offered a graphic expression of the awful atrocities they had witnessed, to a worldwide audience during the course of the trial. In her best-selling book *Eichmann in Jerusalem: A Report on the Banality of Evil*, Hannah Arendt summarised her trial reports, which had originally appeared in the *New Yorker* magazine. She depicted the frail and nondescript Eichmann not as a prime example of Hitler's master-race, nor as an ideologically driven Nazi anti-Semite, but instead as a rather dull, normal-looking 'desk killer' who had carried out the orders he was given by his Nazi superiors for the implementation of 'the Final Solution', and the many bureaucratic tasks associated with it, in a matter-of-fact manner which made his evil seem almost routine. Eichmann came across in the witness box as a sort of bank manager of death. He sorted out the paperwork that ensured millions of Jews were sent by train to death camps.[3] Eichmann explained how he was informed by Heydrich of the 'Final Solution' a few months after the start of the war with the Soviet Union, in June 1941, and he explained how the extermination camps were established and his role in administering the transport of million of victims to their deaths. The massive coverage of the Eichmann trial – during which he was found guilty and sentenced to death – ignited public interest in the Holocaust as never before. The Holocaust now assumed a central place within Israeli politics and society. Ben-Gurion, the Israeli Prime Minister, claimed that if the Jews the Nazis killed in the extermination camps had survived they would have moved to Israel. According to Norman Finkelstein in his controversial book *The Holocaust Industry*, the Holocaust has often been cynically manipulated by Israel and a pro-Israel lobby within the USA in order to bolster Israel's foreign policy.[4] He suggests the underlying aim of the Israeli government for many years after the war was to equate its isolated position in the Middle East with that of Jews during the Nazi era and to contend that the only safeguard against a further outbreak of genocidal anti-Semitism is a very strong Jewish state which requires protection in the Middle East.

But what really brought the Holocaust to the centre of modern public attention more than anything else were popular novels, films, TV dramas and documentaries. Filmmakers had resisted showing the real horror of the Nazi extermination camps for many years after the war. In the 1950s and 1960s there were hundreds of films made about the key battles involving British and US forces in the Second World War. But few of these films ever showed the brutality of the war in eastern Europe and the horrific and genocidal treatment of Russian Jews and Poles. Instead, British and Hollywood movies concentrated on the up-beat story of the defeat of the Nazis in western Europe. One of the most popular films of the 1960s, which was later repeated endlessly on TV, was *The Great Escape*, directed by John Sturges and released in 1963. The story – based loosely on fact – concentrates on a number of British and US soldiers imprisoned in a German prisoner of war camp who plan an audacious mass escape. The camp is run by a rather sympathetically portrayed Luftwaffe officer. All the prisoners look healthy and well dressed, and are treated strictly but fairly. They receive Red Cross parcels, drink coffee, eat chocolate, play football and live in well-kept barracks. They seem on pretty good terms with their Nazi guards, who they call 'The Goons'. There are no Jews and Gypsies in this camp. When a group of Soviet prisoners of war are seen briefly they are portrayed as garden labourers. This sanitised portrayal of a Nazi prisoner of war camp as a quite ordinary and non-violent place in which the prisoners are being well treated under the terms of the Geneva Convention offers the audience a rather distorted view of the brutality of the Nazi camp system. Towards the end of the film, when fifty of the prisoners break out and are hunted down and executed, it is made pretty clear this was done outside the camp by the SS. In another of the most popular films of the 1960s, *The Sound of Music*, directed by Robert Wise and released in 1965, the jolly von Trapp family are helped to escape from Nazi-occupied Austria by a rather naive trainee nun (Maria) played by the sugar-sweet English actress Julie Andrews, who becomes the children's nanny. The climax of *The Sound of Music* features a happy ending for one Austrian family who escape over the Swiss border after another beguiling musical performance. The film completely ignores the brutal anti-Semitism that went on in Austria during the Nazi era.

During the 1960s, the only major Hollywood film that actually focused on the psychological trauma of a Holocaust survivor was *The Pawnbroker*, released in 1964. It was based on the novel by Edward Lewis Wallant, directed by Sidney Lumet and starred the brooding Rod Steiger, who gave a brilliant and riveting performance as Sol Nazerman, a Jewish pawnbroker, living in a down-trodden area of New York, who had survived the Nazi death camps. Sol spends most of his lonely days behind the caged-wire counter of his shop in a deeply depressed mood. He constantly rejects the pleas of the pitiful souls and drug addicts and petty criminals who want 'just a little more money' for the goods they want to pawn in his shop. Behind Sol's detachment from the sorry plight of his poverty-stricken customers is a deeper emotional trauma. This comes to light in a series of flashbacks to the period when he was an inmate in a Nazi camp in which all the members of his family were killed. These memories explain why Sol is a mere shell of a man, who has memories from which he can never escape. Overall, the film offers a very powerful and honest presentation of the difficulties encountered by a Holocaust survivor.

It was during the less optimistic 1970s that the Holocaust came to the centre of popular culture. It was a US TV series called *The Holocaust*, broad-cast on NBC in four episodes between 16 and 20 April 1978, that led the way. It achieved an audience of 120 million viewers. When it was shown in West Germany in January 1979 it attracted an audience of 14 million. This popular series enjoyed success around the English-speaking world. It was directed by Marvin Chomsky, who had previously directed the popular 1977 TV series *Roots*, which had examined the slavery past of African-Americans.

It is no exaggeration to suggest that this TV drama was a seminal moment in emphasising the Holocaust in popular culture as a singular Jewish experience. After this series the murder of the Jews became univer-sally known as 'The Holocaust'. The series used a soap-opera style and portrayed the Holocaust through the experience of the fictional Weiss family of German Jews and a German family which includes a merciless SS officer. The series was filmed on location in Austria and Berlin. It depicts events such as the euthanasia programme, Kristallnacht, the creation of Jewish ghettos and the use of gas chambers. The series won Meryl Streep, one of the leading stars, many awards and propelled her to Hollywood stardom. When it came to light that NBC had made enormous profits from the adver-tisement breaks, it was suggested in some newspaper editorials that TV was simply cashing in on the murder of the Jews. The creators of the series responded by saying it had helped to raise awareness of the Jewish tragedy among young people. The TV series *The Holocaust* began a process which made the murder of the Jews under the Nazis a leading aspect of popular culture.

This process accelerated most noticeably from the 1980s to the present day. The most popular, critically acclaimed and controversial film on the Holocaust produced in the 1980s was unquestionably *Sophie's Choice*. It was based on the best-selling 1979 novel by William Styron, directed by Alan J. Pakula and released in 1982. It starred Meryl Streep, Kevin Kline and Peter MacNicol. Streep won the Academy award as best actress for her mesmeris-ing performance as Sophie Zawistowski, a beautiful but tragic Polish immi-grant who lives with her eccentric and tempestuous Jewish lover Nathan Landau (played by Kline) in a boarding house in Brooklyn, New York. This unlikely couple soon develop a very close friendship with a young writer called simply 'Stingo' (played by MacNicol), who comes from the American South and lives in an apartment upstairs. Stingo is the film's narrator in a storytelling style reminiscent of the novels of Joseph Conrad. The action is contained within the summer of 1947. It uses – like *The Pawbroker* – frequent flashbacks, through Sophie's eyes, which depict her experiences in the city of Krakow in Poland and at the infamous Auschwitz extermination camp. Sophie is deeply troubled by her wartime experience. We soon learn that

Nathan began his relationship with Sophie after he saw her collapse in a near-starved condition in a local library. It is also apparent that Nathan is a jealous, flamboyant, heavy-drinking, violent and mentally unstable Jewish man who is obsessed by the Holocaust. At times Nathan is horribly cruel, vindictive and violent towards Sophie, but he just as quickly apologises profusely for his erratic behaviour and then becomes a sweet and loving partner.

Sophie claims that she was rescued from Auschwitz and then taken to a refugee camp in Sweden before emigrating to America. But Stingo meets someone who knew Sophie's father in Poland and he soon discovers that Sophie is a Polish Catholic. Before the German occupation Sophie's father was a university professor, who was killed by the Nazis as one of the Polish intelligentsia in spite of the fact he was deeply anti-Semitic and had written books and articles that advocated 'extermination' as the best solution to deal with the 'Jewish problem'. We also discover that Sophie – who had two children – was sent to Auschwitz, not as a racial enemy of the Nazis, but as a petty criminal who had stolen cans of tinned meat. Upon arrival at Auschwitz, Sophie is allowed to choose to save one of her children from the gas chamber because the a Nazi guard thinks she looks beautiful and Aryan. After pleading with the guard to let her keep both her children she finally makes her 'choice' and saves her son. In the camp Sophie is given the post of nanny to the children of the camp commandant and she lives in the basement of his opulent home. When she looks out of the window at life in Auschwitz it seems very orderly and peaceful. The camp commandant allows Sophie's son to be placed in the SS *Lebensborn* programme. But when Sophie is caught stealing a radio from the bedroom of the commandant's daughter she is put back in the camps. She never finds out what happened to her son.

Back in the present of this complex tale, Sophie and Nathan get married. But it is soon revealed that Nathan is actually a schizophrenic who has been living a fantasy life for years and avoiding psychiatric treatment. When Nathan goes into another of his drunken and violent rages Sophie decides to run off with Stingo to a hotel and they sleep together. Stingo expresses his love for Sophie but during a long conversation she reveals her secret: the impossible choice she was forced to make by the Nazi guard at Auschwitz. The next morning, when Stingo awakes, Sophie has gone leaving a note which says she thinks Stingo is a lovely man, but that she must go back to Nathan. In a final poignant and deeply emotional scene, Stingo returns to the house where Nathan and Sophie live and he goes to their room, where he discovers them both lying dead in a loving embrace, having committed suicide together in order to escape their mutual mental hell.

Sophie's Choice is not at all an uplifting film with a happy ending. It is a story of guilt, suffering, despair and a 'survivor's guilt' in the character of Sophie, and a tale of the terrible effects of schizophrenia on a brilliant mind in the character of Nathan. The film directly challenges Jewish ownership of the Holocaust by making a Polish Catholic the key victim and depicts her Jewish partner as a complex, violent and mentally unstable character. The writer of *Sophie's Choice*, William Styron, justified his Gentile Holocaust survivor in the following way: 'Although she [Sophie] was not Jewish, she had suffered as much as any Jew who had survived the same afflictions, and – as I think will be made plain – had in certain profound ways suffered more than most.[5] *Sophie's Choice* attempts to suggest the Jewish experience was just one aspect of Nazi genocide, which has been elevated above all others. According to Styron, the Jews were not the primary victims of Nazi genocide, which had millions of targets.

This view of the Holocaust, although frequently discussed in historical debates, was soon challenged in the most important TV documentary on the Nazi murder of the Jews of the 1980s: *Shoah*, a nine-hour epic, directed by Claude Lanzmann. It was first shown in Israel and the USA in 1985, but later broadcast around the world. *Shoah* consists of a number of interviews with people involved in the Holocaust. It also shows many of the sites of the extermination camps, most notably, Chełmno, Treblinka and Auschwitz-Birkenau. The interviews are divided into three categories: survivors, bystanders and perpetrators. Every survivor in the film is Jewish and offers a detailed description of what they witnessed. Many react emotionally to the painful memories. One interviewee breaks down when recalling hearing prisoners breaking into song while being forced into a gas chamber. No one in the film gives a detailed explanation of why they survived. The bystanders are depicted as those who witnessed the events of the Holocaust without being part of it. All the bystanders interviewed are Polish. They offer first-hand accounts of conditions in the Warsaw ghetto, of the gas vans, and recall how little anyone knew about the magnitude of what was happening. The perpetrators interviewed are all German. They describe in some detail the detached implementation of the Final Solution by Nazi officials. Most express ignorance about what they thought was going on, but Lanzmann constantly challenges their assertions with probing questions. Overall, *Shoah* depicts the Holocaust as a singular Jewish experience and it makes very little reference to the other victims of Nazi genocide. Lanzmann's film reveals the utter hopelessness of Jews during the Holocaust. It ends with the poignant words of Simchah Rotem, a survivor of the Warsaw ghetto, who now lives in Israel: 'I'm the last Jew. I'll wait for the morning, and for the Germans.'[6] *Shoah* did arouse some criticism. Many of the Poles who were interviewed later claimed that Lanzmann had edited the documentary to give the impression they willingly collaborated with the Nazis and they alleged he removed from the documentary views that ran contrary to this interpretation.

The major TV drama *War and Remembrance*, which first appeared on the ABC network in the USA in 1988, broke new ground with its graphic visual depiction of the Holocaust. The series – which ran for thirty hours – was based on Herman Wouk's best-selling 1978 novel of the same name, which was a follow-up to his 1971 novel *The Winds of War*, which was made into a TV mini-series in 1983. The two TV adaptations of Wouk's novels focus on a mixture of real and fictional characters. All are connected by family ties and friendship to the main character, a US naval officer Victor 'Pug' Henry (played by Robert Mitchum). The first series concentrates on the period from March 1939 to the Japanese attack on Pearl Harbor in 1941. The second takes up the story in December 1941 and ends on 6 August 1945 with the US atom bomb attacks on the Japanese cities of Hiroshima and Nagasaki. The two major themes in the series are the US war against Japan, and the Holocaust, as seen through the eyes of three members of the Jewish Jastrow family: Aaron (John Gielgud), who is captured by Nazis and sent to the Theresienstadt concentration camp where he dies; Berel (Topol), Aaron's cousin, who is captured with the Red Army in 1941 and sent to Auschwitz but escapes to take part in Jewish resistance; and the beautiful Natalie Henry (Jane Seymour), who becomes a member of the Zionist underground and is sent to Auschwitz but survives. The former concentration camp survivor Branko Lustig was the production designer on the series. The scenes related to the Holocaust include: a visit by Heinrich Himmler to Auschwitz in May 1942, which shows the arrival of Jewish victims in trains, and all the stages to their death in the gas chambers, including the disposal of their bodies in the crematoria; the massacre of Jews at Babi Yar in September 1941; and a mass slaughter of Jews and Czechs outside Prague by machine-gun fire. *War and Remembrance* once more highlights the singularity of the Jewish experience in the Holocaust. It displays the brutality of life in the extermination camps and shows the activities of the Einsatzgruppen in the Soviet Union to a mass worldwide TV audience, in a popular soap-opera format, for the first time.

By the early 1990s the Holocaust had become a popular phenomenon of truly global significance. In the process there had occurred what has been called by some historians as 'The Americanisation of the Holocaust', whereby the Holocaust is viewed as an integral part of US History.[7] Tim Cole suggests there is no greater example of the 'Americanisation' of the Holocaust than the Hollywood film *Schindler's List*, released in 1993 and directed by Steven Spielberg, who had previously produced the major box office hits *Jaws* and *ET*. Not surprisingly, Spielberg's decision to tackle the Holocaust proved incredibly successful and very controversial. *Schindler's List* was adapted from Thomas Keneally's 1982 Booker Prize winning novel *Schindler's Ark* but the title was altered to avoid a potentially offensive biblical reference.

The film tells the story of a German businessman, Oskar Schindler (played by Irish actor Liam Neeson), who in 1939 is just 31 years of age when he makes the short journey from Zwittau in the Sudeten-German region of Czechoslovakia to Krakow in Poland in an attempt to cash in on the German occupation. As a loyal Nazi Party member Schindler is well placed to acquire businesses seized from their Jewish owners. At first Schindler's only aim is to make money and enjoy the good life. As the Nazi persecution of the Jews in Poland escalates, Schindler begins to find Nazi violence extremely frightening. He suddenly decides to save Jews from death by employing them in his factory. By means of a deft process of bribery – and the subtle lobbying of Nazi officials – Schindler turned his factory into a sanctuary which saved over 1000 Jews from the gas chambers.

Spielberg filmed the story entirely on location in Krakow and Kazimerz in Poland using hand-held cameras, in stark black and white. This gives the film the feel of a contemporary documentary. Scenes of graphic Nazi violence in the movie are much less extensive than in the TV series *War and Remembrance*. In one memorable scene – which shows the liquidation of the Jewish ghetto in Krakow – Schindler suddenly sees a little girl, dressed in a bright red coat, who is shown in colour against a black and white background as she wanders through the streets alone while people are shot and killed all around her. From the moment this little girl appears, Schindler's eyes are transfixed upon her and he turns from a cold-hearted businessman concerned only with exploiting Jews for profit into a totally different person. When Schindler later sees the little girl's corpse lying dead on a hand-cart full of bodies he makes a further transformation into a sort of angel of mercy whose primary aim is to save the lives of his Jewish workers.

Before Schindler manages to move Jews to the relative safety of his factory they are incarcerated in a concentration camp in Płaszów run by SS Hauptstürmführer Amon Göth, a brutal SS officer played quite brilliantly by the English actor Ralph Fiennes, who is charged with destroying the Krakow ghetto and building a forced-labour camp nearby. In a chillingly sadistic scene, Göth is seen shooting camp inmates with a rifle from the balcony of his office, seemingly just for fun. In another scene, Schindler's female Jews, with whom the audience now firmly identifies, are seen undressing and being herded into a shower room in Auschwitz. It looks like a gas chamber and we expect they are about to be killed, but water flows from the shower, not Zyklon B. Spielberg directs the scene in a classic Hollywood cliff-hanger style, reminiscent of Alfred Hitchcock's famous shower scene in the thriller *Psycho*. But the audience is extremely relieved when water flows out of the shower and the Jewish women survive and are then transported to his factory. The film ends – as so many of Spielberg films do – in a happy and sentimental way. The Jews Schindler has saved are liberated by the Red Army and we finally see the elderly survivors walking hand-in-hand – in full colour for the first time – towards the present-day grave of Schindler in a Catholic graveyard in Israel.

Schindler's List, which won seven Academy awards, is considered Spielberg's greatest work. It is certainly the most popular and influential Holocaust film of all time. Frank Marchel has suggested that *Schlinder's List* has become 'the most important source of historical information affecting popular perceptions of the Holocaust'.[8] Spielberg took no fee from the film, and some of the profits from the movie financed the Survivors of the Shoah Visual History Foundation, which provides an archive of the filmed testimony of Holocaust survivors. The film has been described as one that is a life-affirming celebration of the indestructible spirit of the Holocaust survivor. It has contributed greatly to the modern-day fascination with the Holocaust. It once more illustrated how interpreting the past through the popular media is now a much more popular pastime than reading erudite works of historical scholarship.

But the film has come in for enormous criticism from many Holocaust historians not because it is poor but because it is so well filmed, so moving and so memorable. *Schindler's List* presents what has been called a 'Hollywood Holocaust', which casts Schindler as the flawed but ultimately redeemed Hollywood hero, and Amon Göth as the cruel and sadistic camp commandant – the archetypal Hollywood 'bad guy'; and most of the Jews are depicted as passive 'survivors'. One of the major problems with *Schindler's List* for a historian is that it tampers with the historical events in order to make the story acceptable to a popular audience. Unlike a historian, who would attempt to show the motivations of all the participants, Spielberg offers no really credible explanation about the racial views of Göth nor does he explain why Nazi ideology viewed the Jews as so dangerous that they needed to be 'exterminated'. Göth – although played brilliantly by Fiennes – emerges as a one-dimensional evil psychopath who kills for pleasure. He is hardly representative of the middle-ranking technocrats in the SS who were at the heart of the Nazi killing machine and feature so heavily within schol-arly debates among historians.

The central figure in the film from beginning to end is Oskar Schindler. He was a member of the Nazi Party, a womaniser and a war profiteer who finally decided to mend his ways. The very last scene in the film shows Schindler making an uplifting and emotionally charged speech to the Jews in his factory. In reality, this speech never took place, as Schindler was making his escape from the camp in a fast car with his wife and mistress and a suitcase full of money, as the Soviet Red Army approached. The film suggests an individual can make a difference. But individuals counted for nothing in the Nazi system and its powerless Jewish victims had little or no chance of resisting or surviving. The noted historian of the Holocaust Raul Hilberg has argued 'there is nothing to be taken from the Holocaust that imbues anyone with hope or the thought of redemption'.[9]

In the aftermath of *Schlinder's List* there has developed a veritable 'Holocaust industry' of novels, poems, documentaries, comedies, pop songs, films, websites, museums, university courses, books, and – in 1996 – even a rather sick Holocaust cookbook. Even Superman has travelled back in time to witness the horrors of the Holocaust and says 'I'm not one to interfere with the governments of the world, but I just can't turn a blind eye and let these fascist bullies exterminate everyone they don't like.'[10]

One important by-product of the 'Holocaust industry' is the rapid growth of a sort of Holocaust tourist trail. Every year more people visit Holocaust museums than actually died during the 'Final Solution'. The death camp at Auschwitz, near the Polish town of Krakow, is visited by over 500,000 visitors every year. Most visitors are aged forty and under. All Polish schoolchildren have to visit Auschwitz as part of the school history curriculum. Above the entrance gates are the words *Arbeit macht frei* ('Work sets you free'), which was the norm at all Nazi concentration camps. But the first words you notice as you enter are 'Those who forget the past are condemned to repeat it.' As was explained in the previous chapter, Auschwitz was one of six extermination camps in Poland that primarily killed Jews. But it has come to be seen in the popular mind as the place where all the Jews died. Within the museum are simple displays of those who came to the camp. There are huge quantities of luggage, vast piles of shoes, human hair, glasses, hairbrushes, and empty Zyklon B canisters. One display shows a series of mug shots of prisoners dressed in their distinctive striped uniforms. Finally, you enter the gas chambers and then see the crematorium ovens.

Before the 1960s 'Auschwitz' was a much less well known camp than the German concentration camps at Dachau, Buchenwald and Bergen-Belsen, which were not death camps associated with the 'Final Solution', but were featured in newsreels that were shown around the world at the end of the war. In 1947, the Polish government decided to make Auschwitz a memorial site of the 'Martyrdom of the Polish nation and other nations'. The Poles had suffered greatly under the Nazis and were not keen to elevate the killing of Jews above their own suffering. Auschwitz was a symbol in Poland of the dangers of fascist aggression to all the people of eastern Europe.

When the museum first opened, visitors were allowed to visit Auschwitz I, where the Poles, Soviet prisoners of war and other Nazi racial enemies were killed, but not Auschwitz II, where most of the Jews perished. Auschwitz II was only opened to the public in the 1960s. The camps at Belsen, Buchenwald and Dachau were also opened to the public after the war but they too emphasised Nazi mass murder on a wide scale and did not concentrate in the singular Jewish aspect of Nazi genocide. Auschwitz is nowadays viewed as the symbolic centre of Holocaust remembrance and of the singularity of the Jewish experience under Nazi rule. In 1979, Auschwitz became a World Heritage site. The actual gas chambers at Auschwitz were reconstructed for the museum in 1948 because the Red Army had destroyed the originals in 1945. A great deal of what tourists now see at Auschwitz is a post-war Polish reproduction of the Nazi original.

Another of the leading Holocaust museums is the Holocaust exhibition in Israel known as Yad Vashem. The major task of this museum, located in Jerusalem, is to perpetuate the memory and lessons of the Holocaust for future generations. It was established in 1953 as 'The Memorial Authority for the Holocaust and Heroism', by an act of the Knesset (Israel's parliament), to commemorate the six million Jews murdered by the Nazis and their collaborators from 1933 to 1945. A crypt directly in front of the memorial contains the ashes of actual Holocaust victims. Approximately 1.5 million children were killed in the Holocaust and they are specially remembered in a poignant Children's Memorial. At Yad Vashem the heroic resistance of Jews in the Warsaw ghetto uprising was initially given great prominence while Auschwitz was viewed as a symbol of destruction and death. The 'Memorial to the Deportees' is an original railway cattle-truck that was used to transport thousands of Jews to the death camps. The stories of the survivors are also given great prominence in the museum. On 15 March 2005 a new Holocaust History Museum was opened on the site. The site also houses the largest historical archive on the Holocaust in the world. The constant theme running through Yad Vashem is an up-beat one of defiance and redemption. It appears to say Hitler may have attempted the 'Final Solution' but he failed. Jewry has survived and Nazism is universally discredited.

It is perfectly natural that Auschwitz and Yad Vashem should exist. After all, Auschwitz was a major site of the Holocaust in Poland and as the Jews were the major victims of Nazi mass murder it is not surprising for Israel to be the location of a major Holocaust museum. But, the place where the majority of Holocaust museums are located is in the USA. From the mid-1980s onwards Holocaust museums opened all over the USA, most notably in Los Angeles, New York, Tampa Bay, Houston and Dallas. The best known is the United States Holocaust Memorial Museum in Washington DC, which is visited by over two million visitors each year. This museum gets more visitors than Graceland, the home of Elvis Presley, America's most famous global pop star. In the 1970s President Jimmy Carter had suggested that because the USA had ignored the Nazi threat in the 1930s it had a modern-day duty to remember the importance of the Holocaust. The Washington Museum gives due emphasis to US indifference to the fate of the Jews during the 1930s. But the major focus is the horror of the death camps. The relics of those who died are displayed extensively. Overall, the Washington Holocaust Museum provides an effective narrative of a horrific period of history, and the photographs and the presentation, as with US films on the Holocaust, are impressive. The museum display ends with the up-beat view that Nazism was ultimately defeated.

In 2001, the Jewish Museum in Berlin was opened to the public and it has become one of the city's leading tourist attractions. A Jewish Museum was originally opened in 1933, but the Gestapo closed it down in 1938. Grim high-rise flats surround the museum, located in the city's run-down but now trendy Kreuzberg area. Set against this bleak urban landscape, the Jewish Museum looks like an alien spaceship which has just landed. What separates this Berlin museum from all the others is the unusual building that houses the exhibition. It was designed by the brilliant Jewish architect Daniel Liberskind. The building creates spaces which tell the story of the Jews in Germany from Roman times to the present day, through a multi-media presentation. It shows Jewish history as a story of achievement, persecution, creativity, survival and regeneration. The section on the Holocaust concentrates less on the horrors of the death camps, but more on Jewish responses. Looked at in this way, the Holocaust is presented as one aspect, but not the whole, of Jewish history.

Although the curators have stressed that the Jewish Museum is not a Holocaust museum, those parts of the building which are linked to the Holocaust are a major attraction for visitors. The zinc-panelled exterior of the building looks like a zigzag puzzle with irregular slashes of glass windows. From above, it can be seen that it is a broken Star of David. Visitors enter the main building up a large staircase which is intentionally tiring to climb so as to give the visitor the feeling of challenge and hardship associated with Jewish history. The building is also full of a series of what Liberskind calls 'empty voids' which commemorate the destruction of Jewish life and culture, which has formed such an important part of Jewish history.

The main building contains the Holocaust Tower, which is an empty space that offers each visitor the chance to reflect on the Nazi Holocaust, but in this dark space thoughts naturally move to the shower rooms in the extermination camps. The Axis of Exile leads outside the building to a courtyard of large concrete columns, known as the 'Garden of Exile', which have been deliberately tilted, leaving every visitor feeling quite off-balance and disorientated. Another remarkable feature is called the 'Memory Void', filled with 10,000 iron faces which visitors are permitted to walk upon, thus creating a loud noise which is filled with deep meaning. It is these incredibly inventive architectural ideas that give the museum such a profound interpretation of the fate of the Jews, not just in the Holocaust but throughout history. Indeed, by presenting the whole of Jewish history this museum explains how the Holocaust happened, how prejudice against the Jews was so ill-informed, and it ends by showing that the Jews have survived this nightmare in their history.

As we have seen, in popular culture the Holocaust began as something that was a peripheral matter, but over the years it has risen to become a dominant event. It is now a staple part of popular novels, films and museums. The desire to view the Holocaust as a universal history lesson that must not be forgotten has been taken up most vigorously by Israel, but much more by the USA, and the elevation of the destruction of the Jews above all other victims of Nazi genocide can, as Tim Cole argues, be attributed largely to US influence. In fact, the 'Americanisation' of the Holocaust has come under some criticism in Israel. Tom Segev, a leading Israeli journalist, has claimed that American Jews have 'stolen the Shoah'.[11] The USA has produced most of the most popular aspects of the Holocaust and, through the dominance of Hollywood over the popular consciousness, is likely to continue to do so.

It could be said that by keeping the Holocaust at the forefront of popular consciousness the 'Americanisation' of Nazi mass murder is helping to ensure it never happens again. Yet a recent poll of schoolchildren in the USA revealed that 53 per cent of American high school children could not even define what the Holocaust was. It seems Americans, who seem to care most about keeping the memory of the Holocaust alive, appear to have little historical knowledge or understanding of it. There is even a danger that because the history of the Holocaust, produced by historians, is actually now at the margins of popular consciousness, it is possible for Holocaust deniers to suggest the Holocaust is just another US conspiracy, to be ranked alongside the conspiracy theories surrounding the death of John F. Kennedy, the Moon Landing and 9/11. Tim Cole contends that 'Shoah business may actually produce denial' because it is only since the period when it became a major popular event that it was 'deemed worth denying'.[12]

These modern-day 'Holocaust deniers' suggest the Nazi regime did not use gas chambers to murder Jews. Some claim those facilities described as 'gas chambers' by most historians were delousing units, designed to contain the spread of contagious diseases among inmates of all the concentration camps. As for the crematoria ovens, visible in most camps, the Holocaust deniers claim they were not large enough to kill millions of people and were used for the 'innocent' purpose of cremating those who died from disease or natural causes. Most controversially of all, Holocaust deniers suggest that Adolf Hitler never even issued any order to kill Europe's Jews and that he did not know that such a policy was even being carried out.[13]

Deborah Lipstadt, in a detailed examination of the modern phenomenon of Holocaust denial, shows the first supporters of this idea were the Nazis themselves as they attempted to downgrade the extent of their crimes in war trials. An American historian, Harry Elmer Barnes, argued – shortly after the Second World War – that the extent of Nazi genocide was exaggerated by Allied propaganda. According to Lipstadt, such views have subsequently only been advanced by extreme right-wing writers and neo-Nazi groups. One of the most well known Holocaust deniers was the American David Hoggan, who wrote *Der erzwungene Krieg* (*The Forced War*), published in 1961, and his even more controversial *The Myth of the Six Million*, which came out in 1969. During the 1970s, Arthur Butz's *The Hoax of the Twentieth Century* outlined what he called a 'case against the presumed extermination of European Jewry' and David Irving, a British historian, produced *Hitler's War*, which claimed Hitler had no knowledge of the Holocaust.[14] In 1979, Willis Carto set up the august-sounding 'Institute of Historical Review' (IHR) with the aim of challenging the 'myth of the Holocaust'. The IHR attempted, without much success, to assert it was not neo-Nazi or anti-Semitic. In recent times the IHR has become a much more strident neo-Nazi discussion forum and claims 'it does not deny the Holocaust', but denies 'many elements of the mainstream view of the Holocaust'.[15]

From the 1980s onwards many governments have attempted to deal harshly with those who continue to publicly deny the Holocaust. The Canadian authorities convicted James Keegstra, a history teacher in a high school, of 'Holocaust denial' in 1984 because he handed out course material to students which reportedly 'denied the Holocaust'. But the charge was later overturned in the appeal court because it was claimed his view was part of the 'freedom of expression' granted to all academics. A more notorious case involved a book called *Did Six Million Really Die?* by Richard Harwood (pseudonym for Richard Verrall, a British 'neo-Nazi'). In 1985, the Canadian publisher of this book, Ernst Zundel, was sentenced to fifteen months in prison for 'publishing material denying the Holocaust'. Once again, a

Canadian appeal court overturned his conviction after many people had claimed he had the right to publish even very controversial views concerning the Holocaust.

The most notorious court case involving a Holocaust denier was a libel case which David Irving brought against Deborah Lipstadt, an American Jewish writer, and Penguin Books, which had published her book on Holocaust denial in 1994. Lipstadt had claimed that David Irving had constantly misinterpreted evidence to support his views on Hitler and the Holocaust. Irving had long been a controversial figure. He had never held an academic post as a historian and was never considered a mainstream historian and yet his books on Hitler and Nazi Germany had sold in large numbers. He always denied he was a Nazi 'sympathiser' but he was constantly giving lectures to far-right groups, and newspapers reported that he associated with many prominent figures within them. In one book he claimed that Hitler had not ordered any organised killing of the Jews and was not informed of any Jewish loss of life until 1943 when he was told of it by Himmler.

When the libel trial began in January 2000, Irving seemed pretty confident of victory. But Lipstadt was determined to defend her view that Irving was a 'Holocaust denier'. She hired Anthony Julius, the well-known British lawyer, to defend her on the libel charges. A number of eminent independent historical experts on the Holocaust and German history gave evidence at the trial, including Professor Richard Evans, Professor Peter Longerich, and Professor Christopher Browning. Irving decided to conduct his own defence. Richard Evans spent two years painstakingly looking at the work of Irving and then compared the evidence he presented with the actual documents from the German archives. Evans showed that Irving had misrepresented evidence on a monumental scale in all of his books. The judge, Charles Gray, found in favour of Lipstadt and pointed out in his judgement Irving's support for neo-Nazi movements in Germany and the USA, and he added that Irving's work aimed to attack the Jewish 'race' and people rather than act as a legitimate questioning of the evidence for the Holocaust.

In a very revealing book, which explains his role in the case, Richard Evans makes clear that the trial verdict was dependent upon the credibility of the historical evidence for the Holocaust. What really brought Irving down was his omission of incontrovertible evidence for the mass killing of Jews and his cavalier treatment of the original sources.[16] What Evans showed is that professionalism and intellectual integrity must govern the handling of historical evidence and there must be eternal vigilance to ensure that expediency does not destroy credible historical insight and judgement. In 2006, Irving pleaded guilty to Holocaust denial in Austria – where it is a criminal offence – and he was sentenced to a prison term. At his Austrian trial Irving admitted: 'The Nazis did murder millions of Jews,' and he said he could no longer deny Hitler knew about the Holocaust. Lipstadt claimed that she was not happy that Irving had gone to prison because 'censorship wins' and 'the best way of fighting Holocaust deniers is with the truth'.[17]

More recently, the denial of the Holocaust has grown in some Muslim countries – especially in the Middle East. In December 2005, Mahmoud Ahmadinejad, the Iranian President, said the Holocaust was a 'fairy tale' used to protect Israel. On 11 December 2006, in Tehran, he opened an international conference to review the historiography of the Holocaust. The participants at the conference included David Duke, the Ku Klux Klan leader, and Frederick Toben, an Australian Holocaust denier who was jailed in Germany in 1999 for casting doubt on the extermination of the Jews. Duke told the conference, 'In Europe, you can freely question, ridicule and deny Jesus Christ. The same is true of the Prophet Mohammed and nothing will happen to you. But offer a single question on the smallest part of the Holocaust and you face prison.' Also present were members of a group called 'Jews against Zionism', which rejects the creation of Israel on the grounds it violates Jewish law.[18]

Holocaust denial is now illegal in a number of countries, including Austria, Belgium, the Czech Republic, France, Germany, Spain, Israel, Lithuania, Romania, Poland, Slovakia and Switzerland. Many prominent figures have recently spoken out against it. In 2006, Kofi Annan, the United Nations General-Secretary, said Holocaust denial was 'the work of bigots'. Elie Wiesel, a famous Holocaust survivor, called the Holocaust 'the most documented tragedy in recorded history'. Never before has a tragedy elicited so much witness from the killers, from the victims and from the bystanders. Unfortunately, given the open nature of the worldwide web and the modern fascination with far-fetched conspiracy theories, the denial of the Holocaust is likely to continue even though the evidence from the historical archives leaves absolutely no doubt that the Holocaust most certainly did occur and close to six million Jews really did die.

6

The Historical Debate on the Holocaust

Historians, psychologists, sociologists, post-modernists, literary critics and philosophers have all attempted to explain the most irrational act of modern Western civilisation. The cherished Western concepts of progress and civilisation were called into question by what one historian called 'the German catastrophe'. Wilhelm Reich blamed the Holocaust on the obedience of the German people to the 'Mass psychology of Fascism', while Hannah Arendt blamed Nazi genocide on a 'totalitarian system in which Adolf Hitler could say "the individual must perish anyway, all that matters is the state"'. Some writers have suggested that the de-humanising effects of European imperialism against so-called 'primitive' people in Africa and Asia during the late nineteenth century made racial-superiority, biological and eugenic theories popular, and these 'master race' views became embedded within Nazi ideology. Enzo Traverso has described Auschwitz as an 'authentic product of Western civilisation'. The end product of Nazi genocide was not a product for sale in the marketplace but death. This would seem to suggest it was modern technology which made death possible on an industrial scale.

The best known supporter of the view that a Holocaust on the scale carried out by the Nazis could only have happened in a modern industrial society is Zygmunt Baumann, a Polish-born Jewish sociologist, who has spent most of his academic life in Britain. In *The Holocaust and Modernity*, published in 1989, Baumann explained how the mass murder of the Jews was a natural consequence of the de-humanising influence of a modern, advanced society, bewitched by the powers of new technology and efficient bureaucratic administration. The middle-ranking Nazi bureaucrats in neat and tidy modern offices administered the killing. Highly trained chemists and doctors worked out how much gas was needed to kill a set number of victims. A modern railway system transported the victims to the death camps. Architects, trained in top universities, designed the camps and the crematoria. The possessions of the victims were recycled for profit by modern industrial companies. In sum, the implementation of the 'Final Solution' by the German authorities was an immensely efficient operation. The Nazi regime judged its success not in monetary profits as in a modern industrial enterprise but in numbers killed. Once the German government gave the go-ahead to the mass killing, modern ideals of professionalism and micro-management took over. The war trials of many of the Nazi perpetrators not only revealed a great degree of job satisfaction in what they were doing but also showed how they felt their efficient carrying out of the genocide policy against the Jews might help their promotion prospects. In Baumann's view, the Holocaust arrived

> in a factory-produced vehicle, wielding weapons only the most advanced science could supply, and following an itinerary designed by scientific organisation. Modern civilisation was not the Holocaust's sufficient condition; it was, however, most certainly its necessary condition. Without it, the Holocaust would have been unthinkable. It was the rational world of modern civilisation that made the Holocaust thinkable.[1]

But Baumann's work has been criticised for ignoring the importance of ideology in promoting genocide and for failing to explain why most of the primary examples of modern genocide have not used modern industrial techniques and occurred in less technologically advanced societies. It has also been suggested that Hitler's racial ideas were developed and pursued more or less independently from pure economic motives.[2]

Over sixty years after news of the horrors of the extermination camps reached the outside world, leading historians remain in fundamental disagreement on most of the key issues surrounding the Holocaust. The historical debate has produced a huge amount of controversy and has been infused with passion, recriminations and often highly moralistic judgements. The modern debate on the Holocaust only really began in earnest from the early 1960s onwards. In the beginning the debate concentrated on trying to explain the origins of the Holocaust and revolved around two key questions: Did Hitler have a 'master plan' for the Holocaust? (known as the 'intentionalist' view), or: Did the Holocaust emerge incrementally from within the German bureaucracy? (the 'functionalist' interpretation).[3] Neither side disputed the reality of the Holocaust and both acknowledged the strength and importance of Hitler's virulent anti-Semitism and his importance in driving the process which led to the mass murder of the Jews.

One of the most famous supporters of the intentionalist view of a clear and straight path to Auschwitz is Lucy Dawidowicz, who was born in New York City in 1915, the child of secular Jewish parents. Dawidowicz, who died in 1990, did not attend a synagogue until 1938. In 1948, after working in Germany at various displaced persons' camps, she married a Polish Jew, Syzmon Dawidowicz. During the 1950s Lucy Dawidowicz was a passionate Zionist and a talented leading writer on the *New York Times*. In her writings on the Holocaust, Dawidowicz argued that Hitler had a 'grand design' for the destruction of the Jews which dated back to 1918 when he first heard news of the Armistice. Everything Hitler did and said from that point onwards aimed to avenge the German defeat and to punish those he held the most responsible: the Jews. To support this interpretation Dawidowicz cited many anti-Semitic passages from Hitler's speeches and writings in order to explain the consistency of his views on the 'Jewish Question'. She portrayed Hitler's Germany as a well-oiled totalitarian regime which carried out Hitler's master plan for the destruction of the Jews from beginning to end.[4] Dawidowicz stuck doggedly to this 'straight path to Auschwitz' thesis all her life; but her extreme intentionalist interpretation has been systematically challenged. There is no problem showing a basic consistency in Hitler's deep hatred of the Jews from the beginning to the very end of his political career. But to view a highly complex policy development such as the Holocaust as the linear result of the earlier declared intentions of a single individual is to beg serious questions about a wide range of factors and contingencies that affected the actual implementation of anti-Semitic policy in the Third Reich. Many of Hitler's speeches which Dawidowicz quotes in her work make little reference to 'killing' or 'exterminating' all the Jews even in Germany – let alone all of Europe.

The question of whether anti-Semitism was the most virulent hatred Hitler harboured has also been disputed. Arno Mayer claimed the major chosen victims for mass 'extermination' were not the Jews, but communists and the state most associated with communism: the Soviet Union. Adolf Hitler was, more than anything else, a fervent anti-communist. In 1941, he ordered the Holocaust as a gesture of despair, after it became clear that his plan to destroy communism in the Soviet Union was doomed to failure. According to Mayer, without the invasion of the Soviet Union and the lawless actions committed against the Russian people which accompanied it, the essential preconditions for the escalation towards a Final Solution of the Jewish Question would probably not have taken place. Many historians have suggested that Mayer plays up anti-communism at the expense of anti-Semitism and fails to appreciate that Hitler's conception of 'Marxism' and 'Soviet Bolshevism' viewed both as essential parts of the 'Jewish world conspiracy'. Hence, a crucial means of weakening perceived Jewish power in the world was to destroy the 'Jewish' Soviet regime.[5]

Even so, no serious historian would today support the view that Hitler planned the Holocaust before the Second World War. But the intentionalist view does survive if in a somewhat radically modified form. Klaus Hildebrand, a German historian, maintains that Hitler was the central driving force behind the 'Final Solution', and he suggests that competing bureaucracies within the regime enabled Hitler to sustain a dominant role over the Third Reich.[6] Richard Breitman has recently argued that Hitler had decided upon the Holocaust by the late 1930s and certainly no later than the summer of 1941. According to Breitman, Hitler's much quoted speech on 30 January 1939 when he stated that if Jews started another world war it would result in 'the annihilation of the entire Jewish race in Europe' was a real promise and not an idle threat.[7]

On the other side of this debate are the more prominent and influential structuralist (or functionalist) historians who insist the Holocaust was not part of Hitler's grand plan. One of the first notable advocates of this position was Karl Schleunes, who argued that there was a *Twisted Road to Auschwitz* which developed in incremental stages.[8] It was accepted by Hitler that the Jews had no place in the long-term future of Germany. But other options to deal with the 'Jewish Question', such as emigration, deportation and forced resettlement, were all attempted before Hitler finally went ahead with the policy of genocide. Schleunes suggested there was no 'grand design' to exterminate the Jews before 1939. A great deal of research by structuralists, on the Third Reich, has confirmed the complexity of the regime's political and administrative structure and has revealed how 'top down' linear bureaucratic decision making was at best difficult and possibly infeasible within Nazi Germany. Attempting to locate Hitler's role within the process of genocide is not straightforward. It has been shown that Nazi Germany was a maze of competing agencies which were often in competition with each other. This polycratic system of government in which there was a multidimensional power structure made central policy implementation at the local level extremely difficult and allowed for great diversity in how policies derived from the centre were actually carried out. The progressive demise of a collective centralised government during the 1930s led to a mushrooming of different departments and ministries who worked largely independently of each other. According to Ian Kershaw the overall structure was reduced 'to a shambles of shifting power-bases and warring factions – but a shambles which unleashed immense energy and contained its own inbuilt destructive momentum'.[9]

The functionalist view was most extensively advanced in the pioneering work of two West German historians: Martin Broszat and Hans Mommsen. According to Broszat, it was internal rivalry between competing groups – not Hitler – that provided the real driving force behind the genocidal policies adopted by the regime. Mommsen called Hitler a 'weak dictator' who was unwilling to take decisions and constantly arbitrating over domestic power struggles within the 'chaotic' Nazi system, which allowed the normal institutions of the old conservative German state to operate alongside the new radical institutions of the Nazi Party. Broszat was an expert on the domestic policies of the Nazi state, but in a deeply influential and much debated essay entitled 'Hitler and the Genesis of the Final Solution', published in 1977, he argued there was never any written Hitler order for the Holocaust. It was only after various plans to expel the Jews from Europe between 1933 and 1941 had failed that Hitler finally approved of radical measures for the 'Final Solution' which had been put forward and carried out by lower middle-ranking officials. Broszat could find no evidence of a comprehensive Nazi plan in place before 1941 to exterminate the Jews, and even when Hitler did approve of the Final Solution, sometime during the latter months of 1941, he left the major decisions for its implementation to the two leading SS leaders Himmler and Heydrich. Broszat (who died in 1989) was deeply critical of intentionalist historians. He believed that they put far too much emphasis on Hitler and his beliefs as the dominant explanation of what happened in the era of the Third Reich.[10]

Hans Mommsen is another deeply influential supporter of the 'functionalist' view of the Holocaust. In the view of Mommsen, Hitler, obviously a fanatical anti-Semite, had no clear idea about what 'the Final Solution' to the Jewish Question should be and he played little or no role in the development of the Holocaust, which came about because radical Nazis competed with one another to implement more and more radical measures in Nazi-occupied eastern Europe between 1939 and 1941. These competing factions brought about a 'cumulative radicalism' on the Jewish Question within the Nazi regime. This led by incremental stages to the realisation of the 'unthinkable' during the Second World War. Mommsen suggests the policy of attempting to kill all of Europe's Jews can by 'no means be attributed to Hitler alone' even though he accepts that the Nazi dictator fully endorsed the policy. Mommsen has faced a number of criticisms, most notably, for underestimating the importance of Hitler and Nazi ideology, for concentrating too much on initiatives for the 'Final Solution' coming from the middle ranks of the German bureaucracy and for not attaching due importance to the policies coming from Hitler and the central government in Berlin.[11]

Götz Aly, using extensive documents from the bureaucracy of the Generalgouvernement in Poland, has recently shown that the Nazi leadership in Berlin had very little to do with initiating the Holocaust. Instead, Aly suggests that the Final Solution grew out of the increasingly radical solutions to de-population policies being enacted by local middle-ranking Nazi bureaucrats in Poland.[12] These local 'men on the spot' were allowed much greater flexibility in carrying out policies of de-population and genocide than has been generally understood. He shows that Nazi officials in Poland between 1939 and 1942 were concerned with the 'Jewish Question', but they had far more lengthy discussions about reducing the 'Slavic population' in eastern Europe. These hard-pressed officials had to cope with a constant flow of different 'territorial' measures being proposed by Himmler, Heydrich and Eichmann. Some of these were concerned with the Jewish Question, but a great many others related to the policy of the 'Germanisation' of occupied Poland. The attempt to implement these differing measures often produced local conflicts and rivalries, which led these Nazi bureaucrats constantly to modify their plans and to instigate others within a process that became ever more complicated. In such a complex situation, Aly believes it is extremely doubtful whether these officials were prioritising a 'single order' from Hitler or the central government to carry out the Jewish Holocaust and so he concludes that the killing of Jews developed gradually within a broader genocidal framework. Aly suggests that the extermination programme directed at Jews began experimentally in Poland, with the mass deportation of Jews in September 1941, and then escalated in stages to the summer of 1942. During this vital period, the attraction of physical annihilation as the best way to deal with the 'Jewish Question' and ease the over-population problem within Poland became a consensus view among the increasingly radicalised middle-ranking Nazi bureaucrats in Poland.[13]

The functionalist interpretation of Götz Aly is based on the examination of previously neglected sources from Russian, German and Polish archives. But it actually comes to similar conclusions to those advanced many years earlier by Hans Mommsen and especially Raul Hilberg, whose three-volume study entitled *The Destruction of the Jews*, published in 1961, remains the most comprehensive study of the Final Solution ever written.[14] When Hilberg's book came out in 1961 it was published by Quadrangle Press, a very small and then little known academic publisher. It has recently come to light that Hannah Arendt advised Columbia University Press not to publish Hilberg's PhD on the grounds that it was not an important contribution to the subject. Lucy Dawidowicz does not even mention Hilberg's work in her 1981 study *The Holocaust and the Historians*.

Raul Hilberg's important study begins with what could be termed an overtly 'intentionalist' slant as he outlines the development of Hitler's anti-Semitic views, but he then goes on to present the evolution of Nazi policy towards the Jews in a functionalist manner. In the fully revised 1985 version, Hilberg shows that Hitler was only very infrequently involved in the actual decisions surrounding important phases of the killing. Hilberg reveals that the key figures were the mid-level officials – who were taking orders from officials directly above them – who came to realise – by a process of trial and error – that a radical programme of killing millions of Jews was attainable during the Second World War. It was these 'men on the spot' who took the major initiatives in the implementation of the Holocaust. Hilberg outlines what has now become an accepted stage-by-stage persecution of the Jews, beginning with legal discrimination between 1933 to 1939, then moving on to the more brutal ghettoisation from 1939 to 1941 and the final extermination of the Jews in a systematic fashion between 1941 and 1945 in the Soviet Union and Poland. During the early stages in this process, Hilberg emphasised that the Nazis regarded the Jews as 'sub-human' but with a right to live. But from late 1941 onwards, the extermination of Jews became an urgent necessity. Hilberg suggests that as genocide developed within the Nazi regime, legality become simply a matter of knowing what to do in relation to a general order concerning the murder of the Jews rather than seeking any ideological or legal clarification 'from above'. What is most controversial in Hilberg's work and aroused particular criticism from Jewish historians is his contention that key elements within Jewish society in Germany and elsewhere in Nazi-occupied Europe were complicit in their own fate. He suggests that an implicit Jewish trust in God, law and contracts led to a mind-set which fatally miscalculated that the Nazis would not destroy them, but would use them for economic purposes. The prevalence of this view – particularly among Jewish leaders – helps to explain the absence of widespread resistance during the mass murder. In Hilberg's controversial view, most Jews went to their deaths like 'lambs to the slaughter'.[15] He described Jewish leaders in the ghettos as 'intoxicated' with the powers given to them by their German rulers. He suggested many were more concerned for their own image and dictatorial powers rather than aiding Jewish salvation.[16] Hannah Arendt conceded that without Jewish help in the administrative and police work surrounding the Holocaust, 'there would have been either complete chaos or an impossibly severe drain on German manpower', and she described the role played by some Jewish leaders as 'undoubtedly the darkest chapter of the whole dark story'.[17] But recent studies of the *Judenräte* have been more sympathetic to Jewish leaders and have highlighted the often appalling decisions that had to be made by these organisations under extreme pressure from merciless and brutal Nazi conquerors. In the view of Yehuda Bauer there was resistance to the Nazis by Jews, which not only consisted of physical opposition, but also applied to any activity that gave the Jewish people dignity and humanity. Given the appalling and brutal conditions in which Jews in eastern Europe had to live, it is remarkable just how much resistance there was.[18] Survivors of the camps have written about the many and varied strategies of survival that prisoners adopted to try and prolong their lives.

The debate concerning the decision to launch the Final Solution has also been the subject of a wide variety of conflicting historical interpretations. There is some agreement that the decision to launch the Europe-wide Holocaust of the Jews unfolded in the latter months of 1941. Jäckel suggests that genocidal plans against the Jews were certainly being discussed by Hitler and his close aides before 1939, but the actual plans for the implementation of the Holocaust were only finalised in the months before the invasion of the Soviet Union. These plans were a logical development of the murderous assaults on Jewish communities which had begun as soon as the war began. The month of March 1941 is cited by some historians as being particularly important. During that month Hitler held meetings with Himmler, Rosenberg, Hans Frank, the Governor of the Generalgovernement, Goebbels, the Propaganda Minister, and Eichmann, in which a 'Jew-free' Poland and the 'final evacuation' of the Jews 'east' were all discussed. Richard Breitman, the biographer of Himmler, suggests that there is evidence for the fateful decision taking place in meetings between Himmler and Hitler in January 1941 and in several other meetings prior to the attack on the Soviet Union.[19]

A more substantial group of historians have suggested that the decision to order the Holocaust took place between the summer and autumn of 1941. Christopher Browning suggests that the attack on the Soviet Union opened the door to a wave of mass murder programmes and methods, most notably starving Russian prisoners of war, engaging in mass shooting of Jews and undertaking experiments with Zyklon B and gas vans. The monumental scale of the killing in the Soviet Union encouraged the Nazi authorities to go further. In Browning's view, Hitler ordered the preparation of an extermination plan by Heydrich at the end of July 1941 and then gave his full agreement to the mass killing of Jews throughout Europe in October or November 1941. Browning specifically refers to Heydrich's meeting with Eichmann in 'late September' at which Hitler's order for the 'physical destruction' of European Jews was confirmed. Browning is also keen to emphasise that Hitler took the decision to exterminate the Jews not as an act of vengeance due to the failure of the Soviet campaign, but as part of a euphoric belief in the ultimate victory of Germany in the Second World War.[20] Phillipp Burrin takes issue with this interpretation and suggests that during the very peak of Hitler's military success – after the defeat of France in the summer of 1940 – Hitler was still prepared to send Europe's Jews overseas, and he only finally decided to kill the Jews in September 1941. According to Burrin, this decision was prompted by an unexpected downturn in the German campaign in the Soviet Union. The possibility of defeat in war filled Hitler's mind with a vengeful rage against the Jews and so he decided to sanction the 'Final Solution', hoping that – whatever happened on the battlefield – the Jews would not survive.[21] Martin Broszat placed the decision as late as November 1941 but his reasoning is similar: the Nazis began the systematic killing of the Jews as 'a way out of a blind alley' which was caused by the deterioration in the military situation in the struggle against the Soviet Union.[22]

Christian Gerlach has recently argued that it was the German declaration of war on the USA on 12 December 1941 that signalled Hitler's official decision to launch the systematic extermination programme. Gerlach suggested that Hitler had already agreed to kill Jews in the Soviet Union prior to Barbarossa and had ordered Heydrich to draw up plans for a Final Solution in July 1941, but that he had hesitated to make a final decision about sanctioning this plan. The Japanese attack on Pearl Harbor on 7 December 1941 and then Hitler's rash decision to immediately declare war on the USA finally brought about a truly global war. In the same period, the German attack on the Soviet Union was becoming bogged down. Hitler knew the German economy was not prepared for a long war. Gerlach argues that Hitler – in a spirit of vengeance – decided to fulfil a promise he had made many times before, namely, that in the event of a global war he would ensure the Jews were annihilated. After sustained criticism of this view, Gerlach has modified his opinion and he now suggests there was no 'big bang' date but an incremental evolution towards the Final Solution developing in the latter months of 1941 and then given added impetus by the Wannsee meeting in January 1942.

This idea of a gradual move towards physical extermination between 1939 and the summer of 1942 is most persuasively advanced by Peter Longerich, who rejects the polarisation of the old intentionalist–structuralist debate and now favours a synthesis of these two positions in order to give a more nuanced interpretation. Longerich shows how the Nazis downgraded anti-Semitic propaganda in the years before they came to power in order to broaden their appeal to German voters. He also rejects the view that anti-Semitism was popular with the general German population. It is the development of Nazi extermination policy as it emerged after the occupation of Poland in September 1939 that lies at the heart of Longerich's thought-provoking interpretation. The outbreak of the war in 1939 – not Operation Barbarossa in 1941 – is the decisive moment in the gradual emergence of an extermination policy. According to Longerich, the ambitious Nazi plans to resettle and deport Jews to an underdeveloped part of Poland that developed between 1939 and 1941 were genocidal from the beginning and contained the idea that the Jewish race would wither away over several generations. He suggests the T4 programme which began in September had already shown the willingness of the regime to institute a programme of systematic killing of a 'racially united' group. But Longerich rejects the idea that this was part of a clear-cut stage-by-stage plan for the 'Final Solution' and instead opts for the idea of a gradual and by no means inevitable evolution of policy, which moved through the discussion of various resettlement and emigration schemes towards the escalation of mass murder of Jews in the Soviet Union, and gave way – in further incremental stages – to a mass extermination policy in the summer of 1942 in the death camps. For Longerich even the rapid escalation of the killing of Jews in the Soviet Union in summer 1941 did not yet imply that a clear policy of killing all the Jews in Europe was underway. The building of the first gas chambers in late 1941 was – according to Longerich – experimental and not the beginning of an already decided and clearly coordinated policy of mass physical extermination. Even at the end of 1941, when most other historians argue the Holocaust was most definitely underway, Longerich once more questions whether there is really conclusive evidence that any comprehensive decision to kill the Jews on a Europe-wide scale had already been taken. Even at the Wannsee Conference in January 1942 it was assumed that many Jews would die of starvation through the consequences of hard labour, not by a clear-cut and swift extermination policy in purpose-built camps. In the view of Longerich it is only after April 1942 that the final decision was taken to kill all the Jews in Europe. By suggesting a much longer time line for the Holocaust, beginning in 1939 and moving through gradual stages to the summer of 1942, and being driven by the 'men on the spot', Longerich is suggesting that it was circumstances in Poland that led towards a consensus emerging among Nazi officials in Poland which ended with advocating a policy of mass extermination as the 'Final Solution'.[23]

Longerich's analysis has the advantage of locating the gradual move towards mass extermination in the ruthless and de-humanising occupation of Poland, but the idea of 'detached' mid-level officials taking such a bold path towards mass murder independently of the centre does not appear wholly convincing. Some historians are sceptical as to whether the policy of mass murder of the Jews could have evolved between September 1939 and April 1942. Christopher Browning has suggested that the consensus to murder the Jews occurred at the centre in conversations between Hitler and Himmler during the planning and early stages of the attack on the Soviet Union and was filtered down the system by the SS in a period beginning from the late summer of 1941 onwards. Christoph Dieckmann has asserted that the plans for Operation Barbarossa were so murderous as to constitute a decisive step towards extermination.[24] The officials in Poland were either implementing policy or were allowed to devise it to their own increasingly radical specifications.

The Wannsee Conference of January 1942, which was once viewed as the crucial moment when the Final Solution was launched, has been increasingly regarded as of much less importance, in recent studies. The specialist historians at the Wannsee Museum support the idea of a gradual evolution towards mass murder, and play down the significance of the conference as 'the key turning point'. But Mark Roseman, who has recently reviewed the importance of the Wannsee meeting as a key factor in the development of the Final Solution, has concluded that it was far more important than has recently been suggested. Heydrich's aim was to propel the extermination process forward under strengthened SS coordination and Roseman argues he succeeded in this objective because it was soon after the meeting that the scale of the killing increased most dramatically.[25] Christian Gerlach has also suggested that Wannsee represented a 'new acceleration' of the Final Solution, and that after being informed in Riga of the outcome of the Wannsee Conference, the Commander of the Security Police and the SD in Minsk, Walter Hofmann, announced on 29 January 1942 that he wanted to initiate a 'vigorous schedule of executions' in the spring.[26]

Overall, the intentionalist–functionalist debate has reached a compromise position. Few intentionalist historians now argue that Hitler's frequently aired hatred of the Jews actually caused the extermination of the Jews. Before 1941, the evidence that Hitler planned the mass extermination of all of Europe's Jews is totally unconvincing. The key to solving why the Holocaust occurred seems to lie increasingly with how Hitler's vague intent 'to get rid of the Jews' was interpreted and turned into a reality by the various agencies and officials who carried it out. Most structuralist historians now accept that Hitler maintained a violent hatred of the Jews throughout his political career, and acknowledge that his personal animosity towards them determined the climate in which the escalating radicalisation of policies towards the Jews took place. It seems the future research agenda is moving beyond the old 'intentionalism versus functionalism' debate. The idea that officials were 'working towards the Führer' has been utilised by Sir Ian Kershaw to explain why subordinates acted in an extremely radical manner on the Jewish Question. Most believed ever more de-humanising policies would be approved of by the Nazi leader and this ingrained view had a momentum that culminated in genocide.[27] The major problem with many 'structuralist' examinations of the Holocaust is that they fail to fully acknowledge the limitations of the sources upon which their arguments are based. They are seldom extensive enough to allow for a detailed reconstruction of the process of decision making in Nazi-occupied regions of Poland or the Soviet Union to be fully evaluated. Many official German documents relating to the Holocaust were destroyed. A great quantity of material relating to decision making surrounding Hitler and the central government in Berlin were either never committed to paper, or were also destroyed before the end of the war.

There has now developed what has been termed a 'new synthesis' between the two positions. This new thinking accepts that Hitler – although he lacked a 'master plan' – was the decisive ideological force behind the Holocaust, and that through a dynamic mixture of influences from above and below there was an incremental movement from the summer of 1941 onwards towards the eventual murder of the Jews on a Europe-wide scale. One of the most important adherents to this 'new synthesis' on the Holocaust is the Jewish historian Yehuda Bauer, who originally supported the intentionalist position, but now rejects the idea that Hitler had a master plan to exterminate the Jews. At the same time, he disagrees that Hitler played only a minor or 'shadowy' role or that the Holocaust was primarily due to initiatives taken by middle-raking bureaucrats. Bauer suggests Hitler was the decisive figure in the Holocaust and that during 1941 he gave a series of verbal orders to Himmler to order the genocide of the entire Jewish people in Europe. Bauer suggests the Holocaust was not just another example of genocide but was the most extensive and unique, because every Jew was designated for extermination.

Another important supporter of the 'new synthesis' is the Jewish scholar Saul Friedländer, who views Nazism as the negation of all life and the Holocaust as a unique event in history. He was also a firm supporter of the intentionalist view, but he now suggests that Hitler did not have a master plan to kill the Jews dating back to *Mein Kampf*. He believes the old 'straight road to Auschwitz' thesis as no longer tenable as Hitler's policies towards the Jews contained no clear plan for extermination before 1941. Friedländer has conceded that the functionalists have convincingly shown the complex nature of decision making in the Nazi regime, but maintains that they did so by reducing Hitler's role to relative insignificance. What needs to be accepted by functionalists – claims Friedländer – is that Hitler saw himself as involved in a war with the Jews. Once the German army was losing the initiative in the Second World War, Hitler's 'war against the Jews' became a dominant aim and so he pushed ahead with the murder of the Jews. Until the autumn of 1941, Hitler had only ordered the killing of Jews in the Soviet Union, but from that point onwards he gave the go-ahead to an overall plan he already had in mind before the attack on the Soviet Union – to kill all Europe's Jews. During the last months of 1941 there are numerous examples of this plan being implemented.[28]

Sir Ian Kershaw, after recently surveying the current state of historiography on Hitler's role in the decision for the Final Solution, concludes that 'Hitler's direct actions are still difficult to locate.' Kershaw suggests Hitler's ideological aim of 'getting rid of the Jews' and finding a solution to the Jewish Question was already enshrined within the Nazi bureaucracy. Without Hitler's fanatical will to kill the Jews, there would have been no Holocaust. But in Kershaw's view it was the competent administrators such as Eichmann, Heydrich, Himmler and Höss who turned Hitler's desires into a systematic killing machine, and the gradual 'process of depersonalisation and dehumanisation of Jews' which took place between 1933 and 1941 prepared the ground for the mass killing during the Second World War. Once mass shootings were used by the *Einsatzgruppen* to kill Jews in the Soviet Union, the idea of extermination quickly became the 'Final Solution' for all Europe's Jews. For Kershaw, the movement towards a Final Solution was an incremental process, pushed ahead by Operation Barbarossa and gradually moving to the fully operative 'Final Solution' by the summer of 1942.[29] Once again, the inadequacy of the sources and the secrecy of the killing operations have led to various dates being suggested for the decision to launch the 'Final Solution'. It is the 'balance of probabilities' that determines which date historians opt for when discussing the date or period when the 'Final Solution' was launched but the period from May to October 1941 appears the most likely, based on the current state of the interpretation of the largely circumstantial evidence.

The massive concentration in the historical debate on the timing of the Holocaust tends to relegate a consideration of the testimony of those who survived the Nazi death camps to a position of relative insignificance. Many studies of the Holocaust actually contain very little examination of the reality of life and death in the extermination camps. By focusing on the victims of the mass murder of the Jews, the reality of the Holocaust becomes clearer. The most widely known testimony of a Holocaust survivor is *If This is a Man* by Primo Levi, a Jewish Italian chemist who spent eleven months in Auschwitz between February 1944 and January 1945, when the camp was finally liberated by the Red Army. Levi claimed that he survived for a number of disparate reasons. He learnt German, he tried to keep a low profile, and his professional qualifications as a chemist enabled him to get a job in the Buna laboratory that produced synthetic rubber, which allowed him to avoid the hard labour in freezing conditions. Even when he became ill with scarlet fever, this worked to his advantage, as when the SS hurriedly evacuated the camp in January 1945 he was left behind. Levi's story showed how, through a combination of luck and skill, someone could survive. Levi rejected the idea that Stalin's gulags, where 30 per cent of inmates perished, could be remotely compared with the Nazi extermination camps, in which 90 per cent of Jewish inmates died.[30] The vivid testimony of Holocaust survivors provides evidence of the alien world of the camps. It gives some insight into what it was like to be trapped in one. In this tradition Anna Pawełczyńska, a political prisoner in Auschwitz, produced a pioneering study of 'values and violence' in the camp, revealing that even within the brutalising context of Auschwitz remnants of personal integrity could be salvaged.[31]

One of the most important recent developments within the historical debate is the publication of new pioneering studies on the role of women and children in the Holocaust. These studies are mostly based on the evidence of Holocaust survivors. At Auschwitz, women constituted more than half of those murdered. The camp had a special women's section to facilitate forced labour and many would die in the factories and satellite camps. Irena Strzelecka has written a chilling account of women in Auschwitz. Women were not just physically abused but were subject to widespread sexual abuse in much larger numbers than male inmates.[32] But, there is another side to the role played by women in the Holocaust. Claudia Koonz has revealed that many women in Nazi Germany and in the occupied territories were complicit in Nazi crimes. Many women were supporters, leaders, organisers and promoters of anti-Semitism.[33] Jill Stephenson agrees that the indictment of German women for preparing the ground for the promotion of anti-Semitic ideas is now extensive. Women schoolteachers bullied Jewish children, and peddled anti-Semitism at their own children. In addition, women proved useful to aid the Gestapo in tracking down Jews who were in hiding.[34] Much recent work has focused on women as agents of Nazi racial policy in the eastern occupied territories. There were many leading female perpetrators. The Allies hanged Irma Griese for her barbarous treatment of inmates in a number of camps, including Auschwitz, Belsen and Ravensbrück. She joined the SS at 19 years of age and was so vicious in her treatment of inmates that Peter Phillips, a British POW and camp survivor, writes that 'her name spells nightmare. It means once again feeling her lash on your back or face; it means again seeing her kill a friend whom you had spoken to or touched a minute before; it means staring petrified at her finger as it moved slowly past you pointing out those to be exterminated.'[35]

The fate of children in the Holocaust is another important new area of historical research. Most children were killed immediately as a priority because they were considered to be the future 'gene pool' of the Jewish 'race'. At Auschwitz, there was a special *Kinderlager* or Children's Camp, which held the child labour until they were exterminated.[36] Debórah Dwork's comprehensive study of Holocaust children lays out the horrific extent of slaughter of Jewish children in graphic detail. A staggering 1.5 million Jewish children – comprising 91 per cent of all Jewish children alive in Europe in 1939, perished during the Holocaust. Using extensive survivor testimony, Dwork examines how children lived and died. In this distorted world the young held more tightly to brothers and sisters, attached themselves to other children or joined another surviving family. If a child's family had been killed, older, more experienced children would adopt him or her. Dwork discusses the incredible strength of many of the children. They fed each other, looked after sick friends and protected their surrogate families. According to Dwork, the evil and bestial environment within the camps often meant vast numbers of children were numbed and retreated into silence, unable to act to save themselves or others.[37] Many children proved incapable of surviving the appalling conditions in Jewish ghettos. Starvation and disease were physical horrors, but children also suffered the trauma of seeing parents and siblings die. They lived in a frightening bewildering world in which vicious and unpredictable violence became routine. Jane Marks has described how children often tried to pass themselves off as 'Aryans' in Nazi-occupied countries, but feared betrayal at any moment.[38] Life in the camps and the ghettos often affected children's play. Many games attempted to make sense of what was happening to them. The children's play-acting included the impersonation of Nazi guards and featured games concerning torture and death.[39]

Over recent years a great deal of Holocaust research has dwelled extensively on the Holocaust in the east as well as in other parts of Europe. One key aspect of this research is to examine the number of non-Germans who took part in the killings or collaborated with the Nazis in carrying them out. Hilberg identified a vast 'semi-circular arc' of territory that became the German killing grounds in Europe, from the Balkans to Poland and the Soviet Front. In recent times, historians have explored these regional perspectives in depth and they have become a valuable part of Holocaust studies. Ulrich Herbert has examined Nazi extermination policies in Galicia, Lithuania, Byelorussia, Serbia, Upper Silesia and the area surrounding Auschwitz itself. In the past, these regions have been regarded as peripheral to the German and Polish nucleus of the Holocaust, but they are now viewed as part of a wide perspective on the vast scope of the Holocaust.[40] Similarly, Sandkühler's work on south-east Poland has revealed how SS personnel in the camps there determined the pace of the extermination programmes. It was subordinates who made the decisions driving anti-Jewish policy in south-east Poland, rather than any directives handed down from the central government in Berlin.[41]

The extensive collaboration of local populations in eastern Europe in the Holocaust has also been extensively researched, as Martin Dean's work on the Ukraine amply demonstrates. Of course, *Einsatzgruppen* involvement in the mass shootings at the outset of Operation Barbarossa is well documented. What is less understood is what Dean describes as the 'Second Wave' of annihilation in the Soviet Union during 1942, which is now recognised as even more murderous than the first. Dean shows that the collaboration of local people and institutions of government was a far greater factor in their efficient operation than was previously understood. Dean's research into 'Second Wave' extermination in Byelorussia and the Ukraine demonstrates this effectively. As well as German SS and police units, pivotal roles were also played by local police volunteers in units called *Schutzmannschaften* (policemen). These men were tireless in their pursuit and murder of Jews and they hoped their reward would be a Ukrainian state. Most locals viewed these local police units as more vicious in dealing with Jews than the Nazis. Dean looks at the motivation of these 'ordinary men' and reveals they were not all rabid anti-Semites. Some had joined for a regular income, free alcohol, and because of peer pressure. Ukrainians had been opposed to the Soviet regime since its inception and thousands of Ukrainians willingly volunteered for SS regiments, special army groups and the death camp units. They were conspicuous as guards in the 'Operation Reinhard' death camps of Sobibór, Belzec and Treblinka. Of course, traditional anti-Semitism in the Byelorussian and Ukrainian regions played some part, but these men just as willingly killed non-Jews and they were more 'murderers for pay' rather than ideologically inspired Aryan warriors. There are implications in this work for other attempts to explain the Holocaust. The focus on local collaboration strengthens criticism of the view that the Holocaust was carried out exclusively by Germans conditioned by a unique, pervasive, eliminationist anti-Semitism. But Dean's important study also qualifies Hannah Arendt's 'banality of evil' model. Many of the local auxiliary units he examined actually knew their Jewish victims. Dean refers to the 'gruesome intimacy of the massacres', carried out by men who were hardly 'desk-bound' bureaucrat–murderers, dealing with anonymous victims as so many items in a ledger.[42]

Extensive collaboration in Nazi mass murder was also significant in Lithuania, where Jews were the first to die following the German attack on the USSR. Lithuanians killed Jews indiscriminately and were actually organising pogroms of Jews shortly after the German assault on the Soviet Union, and were including women and children in their mass killings before the *Einsatzgruppen* did so. By December 1941, 265,000 of Lithuania's Jews (making up 96 per cent of the Jewish population) had been killed. The presence of Germans was superfluous in these murders as over half the killings were carried out by local Lithuanian auxiliary units. Arno Mayer has noted that SS Colonel Karl Jäger, head of *Einsatzkommando* 3 (*Einsatzgruppe* A), reported in July 1941 that at Kovno he had encouraged Lithuanian partisans to massacre Jews. Mayer comments that the partisans needed no encouragement: they were quite happy to take the initiative. The notorious IXth Fort at

Kovno was frequently used by Lithuanian gunmen for numerous 'actions', in which thousands of Jews lost their lives in horrific circumstances, and Avraham Tory, a survivor of Kovno, has left a frightful, indelible picture of the fort where Jews were held in filthy cells before torture and mass execution. Recent studies have indicated that the part played by the local population was even larger than had been previously indicated. The parallels with the Ukraine are strong. There was sympathy for anti-Semitism and anti-Soviet nationalism, which welcomed Nazi eliminationist policies. It has also been revealed that the Lithuanians did not need recruiting.[43] Even more crucial in the Soviet Union than local collaborators was the role of the regular army, and a great deal of recent research has dealt with Hitler's conscripted soldiers. The active support of the Wehrmacht, especially in supporting the activities of the Einsatzgruppen, often made the mass murder of Jews more of a 'job share' scheme between the SS and the army, as has been shown in the work of Hannes Heer and Omer Bartov.

The implementation of the Holocaust across Europe was hardly a controlled experiment. It was disfigured by the complexities of local politics, the variable nature of anti-Semitism and the overriding influence of the diplomatic concerns of national leaders. Hilberg suggested that the unevenness of the implementation of the Final Solution in Germany's periphery was not an accident. Most of Germany's neighbours, whether allied or conquered nations, had to balance a variety of considerations in their decision making. The result was a spectrum of reactions ranging from non-cooperation, through to some forms of participation, and to heavy involvement, which – with the possible exception of the Ukraine and the Baltic states – fell short, in one aspect or another, of reaching the exacting German standard.[44]

As the enormity of the killing during the Holocaust became widely known after 1945, questions were asked about why the Allies had not intervened. Many historians have made a distinction between 'knowledge' and 'information'. Information about Nazi genocide reached the Allies very early in the war. David Wyman showed that the Allies could have bombed Auschwitz and the railways which serviced it. Martin Gilbert has revealed that the Allies had detailed knowledge of what was going on at Auschwitz, due to reports they received from escapees in 1944, most notably, Alfred Wetzler and Rudolph Vrba. There were no technical reasons why the RAF, or the US long-range bombers using Italian bases, could not have reached Auschwitz, especially in the latter stages of the war. Allied planes were able to drop supplies to Polish forces in Warsaw as they rose against the Nazis in August 1944, and Allied aircraft had already bombed the I. G. Farben works at Auschwitz.[45]

It is also now known that the British secret service had broken German secret codes very early in the war. Richard Breitman has demonstrated that the British were reading the confidential messages of the German Order Police from September 1939 and they had broken the code of the German 'Enigma' machine by May 1940. By the time of the German invasion of Russia occurred, experts at Bletchley Park – the headquarters of the British Government Code and Cypher School – were fully aware of the mass shootings by the *Einsatzgruppen* in occupied Poland. The routes of the Jewish deportations across Europe to the killing camps in the east were also documented by the British secret service. *Einsatzgruppen* reports on the mass killing of Jews in the Soviet Union were also being read at Bletchley Park.[46] Even SS reports on the daily number of Jews killed were being read by the British. Bernard Wasserstein, in a controversial analysis, suggests that the inaction of the British government in response to the plight of the Jews during the Holocaust was due to a British reluctance to sanction a major influx of Jewish refugees to Palestine after the war. He argued that the British government preferred Arab support in the Middle East to buttress British control of the Suez Canal rather than supporting the establishment of a Jewish state.[47] But this analysis does not give due regard to the fact that when the British government publicised the hostile treatment of Jews in Nazi Germany, during the war the British public thought it was propaganda. The US government thought bombing Auschwitz would give the impression that the war was being fought on behalf of the Jews. According to Breitman, the US State Department believed that if a public campaign was mounted to 'save the Jews', this would be used by Nazi propaganda to portray the US as a 'Jewish state' and part of Hitler's much quoted 'worldwide Jewish conspiracy'.[48] Hilberg emphasised that the Allies were far more concerned to defeat Germany on the battlefield rather than diverting bombing resources to the defence of the Jews. But Morse directs criticism at what he calls an 'anti-Semitic US administration' and he notes the frustrations of senior government figures like Secretary of the Treasury Henry Morgenthau (himself a Jew), who criticised the State Department for obstructing efforts to help the Jews.[49] Defenders of Allied inaction during the Holocaust pointed out that only by hastening the end of the war could more Jews be saved. During the latter part of 1944, British and US air forces were heavily engaged in the western offensive which had began with the D-Day landing on 6 June 1944.[50] It was not really possible for the Allies to have bombed the death camps in Poland before June 1944. It is also questionable whether an attack on Auschwitz at that date would have made a significant difference to the death figures as most of Europe's Jews had already perished. William Rubinstein has vigorously defended Allied inaction and dismissed the idea of bombing Auschwitz as totally impracticable. David Cesarani has convincingly and impressively demonstrated that Allied bombing in eastern Europe would not have made a significant difference to the final large-scale murder of Jews which took place in Hungary.[51]

It has also been suggested that the Vatican and the Roman Catholic Church in general can be heavily criticised as 'Bystanders' during the Holocaust. Günter Lewy showed in a study in 1964 that Pope Pius XII did not have any fundamental objection to anti-Jewish discrimination, and he judged his response to the mass murders of the Jews as wholly unsatisfactory.[52] More recently Daniel Goldhagen has suggested that the German Catholic hierarchy did very little to oppose Nazi crimes against the Jews and he bitterly accuses Pope Pius XII for his failure to condemn the Final Solution. For Goldhagen, the Roman Catholic Church had sympathy with much of Nazi policy towards the Jews, as anti-Semitism had been common for centuries in Christian communities. In Goldhagen's view, the Roman Catholic Church in Germany constantly promoted these views and deliberately ignored the extermination campaigns.[53]

A major focus on the Catholic response to the Holocaust revolves around Pope Pius XII's actions. As Eugenio Pacelli he had served as Papal Nuncio in pre-1933 Weimar Germany and he was the architect of the Concordat that in 1933 had placed Nazi–Catholic relations on a formal footing. John Cornwell, using many contemporary sources (including the diary of Harold Tittmann, US Ambassador to the Holy See, and the dispatches to the British Foreign Office of Francis D'Arcy Osborne, Britain's representative to the Vatican), highlights the Pope's unwillingness to declare publicly his knowledge of the Final Solution. John K. Roth and the collaborative research by Susan Zuccotti and Carol Rittner have also been critical of the Pope's inaction over the Holocaust but they stop short of suggesting he endorsed the policy. Anthony Rhodes has attempted to show that Pius XII's failure to make public any opposition to Nazi anti-Semitic policies was due to his concern about possible Nazi reprisals against Catholics in Europe. Rhodes also points out that concentration on the attitude of the Vatican fails to give enough acknowledgement of the brave rescue work undertaken by many individual priests and nuns of the Catholic Church, who helped to save thousands of Jewish lives.[54] In two important recent studies both Dalin and Marchione have argued that the long-standing negative attacks on Pius XII's role in the Holocaust are not wholly justified and they reveal some of the vigorous efforts he made – particularly behind the scenes – to protect Jews.[55] It is probably worth adding that the Catholic Church voiced strong public opposition towards Nazi euthanasia policies, as has been emphasised in a recent study by Michael Burleigh.

In more recent times, the reaction of 'ordinary Germans' towards the

Holocaust has been subject to extensive examination and has aroused enormous controversy and public debate. Christopher Browning, an American historian, who has been called a 'moderate-functionalist', has emerged at the centre of this discussion. Browning's most influential study on the Holocaust is *Ordinary Men*, published in 1992, which concentrates on a civilian German police unit, Battalion 101, which formed part of the Order Police (*Ordungspolizei*) who were involved in the forcible deportation of Jews to the death camps in Poland in 1942. Browning's research resisted the temptation to stereotype the Nazi perpetrators as uniquely evil and beyond humanity. His work is greatly influenced by Stanley Milgram, a psychologist who, in a series of psychological experiments beginning in 1963 and culminating in his book *Obedience to Authority*, published in 1974, showed that many very 'ordinary people' drawn from a wide range of occupations and social and educational backgrounds will participate in the torture and even the murder of other human beings when ordered to do so by those they regard as being in a position of white-coated authority.[56] In Milgram's novel experiments, a group of volunteers were ordered to apply ever more powerful electrical shocks to a man strapped into an electric chair. A very high proportion applied shocks that would have killed the man, and did so not knowing for sure if electricity was being used. Milgram concluded that his experiments proved the 'essence of obedience' was the feeling that a person was carrying out someone else's orders. Many other psychological experiments have confirmed the willingness of human beings to carry out sadistic acts in the name of obedience.

Browning reveals in *Ordinary Men* that the policemen who carried out genocide in Poland were not usually Nazi fanatics, but randomly recruited German middle-aged men of working-class origin, mostly from Bremen and Hamburg. These men had been drafted into the German civilian police force because they were deemed unfit for military service. Most of them were not disturbed or pathological individuals. They simply did what they were asked to do. In Poland, they were asked to round up Jews and to deport them to the death camps. They were also asked to participate in mass shootings when required. The commander of the police unit gave all the men the option of not killing, and so the majority participated willingly. Browning concluded that those who killed did so, not because of some anti-Semitic desire to kill Jews, but because of the desire to conform and remain part of the group.

On the broader dimensions of Nazi genocide, Browning suggests there was no premeditated murder programme aimed at the Jews, but an 'evolving policy' that responded to the changing circumstances and opportunities created by the German occupation of Poland between 1939 and 1942 and by the killing operations of the Einsatzgruppen in the initial phase of the attack on the Soviet Union in the summer of 1941. Between 1939 and 1941 the

Nazis were engaged in a programme of general 'ethnic cleansing' which involved decimating some populations and Germanising others. It was taken for granted that the resettlement programmes would involve many people perishing. Within the complex framework of a group of Nazi officials dealing with a vast influx of people within Poland, there remained the problem of how to deal with the Jews who were also congregating there in ever increasing numbers. Browning claims that two factions within the Nazi-run Generalgouvernement – mostly composed of middle-ranking Nazi bureaucrats – advocated two different 'solutions' to the Jewish problem. One group, the 'Productionists', wanted the Jews to be used as slave labour in order to bolster the German war effort. A second faction, dubbed the 'Attritionists', favoured letting the Jews starve and die while undergoing slave labour. Once it was decided that the Jews in Poland would not be expelled to the east – during the autumn of 1941 – the question then arose about what to do with the Jews in Poland, and out of this dilemma came the decision to annihilate the Jews on a Europe-wide basis. For Browning, the Final Solution was due to rivalry between competing factions within the unstable power structure of the Nazi state, and the mass murder of the Jews was a last resort after emigration schemes had proved impracticable and it seemed there was no end to the over-population problems in Poland. In the end, the policy of forced labour and starvation ran hand in hand with systematic extermination during the Holocaust. In Lodz, the high productivity of industry ensured Jews were able to survive until the summer of 1944, but in other ghettos such economic consid-erations played a less significant role in preventing mass extermination.[57]

When it was first published, *Ordinary Men* was viewed as a path-breaking work of historical research, but the Browning interpretation of the Holocaust was immediately attacked by a young Jewish American political scientist, whose family had suffered during the Holocaust. His name was Daniel Goldhagen and he attempted to re-invigorate the seemingly moribund inten-tionalist position. Goldhagen accused Browning – in a book review of *Ordinary Men*, published in *The New Republic* in 1992 – not only of manufac-turing evidence, but of writing a book of 'no scholarly value'. Goldhagen went even further in his bitter attack on Browning by producing a book based on his Harvard PhD political science thesis entitled *Hitler's Willing Executioners: Ordinary Germans and the Holocaust*, in 1996. This much-hyped book attracted enormous media interest and ignited one of the most contro-versial debates since 1945 among historians concerning the Holocaust.[58] Goldhagen argued that there was a 'straight path' to the Holocaust. It was the inevitable outcome of a long-held desire to 'eliminate Jews' from German society that was not merely held by Hitler but shared by the great majority of 'ordinary Germans'. Goldhagen's study focused on the personal involvement of thousands of German murderers. He looked at those who pulled the triggers, those who set fire to the barns, the houses and the churches, and those who laughed as they smashed babies' heads into walls. A very lengthy section of Goldhagen's book is full of extremely graphic and harrowing descriptions of eyewitness accounts of the terrible cruelty inflicted on Jews by the 'ordinary men' in the 'Order Police' and their Reserve Police Battalions. Goldhagen suggests the role of this German civilian police force in the Nazi extermination of the Jews is as important as the much more extensively researched roles of the SS and the *Einsatzgruppen*.

For Goldhagen the Holocaust has a mono-causal explanation. All Germans in the Nazi era were imbued with a deeply in-bred eliminationist anti-Semitism. Every class of society and every political and social institution in Germany regarded the Jew as a threat to Germany's very existence. The Jews – according to Goldhagen – were a race apart in Germany: the source of 'race-defilement', the root of criminality, conspiracy, communism, economic corruption and immorality. Germans had been acculturated into believing that only by cutting out this carcinogenic human material could they hope to retain racial dignity, national strength and vigour. By the 1930s, Goldhagen believed, most Germans had accepted as a necessity the removal of the Jews.

The whole thrust of Goldhagen's controversial thesis is to emphasise that Germans cannot hide behind the myth that the Holocaust was a secret, clandestine activity carried out by selected and fanatical members of the Nazi elite. Instead, Goldhagen suggests the Germans must finally face up to the broader reality and responsibility for the enormity of what happened. Hitler was merely the catalyst who unleashed long-standing desires within German society to exterminate the Jews. The German perpetrators treated the Jews in the brutal way they did, not because they were ordered to do so, but because they enthusiastically agreed with what they were doing. This was a very challenging interpretation. It raised the question of the relationship between anti-Semitism in German society and the persecution and killing of Jews. The deeply moralistic and strident polemical tone of Goldhagen's book attacked the long-held assumption that most Germans did not know nor would they have approved of the Holocaust. Not surprisingly, Goldhagen's book created enormous interest in Germany. Newspapers were full of what became known as 'the Goldhagen Controversy'. This was no dry academic exercise but rather, a battle for the very soul of Germany. The book attacked the carefully constructed functionalist arguments which had increasingly downgraded the importance of anti-Semitism and ideology as significant factors in explaining the Holocaust. The book, with its clear and simply understood interpretation, was a best-seller overnight in Germany, the USA, and Britain. The German magazine *Der Spiegel* ran a thirty-page report on the book under the headline

'A Nation of Demons'. The youthful looking Goldhagen – who did not even hold a full-time academic post at the time his book came out – was thrust into major debates with most of the leading historians of the Holocaust on British, German and American TV. Goldhagen showed a great deal of media savvy in these debates. A number of opinion polls of young Germans who had seen his debates on TV were very attracted by his argument.

But the academic criticism of Goldhagen by historians was sustained, savage and generally dismissive. To begin with, it was suggested his argument was too simplistic and rested on the flimsy foundation of a highly selective analysis of primary and secondary sources used to sustain a flawed argument. Norman Finkelstein claimed the study was full of gross misinterpretations of the secondary literature accompanied by a flawed analysis of the original sources.[59] The eminent British historian of Nazi Germany Sir Ian Kershaw agreed with the leading German historian Eberhard Jäckel that Goldhagen had simply produced a 'bad book' which was supported by a flawed reading of sources.[60] Ruth Bettina Birn, a leading expert on the scholarly files of the Order Police on which Goldhagen had based his book, claimed that Goldhagen had placed a one-sided slant on much of the evidence he had examined.[61] The highly respected Jewish historian Yehuda Bauer pointed out that Goldhagen ignored many Polish and Israeli sources and that he did not attempt to compare the so-called 'unique' German anti-Semitism with other examples in Europe.[62] Many critics were deeply troubled by Goldhagen's anthropological style. The killers in Goldhagen's book murdered Jews because this was part of their cultural and genetic make-up. In other words, if they had not been born German they would not have killed Jews. According to Jäckel, this is a massive generalisation, attributing genocidal, biological, psychological and intellectual traits to the citizens of an individually defined nation state.[63] Hans Mommsen accepts that anti-Semitism was a conditioning factor in the Holocaust and was apparent within German society from the late nineteenth century onwards, but he rejects Goldhagen's notion that it was the only cause. According to Mommsen, the structure of the Nazi regime, aligned around permanent competition among self-dissolving institutions, fuelled a process of cumulative radicalism whose inevitable end point was the liquidation of the Jews.

Geoff Eley has continued the general scholarly demolition by historians of Goldhagen's study. He castigated Goldhagen for ignoring important research on German slave-labour policies which were not confined to Jews. The treatment of slave labourers under Nazi rule reveals a complex range of factors in the development of Nazi violence, including the tensions arising from the eclectic national mix of the labour force, pressures for increased output brought by apolitical technocrats oblivious to human suffering, and increased fears concerning impending military defeat. Within this frame-work, hatred of the Jews was not always the most significant factor or the only priority. More generally, scholars now take a more sophisticated view of the complicity of 'ordinary Germans' in the regime's crimes. Responses to the regime were articulated in infinite gradations ranging from enthusiasm, acceptance, indifference, even resistance.[64] Hans-Ulrich Wehler dismissed the simplistic demonisation of Germany and notions of a 'special path' (or *Sonderweg*) to explain Germany's unique historical development and he views Goldhagen's 'collective guilt' thesis as a kind of 'racism in reverse'. He also suggested Goldhagen failed to evaluate the varied social, political, economic and cultural factors central to understanding the Holocaust, most notably, the hugely complex conditions that brutalised the personnel involved in policy making, both in the Nazi bureaucratic elite and during the dislocation, created by the Polish and Russian campaigns, 'of the connec-tions between concepts of orders and obedience, authority and duty; of the distortion of reality; of the impact of specific circumstances; of group pres-sures; of the despotic power wielded by middling and petty authorities; or of the extent to which people could become acclimatized even to daily mass murder'.[65] Wehler also points out that some of the worst genocidal atrocities in Nazi-occupied Europe often involved very willing helpers including Croats, Hungarians, Romanians, Poles, Lithuanians, Latvians and Ukrainians. Myriad examples from recent history show Germans are not uniquely genocidal. It is probably worth adding that Germans did not just kill Jews, but also thou-sands of Gypsies, Poles, Russian prisoners of war, homosexuals, political opponents, the mentally ill, the physically deformed, Slavs and other nation-als in Europe. In Himmler's far-reaching genocidal plans, Jews were only a percentage of the planned 30 million murders.

But the 'Goldhagen controversy' did focus attention on two important issues that had festered within German society since the end of the war, but were never fully addressed: how many ordinary Germans were violently anti-Semitic, and what role did Nazi propaganda play in fomenting anti-Semitism in German society? For too long the totalitarian model of Hitler as 'Master in the Third Reich' had rendered most Germans seemingly guiltless as the 'victims' of a criminal regime. It was assumed – especially in West Germany – that very few 'ordinary Germans' were actively involved in Nazi genocide. Even those who had participated were seemingly 'obeying' a supremely powerful government machine. But the extensive modern research into the Holocaust revealed the large number of different civilian agencies involved in the killing process. Klaus Fischer has constructed an indictment of the Germans on the evidence of the administrative require-ments of the Nazi killing machine. Officials at many levels were crucial to the operation of the Final Solution. The list is extensive: main government departments at local and national levels, academics at the leading universities, all legal and justice agencies, military commands, police battalions, transport executives and operatives, Party and SS leaders, field personnel, concentration camp staff, and extensive business interests. Fischer estimates that this involved the direct involvement of at least 300,000 people.[66] It is now more fully understood that the Gestapo and the police system depended on the active collaboration of the German public in order to ensure the smooth running of its anti-Semitic policies. Gellately has revealed that without substantial public collaboration 'it would have been next to impossible for the Gestapo to enforce these kinds of racial policies'.[67]

The recently published diary of Victor Klemperer, a Jew who survived precariously in Dresden during the war by virtue of his marriage to an 'Aryan' wife, provides an unrivalled chronicle of Jewish courage in the face of incredible privation and the constant fear of imprisonment and transportation to the east. Klemperer records that knowledge of *Einsatzgruppen* atrocities in Poland was in wide circulation in Germany immediately after the attack on Warsaw in 1939 and that the appalling outcome of the Jewish deportations from Germany was a matter of public awareness as early as October 1941. On 25 October 1941, he notes, 'Ever more shocking reports about deportations of Jews to Poland.' On 18 November 1941, he writes, 'The news of the Jewish deportations to Poland and Russia sounds catastrophic from several sources.'[68] The frequent post-war mantra 'We did not know' is now impossible to sustain. The German population was extensively leafleted about German atrocities in the east by the Allied air forces. German soldiers, policemen, train drivers and members of the Nazi bureaucracy all passed on information of the killings to their families in Germany in letters and on visits home.

Many recent studies are now emphasising that anti-Semitism was by no means a marginal feature of life inside Nazi Germany. Gretschen Schafft's *From Racism to Genocide*, which examines anthropologists in Nazi Germany, amply demonstrates the widespread permeation of Nazi racist and eugenicist values within the legal system, the medical profession, the scientific community, administrative bureaucracies and the universities. Anthropologists were key figures in every phase of the Holocaust: as anti-Semitic racist propagandists; taking leading roles in concentration camp medical experiments; as key officials in the racial courts; and in implementing the killing during the 'Final Solution' in the extermination camps.[69] Marion Kaplan has shown that Jews were frequently attacked in public during the Second World War because many Germans held them responsible for the British and US air raids dubbed the 'Jewish Sky Terror'. Kaplan also notes that Germans did not demand extermination, but she emphasises that anti Semitism was 'widespread, deep and invidious' within Nazi Germany. Most Germans wanted Jews simply to 'disappear' and were prepared to avert their eyes when this process escalated into murder.[70] According to Fischer, 'most of the anti-Jewish terror was widely known by the German people. After all, the endless lines of trains from every part of the Reich and all over Europe, packed with hungry, thirsty and dying Jews and heading eastwards, were scarcely concealable.'[71]

The role played by propaganda in helping to make anti-Semitic discourses acceptable in German society during the Nazi era is now being subjected to increasing analysis. Nazi racial ideology featured prominently in the propaganda of the regime. Serious consideration is now being given as to whether this propaganda contributed to the 'cumulative radicalisation' of policy towards the Jews that occurred during the war. Standard works on the effectiveness of Goebbels' Ministry of Propaganda in promoting anti-Semitism have mostly concluded that the 'hypodermic syringe model', in which a passive audience is injected with the required propaganda message to become overnight believers in radical anti-Semitism, is too far-fetched. Nazi propaganda was most effective where it built on pre-existing prejudice. Anti-communism was already a largely unquestioned, central popular prejudice among large sections of the German population and Nazi propaganda was able to strengthen this prejudice. But the forging of a widespread, virulent, aggressive anti-Semitism in Germany required a more fundamental reconstruction of existing values and encountered more difficulties gaining popular acceptance. It seems anti-Semitic films such as *Der ewige Jude* (*The Eternal Jew*) and the extensive treatment of the 'Jewish Question' in newsreels and newspapers, such as the party newspapers the *Völkischer Beobachter* and the virulently anti-Semitic *Der Stürmer*, proved more popular with Party activists than with the general public.[72] But recent oral history studies have indicated that the ceaseless effort of the regime to promote anti-Semitism in every aspect of life did influence many younger educated members of German society through school and within the Hitler Youth. These were the very same people who came to prominence in the SS, the police, the bureaucracy and the army during the Second World War.[73]

A number of important recent studies have also examined the activities of the leading middle-ranking Nazi perpetrators of the Holocaust, most notably Michael Thad Allen's work on the role of the SS in slave-labour policies, Isabel Heinemann's study of the Race and Settlement Office (RuSHA) and Andrej Angrick's impressive work on *Einsatzgruppe* D. Most of this recent work on the Nazi perpetrators comes from young, talented German scholars. Two of the most impressive new German studies are by Michael Wildt and Ulrich Herbert. Wildt's massive and impressive study of the Reich Main

Security Office (RSHA), called *The Generation of the Unbound*, published in 2003, offers a very detailed examination of the mind-set of the leading bureaucrats who ran the 'Final Solution' under Himmler and Heydrich. Wildt's study uses a number of mini-biographies of the leading figures in the RSHA to build up a picture of the mind-set of the leading figures in the RHSA. He shows they all believed in the 'stab-in-the-back myth' concerning the German defeat in the First World War. Most had fought in the paramilitary *Freikorps* in the early 1920s. All valued the soldierly values of toughness, action and ruthlessness. Every one of them was a strident anti-communist and all were anti-Semites during the Weimar period. For this group, the political and economic chaos in Weimar Germany in the early 1920s was the major influence behind their desire to support the building of a 'new Germany'. But these men – unlike the leading Nazis of the 1920s – valued and gained academic qualifications in the German university system. In fact, Wildt argues that these men were not predestined to join the Nazi Party and their fervent nationalism developed separately from the Nazi ideology or influence during the 1920s. But it was fervent German patriotism that allowed them to support National Socialism after Hitler came to power. The highly educated elite group who ran the RSHA were – according to Wildt – equally at home in drafting the administrative details of Nazi anti-Semitic legislation in the mid-1930s, and in taking an active part in the mass shootings by the *Einsatzgruppen* in the 1940s. They became fixated on the goal of achieving the racial aims of the Reich at home and within the Nazi-occupied territories. Although it might be questioned whether the artificial process of selecting certain individuals to represent the entire mind-set of the RSHA is a sound methodological approach, Wildt's massive study does provide so much new evidence to support the view that what is presented is a representative sample of the thinking of the RSHA.[74]

Ulrich Herbert's biography of Werner Best examines the impact of a number of key aspects of Nazi rule on Best's career. Best was also a solid member of the German middle class. His political outlook was shaped by the German defeat in 1918. He went to university in the 1920s where he encountered strong German nationalist sentiments among the students. He strongly supported the drive to exclude Jews from membership of student unions, which took place in many German universities before Hitler came to power. By the time he joined the Nazi Party in 1930 he was already a very passionate German nationalist. The reason he had resisted joining the Nazi Party earlier was because he felt it contained too many members of what he regarded as 'the uncouth working classes'. In 1933, Himmler appointed him as chief of the SD and he later became Heydrich's deputy – after a period working for the Gestapo. Best rejoiced in the 'Night of the Long Knives' as it purged the party of the vulgar, rowdy elements that he so despised. In the late 1930s he became an avid supporter of Himmler's drive to promote 'racially superior' individuals within the SS and the RSHA. These policies greatly accelerated the career prospects of university-educated members of the middle class, who had been fervent nationalists in the 1920s but not Nazis. Heydrich viewed Best as a potential political rival and he tried to sideline him by sending him to France to run the German occupation force in 1940. After Heydrich was assassinated in May 1942, Best became Germany's plenipotentiary in Nazi-occupied Denmark. After the Second World War, Best portrayed himself as someone who had been 'taking orders' from the Nazis and he actually testified against many leading Nazi perpetrators at the Nuremberg trials. In reality, Best had always supported and promoted the planned and orderly violence that occurred in the extermination camps. Herbert even reveals how Best attempted to resolve his personal rivalry with Heydrich by trying to suggest both men were essentially on the same wavelength and shared a similar outlook.

It is now apparent that the old and now tired intentionalist–functionalist debate has largely been replaced by a more nuanced and multi-faceted historical debate on the Holocaust. Hitler is now increasingly viewed as passionately committed to his racial policy. He is no longer viewed as a 'coffee house dreamer' or a 'power mad opportunist' whose only interest was power. Hitler's racial policy and his mission to 'remove' Jews are now viewed among all serious scholars as central driving forces in the movement towards mass murder. It is apparent that Hitler's anti-Semitism shaped the climate of ideas that led to the murder of the Jews even if the path to Auschwitz was long and winding. The importance of Nazi propaganda and the successful mobilisation of Nazi racial and anti-Semitic ideology through-out German society were of central importance in producing the 'cumulative radicalism' within the Nazi system. The passionate Nazi drive for racial purity and military conquest appears to have appealed most forcefully to the well-educated Germans who came to maturity as the Second World War began. It was these individuals who came to prominence in the leadership and especially within the SS–police system that ran racial policy and the Holocaust. It now seems clear that Hitler played a decisive role in creating the climate in which the Holocaust became a reality. But the functionalists were right in their assertion that the process towards the extermination of the Jews was extremely complex. It was due to a combination of strong ideo-logical leadership, successful propaganda, policy directives from the centre and strong genocidal impulses coming from the 'men on the spot', who not only carried out policy but made important contributions to the process that led to the 'Final Solution'.

Conclusion

There has been so much written about the Holocaust that it is extraordinarily difficult to make sense of it. Historians have tended to investigate separate aspects of the Holocaust as distinct micro-research areas. This explains why finding a satisfactory overall synthesis becomes ever more difficult. The scale of the Holocaust is certainly without precedent. There were nine million Jews in Europe in 1939 and only three million were left alive by the time the Third Reich collapsed in the ruins of Berlin. The killing was not just limited to Jews in the Soviet Union or Germany, but encompassed Jews from all over Europe. Every single Jew was sentenced to death by the Nazi regime simply for existing. No differentiation was made in terms of gender, class, occupation or geographical location. Jews were not defined by the Nazis according to culture, religion or nationality. They were a separate and 'parasitic race' that had to be eliminated. Other potential victims of Nazi genocide might survive by changing political or national allegiance, but for the Jews there was no escape. All Jews were to be first identified then isolated and finally erased.

On the surface, this does appear unique and unprecedented. But it must not be forgotten that at the time the Holocaust occurred Hitler's regime and armed forces controlled or influenced most of the European continent, except for the Soviet Union and Great Britain. So the attempt to kill the Jews could only have been attempted by a dominant power, controlling a vast landmass, with the will and technological capability to carry it out. A great deal of mass genocide has occurred in other nations with vast territorial power, most notably in China and the Soviet Union. At the same time, genocide has taken place in small nations in almost every continent. A similar 'Holocaust' to that inflicted on the Jews could happen in the future and there is no guarantee it will not. What is most startling about Nazi genocide towards the Jews is the lack of pragmatism surrounding the whole project. Vast economic and transport resources were diverted to the killing programme and important labour resources were sacrificed at the very time they were desperately needed.

One reason why the Holocaust has exerted such popular fascination, particularly in post-war western democratic societies, is the shock that a highly efficient and cultured western European state – the birthplace of

Beethoven, Goethe and Mann – could be responsible for it. Western Europe was conventionally viewed – through the Eurocentric lenses – as 'enlightened'. Daniel Goldhagen has suggested that Germany was the ideal candidate for the title of 'murderer of the Jews' because it had a long history of wanting to 'eliminate' the Jews from its territory. But Hitler did not build up his popularity in Germany because of anti-Semitism. Most of those who voted for Hitler were attracted by his passionate devotion to German nationalism. Anti-Semitism was played down in Nazi propaganda election campaigns. In general, anti-Semitism was more pronounced in Tsarist Russia, Poland and France and among Austrian elites before 1933 than in Germany. The mass killing of Jews, given the widespread nature of anti-Semitism in many countries in Europe, could have happened elsewhere.

Yet in a very short space of time Adolf Hitler was able to permeate his own deeply held anti-Semitic and racial-purification views into the fabric of the Nazi regime and then among wide sections of German society. Hitler may have played down his own rabid anti-Semitism to achieve power, but his 'mission' to remove Jews from German society remained a powerful factor within his policy aims and his ideology. As Martin Bormann, the leading Nazi Party official, put it: 'National-Socialist doctrine is entirely anti-Jewish, which means anti-communist and anti-Christian. Everything is linked within National Socialism and everything aims at the fight against Judaism.'

The drive to push Nazi anti-Semitic ideas and racial policy went on at a rapid pace in German society once Hitler came to power. The schools, the mass media and the Nazi Youth organisations all played important roles in promoting racist ideas. These ideas penetrated all levels of Germany society, but especially the traditional middle class. Most of the middle-ranking bureaucrats who carried out the 'Final Solution' were relatively young men who had felt the influence of Nazi racist and anti-Semitic ideology after Hitler came to power. The swiftness with which the existing 'conservative' German bureaucracy carried out one set of rules based on law and then switched to another based on criminality and then genocide does require explanation. For the younger members of middle-class German society who came to maturity when the Second World War was being fought, these ideas were quickly assimilated.

The figure of Adolf Eichmann, the dull 'desk killer' looking out for his own career, the bureaucratic cipher, with no ideological principles, has come to represent all those middle-ranking officials who administered the Final Solution. Eichmann appears as the classic 'go with the flow' pen pusher forced to keep his head down and not 'rock the boat'. But Eichmann's testimony – given at his trial in Jerusalem – when examined in full is mostly self-serving rhetoric which attempts to suggest he was not responsible because he was taking orders from his superiors. Simple reference to Eichmann's detached form of evil cannot explain the extent to which a racist and anti-Semitic outlook had permeated the mind-set of the bureaucratic elites that carried out the Holocaust. Christian Wirth, who ran 'Operation Reinhardt', was a brutal, nasty, vicious anti-Semite who fits the bill of a very 'Willing Executioner'. There were many people similar to both of these figures among the perpetrators of the 'Final Solution' and myriad variations in between. In spreading the gospel of Nazi racial and anti-Semitic ideas within the German bureaucracy and the German police and security forces that carried out the murders, Hitler's regime was extremely successful. If all these people were simply 'taking orders' from above – as so many of them claimed at the war trials – or reacting to 'system pressure', imposed from above and on the ground – then Milgram's experiments on the development of 'authoritarian obedience' do have some relevance when related to Nazi Germany. It is, as Hannah Arendt, pointed out, 'easier to be evil than be good'. But many of those who carried out the killing were not Wirth-like sadistic monsters. Even so, most German officials did adapt very quickly – almost too quickly – to the criminal acts ordered by the regime against the Jews for them simply to have been viewed as banal instructions from 'above'. These people had a loyalty to Hitler, but they retained a problem-solving mentality derived from their solid family backgrounds and elite education. There are many historians who talk of a 'cumulative radicalisation' towards genocide without explaining what this term means. Even the trial in the 1960s of nurses involved in the T4 programme revealed that these 'ordinary' health service workers actually believed in the racist and eugenicist ideas behind the killing they carried out. It is scarcely credible that most of the highly educated bureaucrats who participated in the Holocaust did not vehemently support the radical policies they advocated. They were not simply solving problems of over-population and 'the Jewish Question' in complete isolation from a general ideological framework and a set of ideological tenets they believed in. Micheal Wildt's examination of the RSHA showed that it was individuals from the solid upper middle-class strata who rapidly rose within the SS–police apparatus between 1933 and 1945, while the lower middle-class recruits who had been the backbone of the pre-1933 party suffered a steep decline in numbers and influence. The fortunes of academics and medical men from solid conserva-tive upper middle-class families also prospered within the machinery of Nazi genocide. Whether this was simple traditional bourgeois adaptation to authority or the flowering of a deeper ideological passion for Nazi racial doctrines requires much further critical analysis.

From the beginning, the passionate nationalism of the traditional conser-vatives and Hitler's Nazism was a matter of degree. Hitler provided the opportunity for a new definition of German nationalism. Some members of the German middle class struggled between 'old' ideals and the 'new' Germany. But for most of the younger middle-class bureaucrats who carried out the 'Final Solution', Nazi racist ideology reflected their own strong nationalistic outlook and they did not object to the violent methods that came with it. It was soon accepted – especially in Poland and the Soviet Union – that killing 'racial enemies' was a 'moral national duty' designed to save the purity of the German race. The move towards genocide happened as soon as the war began and escalated most forcefully in the 'east', which had been defined as a region peopled by 'sub-humans' in Nazi propaganda and in the schools and the universities, in which most of the perpetrators were educated within strict Nazi racist doctrines.

The intentionalists argued that it was Adolf Hitler who engineered this descent into murderous criminality and quite deliberately plotted a 'straight road to Auschwitz'. It can be proved that Hitler had a pathological hatred of the Jews and his desire to 'remove' them from Germany can be graphically demonstrated by reference to his writings, his speeches and his actions. Hitler saw the Jews as his central 'race enemy'. They were planning – he thought – a 'world-wide conspiracy' to undermine national unity and promote war. But there is no convincing evidence to support the view that Hitler planned the systematic murder of the Jews – even in Germany, let alone Europe – before the Second World War began. The weight of evidence suggests he genuinely supported the idea of Jewish 'emigration' as a solution to the 'Jewish Question' up until the invasion of the Soviet Union in June 1941.

The functionalists argued there was 'a twisted road to Auschwitz' and suggested Hitler did not plan the Holocaust or even give a written order for it. The functionalists asserted that the programme to kill the Jews emerged by a process of 'cumulative radicalism' within the Nazi system once the war began, and developed thereafter in incremental stages from the ghettoisation in Poland to the escalation of killing by the *Einsatzgruppen* in the Soviet Union to the creation of dedicated extermination camps between December 1941 and the summer of 1942. Hitler just sanctioned a process that was driven by middle-ranking 'bureaucrats', who produced radical solutions to the Jewish Question 'from below' that were later sanctioned and approved by the Nazi dictator. Götz Aly has impressively demonstrated in relation to the carrying out of the Holocaust by ideologically detached bureaucrats in Poland that these officials developed – largely on their own initiative – a radical de-population programme that involved genocide on a wide-ranging scale and was by no means dominated by 'the Final Solution'.

In recent times, it has been conceded that intentionalism is teleologically and methodologically unsound and that functionalism often reduced the whole episode to the imperatives of a modern bureaucratic machine and downplayed the roles of Hitler and Nazi ideology to relative insignificance. The search is now on for a 'new synthesis' on the Holocaust that takes account of factors from both above and below. The middle-ranking bureaucrats who carried out the murder all felt they were 'working towards the Führer'. In practice, this meant finding radical solutions to over-population and the Jewish question that they thought Hitler would approve of. In Poland there was some resistance to pushing ahead with the 'Final Solution' from the autumn of 1941 onwards. The ideological decision makers in Berlin started to impose policy on the 'Jewish Question' from 'above', which some mid-level officials attempt to subvert – not because they wanted to save the Jews, but because slave labour was required for the military needs of the Wehrmacht as the Soviet campaign started to falter. The whole process was much too complicated to be reduced to a simple uniform implementation of a Führer order and is correctly viewed as an evolving process which ultimately became a systematic attempt to murder all of Europe's Jews. Hitler's support for a 'Final Solution' was the engine of the process even though different vehicles were used to come to a consensus that the 'Final Solution' was physical extermination.

The Holocaust was pursued in the latter stages of the war, without any regard for its economic consequences. Outside the Soviet Union, great care was taken to disguise the murder of the Jews. Hilberg has shown how even the language that the Nazis used to describe the 'Final Solution' was elliptical. The killing schemes were discussed behind the closed doors of the organisations responsible for administering and carrying out the murders. The *Einsatzgruppen* kept detailed figures of the number of Jews murdered in the Soviet Union, but in the extermination camps no detailed records were kept. The victims west of the Soviet border were fooled into believing that deportation really meant 'resettlement', work and a future. There was a sense of security felt by the Jews because their cooperation was solicited and it seemed they could be part of the decisions and affect their outcomes. At the killing centres elaborate subterfuges were practised to convince the arrivals that their transit ordeals were over once the shower rooms had been used. The Jewish community leadership in the ghettos believed it could protect Jews by complying with the ever-increasing Nazi economic demands and successive deportations. What was being camouflaged was the total annihilation of the Jewish 'race' wherever it was found across Europe.

Most of the leading perpetrators in the camps implemented the 'order' they were given 'from above', to kill the Jews, with feelings ranging from ideological enthusiasm through to banal indifference. Those Jews and others deemed 'unfit to work' were gassed immediately, with the rest used as slave labour. Within the camps genocide and slave labour ran hand in hand. Every slave labourer within the camps who survived the selection process was treated terribly. In their striped uniforms, with shaven heads and different coloured badges of identification, the prisoners found that the avenues of genocide for the racist–biological–eugenicist and politically motivated perpe- trators who ran the camps were manifold. But there was a very important difference between a Jew and the other prisoners – not in terms of the brutal- ity each suffered, but in the overall ideologically driven policy objective defined by Hitler. Every single Jew in Europe was going to die or be killed and it is the attempt by Adolf Hitler's regime to achieve this goal and the willing- ness of so many seemingly ordinary people to carry this out which makes the Holocaust still the most remarkable example of genocide in spite of all attempts to suggest otherwise.

Notes

● Notes to the Introduction

1 The term 'Holocaust' originally comes from the Greek word *Holókauston*, meaning a burnt sacrifice to a god. From the 19th century, it was used to describe large-scale disasters. The *Oxford English Dictionary* claims it was used to describe Hitler's killing of the Jews as early as 1942. It did not come into widespread usage until the 1950s. Since the 1960s it has been used to refer to the destruction of the Jews, in order to distinguish it from the remainder of Nazi genocide. The term *Shoah*, meaning calamity or catastrophe, is often preferred by many Jewish scholars.
2 See U. Herbert (ed.), *National Socialist Extermination Policies: Contemporary German Perspectives and Controversies* (Oxford: Berghahn Books, 2000).
3 See also J. Ezard, 'The Germans Knew of the Holocaust Horror about the Death Camps', *Guardian*, 17 February 2001.

● Notes to Chapter 1: Hitler and 'the Jewish Question'

1 See R. Binion, *Hitler among the Germans* (Illinois: Illinois University Press, 1984), p. 85.
2 E. Jäckel and A. Kuhn (eds), *Hitler. Sämtliche Aufzeichnungen, 1905–1924* (Stuttgart, 1980), pp. 88–90.
3 Quoted in L. Dawidowicz, *The War against the Jews* (London, 1977), pp. 17–20.
4 Quoted in P. Burrin, *Hitler and the Jews* (London: Edward Arnold, 1989), p. 26.
5 A. Hitler, *Mein Kampf* (London, 1969), p. 60.
6 Ibid.
7 Joseph Goebbel, *The Goebbels Diaries* (New York: Doubleday, 1948), 28 March 1933.
8 H. Krausnick, H. Bucheim, M. Broszat and H. Jacobson, *Anatomy of the SS State* (New York: Waler, 1968), p. 22.
9 Quoted in N. H. Baynes, *The Speeches of Adolf Hitler* ([Oxford, 1942]: Howard Vertig, 2006), pp. 538–9.

10 Quoted in P. Burrin, *Hitler and the Jews* (London: Edward Arnold, 1994), p. 49.
11 Joseph Goebbels' Diary, 30 November 1937.
12 K. Schleunes, *The Twisted Road to Auschwitz: Nazi Policy toward German Jews, 1933–1939* (London, 1970), p. 236.
13 Burrin, *Hitler and the Jews*, p. 60.

● **Notes to Chapter 2: War, Resettlement and Ghettoisation**

1 See the speeches of 22 May 1939 and 22 August 1939 reproduced in N. Baynes, *Speeches of Adolf Hitler*.
2 Quoted in S. Benedict, 'Nurses' Participation in the Nazi Euthanasia Programme', *Western Journal of Nursing*, vol. 21 (1999), pp. 9–10.
3 J. Noakes and G. Pridham, *Nazism, 1919–1945: A Documentary Reader*, Vol. 3: *Foreign Policy War and Racial Extermination* (Exeter: University of Exeter Press, 1997), p. 1019.
4 H. Arendt, *Eichmann in Jerusalem: A Report on the Banality of Evil* (Harmondsworth: Penguin, 1994), pp. 288–9.
5 J. Noakes and G. Pridham, *Nazism, 1919–1945*, p. 1027.
6 Reichskommissariat für die Festigung des Deutschen Volkstums (RKFDV).
7 Quoted in G. Corni, *Hitler's Ghettoes: Voices from the Beleaguered Society, 1939–1944* (London: Edward Arnold, 2003), pp. 23–4.
8 Quoted in G. Aly, *'Final Solution': Nazi Population Policy and the Murder of the European Jews* (London: Edward Arnold, 1999), p. 250.
9 See P. Longerich, *Politik der Vernichtung Gesamtdarstellung der national-sozialistische Judenverfolgung* (Munich: Piper Verlag, 1998).

● **Notes to Chapter 3: From Operation Barbarossa to the Wannsee Conference**

1 J. Noakes and G. Pridham (eds), *Nazism, 1919–1945*, vol. 3: *Foreign Policy, War and Racial Extermination* (Exeter: University of Exeter Press, 1997), pp. 1086–7.
2 Ibid., p. 1106.
3 M. Berenbaum, *Witness to the Holocaust* (New York: HarperCollins, 1997), pp. 121–35.
4 Y. Arad, S. Krakowski and S. Spector (eds), *The Einsatzgruppen Reports: Selections from the Dispatches of the Nazi Death Squads* (New York: United States Holocaust Museum, 1989), pp. vii–ix (hereinafter: *Einsatzgruppen Reports*).

5   C. Browning, 'Hitler and the Euphoria of Victory', in D. Cesarani, *The Final Solution, Origins and Implementation* (London: Routledge, 1994), p. 139.
6   Berenbaum, Witness, p. 114.
7   C. Sydnor, *Soldiers of Destruction: The SS Death's Head Division, 1933–1945* (Princeton, NJ: University of Princeton Press, 1990), p. 153.
8   J. Forster, 'The Relation between Operation Barbarossa as an Ideological War of Extermination and the Final Solution', in D. Cesarani, *The Final Solution, Origins and Implementation* (London: Routledge, 1994), p. 93.
9   Quoted in *Trial of the Major War Criminals*, vol. 31 (Nuremberg, 1949), PS-502.
10 Quoted in A. Hillgruber, *Staatsmänner und Diplomaten bei Hitler*, vol. 2: *Vertrauliche Aufzeichnungen über Unterredungen mit Vetretern des Auslandes* (Frankfurt a.M., 1970), p. 556.
11 Quoted in L. Dawidowicz (ed.), *A Holocaust Reader* (West Oregon: Behrman House, 1976), pp. 72–3.
12 *Einsatzgruppen Reports* [From the Bundesarchiv-Militärarchiv-Freiburg], Operational Situation Report USSR, no. 10 (2 July 1941), pp. 2–3.
13 Ibid., no. 14 (6 July 194)1, pp. 10–12.
14 Ibid., no. 17 (7 July 1941), pp. 13–15.
15 Ibid., no. 19 (11 July 1941), pp. 16–19.
16 Ibid., no. 24 (16 July 1941), pp. 29–33.
17 Quoted in R. Breitman, 'Himmler and the "Terrible Secret" among the Executioners', *Journal of Contemporary History*, vol. 26 (1991), p. 433.
18 C. Browning, *Fateful Months: Essays on the Emergence of the Final Solution* (New York: Holmes of Meier, 1991), pp. 16–20.
19 Berenbaum, *Witness to the Holocaust*, pp. 121–35.
20 Joseph Goebbels, *The Goebbels Diaires* (New York: Doubleday, 1948) 19 August 1941.
21 Noakes and Pridham, *Nazism*, vol. 3, p. 1105.
22 *Einsatzgruppen Reports*, Operational Report, 106 (7 October 1941), pp. 171–4.
23 Nuremberg Document NOKW-3292, quoted in Y. Gutman, Y. Arad and A. Margaliot (eds), *Documents on the Holocaust* (Yad Vashem Publications, 1999), p. 387.
24 Ibid., pp. 264–5.
25 Nuremberg Documents PS-4064 in Gutman, Arad and Margaliot.
26 *Einsatzgruppen Reports*, no. 128 (2 November 1941), pp. 217–20.
27 Noakes and Pridham, *Nazism*, pp. 1097–8.
28 See S. Friedländer, 'From Anti-Semitism to Extermination: a Historiographical Study of Nazi Policies towards the Jews and an Essay of Interpretation', in M. Marrus, *The Nazi Holocaust, Part 3*, Volume 1: *The 'Final Solution': The Implementation of Mass Murder* (Meckler, 1989), p. 340.

29 Quoted in M. Broszat, 'Hitler and the Genesis of the Final Solution', *Yad Vashem Studies*, 13 (1979).
30 Record of a conversation between Hitler and the Grand Mufti of Jerusalem, 2 November 1941, quoted in HMSO, *Documents on German Foreign Policy, 1918–1945*, Series D, vol. XIII: *The War Years June 23, 1941–December 11, 1941* (London, 1964), p. 881.
31 *Das Reich*, 16 November 1941.
32 *Die Zeit* reported on this entry from Goebbels diary on 9 January 1998, shortly after it had been discovered.
33 Noakes and Pridham, *Nazism*, pp. 1126–7.
34 C. R. Browning, 'A Reply to Broszat Regarding the Origins of the Final Solution', in Marrus, *Nazi Holocaust*, p. 182.
35 M. Roseman, *The Villa, the Lake, the Meeting: Wannsee and the Final Solution* (London, 2003), p. 113.
36 Noakes and Pridham, *Nazism*, vol. 3, p.1153.
37 Ibid. p. 143.

Notes to Chapter 4: Life and Death in the Extermination Camps

1 See F. Piper, 'Estimating the Number of Deportees to and Victims of Auschwitz-Birkenau Camp', *Yad Vashem Studies*, vol. 21 (1991), pp. 40–103.
2 Bundesarchiv, Belzec trial transcript, Statement by Joseph Oberhauser, 24 January 1963.
3 G. Sereny, *Into That Darkness: From Mercy Killing to Mass Murder* ([1974] Pimlico, 1995), pp. 163–4, p. 224.
4 Rudolph Höss, *Death Dealer: The Memoirs of the SS Kommandant at Auschwitz* (London: Da Capo Press, [1957] 1992), p. 157.
5 O. Friedrich, *The Kingdom of Auschwitz* (Putnam: Penguin, 1996), p. 45.
6 P. Levi, *Survival in Auschwitz: The Nazi Assault on Humanity* ([1958]; Simon & Schuster, 1996), p. 91.
7 See O. Sofsky, *The Order of Terror: The Concentration Camp* (Princeton, NJ: Princeton University Press, 1993), pp. 131–2.
8 F. Piper, 'The Mass Extermination of Jews in the Gas Chambers', in F. Piper and T. Swiebocka (eds), *Auschwitz: Nazi Death Camp* (Auschwitz: Auschwitz-Birkenau State Museum, 1996), pp. 165–73.
9 F. Müller, *Eyewitness Auschwitz: Three Years in the Gas Chambers* (Dee, Chicago/The Holocaust Museum, 1979), pp. 116–17.
10 Levi, *Survival in Auschwitz*, p. 87.
11 See E. Cohen, *Human Behaviour in the Concentration Camp* (London: Jonathan Cape, 1954).

12   L. Langer, *Holocaust Testimonies: The Ruins of Memory* (New Haven, CT: Yale University Press, 1991), p. 117.

13   See T. Borowski, *This Way to the Gas Ladies and Gentlemen* (Harmondsworth: Penguin, 1996).

14   Levi, *Survival in Auschwitz*, p. 33.

15   D. Ofer and L. Weitzman (eds), *Women in the Holocaust* (New Haven, CT: Yale University Press, 1998), p. 1.

16   See R. Bridenthal, A. Grossman and M. Kaplan (eds), *When Biology became Destiny: Women in Weimar and Nazi Germany* (New York: Monthly Review Press, 1984).

17   See L. Bitton-Jackson, *I have Lived a Thousand Years: Growing Up in the Holocaust* (New York: Simon & Schuster, 1999).

18   See L. Greenman, *An Englishman in Auschwitz* (Vallentine Mitchell, 2001).

Notes to Chapter 5: The Holocaust and Popular Culture

1   *Shoah* is the Hebrew term for the Holocaust.

2   See R. Hilberg, *The Destruction of the Jews* (London: Holmes & Meier, 1948).

3   See H. Arendt, *Eichmann in Jerusalem: A Report on the Banality of Evil* (London: Penguin, 1994 edn).

4   See N. G. Finkelstein, *The Holocaust Industry: Reflections on the Exploitation of Jewish Suffering* (London: Verso, 2001).

5   W. Styron, *Sophie's Choice* (London: Vintage, 2000 edn), p. 264.

6   *Shoah*, 1985.

7   For a more detailed discussion see L. Jick, 'The Holocaust: its Use and Abuse within the American Public', *Yad Vashem Studies*, vol. 14 (1981).

8   F. Manchel, 'A Reel Witness: Steven Spielberg's Representation of the Holocaust in Schindler's List', *Journal of Modern History*, vol. 67 (1995), p. 84.

9   *New York Times*, 12 June 1994, p. 6.

10   'Superman Lands in Holocaust Row', *Guardian*, 27 June 1998, p. 17.

11   See Y. Loshitzky, *Spielberg's Holocaust: Critical Perspectives on Schindler's List* (Bloomington, IN: Indiana University Press, 1997), p. 8.

12   T. Cole, *Selling the Holocaust: How History is Bought, Packaged and Sold* (London: Routledge, 2000), p. 188.

13   For a detailed discussion of the view of the 'Holocaust deniers', see D. Lipstadt, *Denying the Holocaust: The Growing Assault on Truth and Memory* (Harmondsworth: Penguin, 1994).

14   See D. Hoggan, *The Myth of the Six Million* (1969); A. Butz, *The Hoax of the Twentieth Century: The Case against the Presumed Extermination of*

European Jewry (Institute of Historical Review, 1994); D. Irving, *Hitler's War* (1977).

15 *Journal of Historical Review*, vol. 13 (1993), pp. 30–3.

16 See R. Evans, *Telling Lies about Hitler: History, Holocaust and the David Irving Trial* (London: Verso, 2002). This is not just a superb analysis of the Irving case, but it also shows how a historian constructs an interpretation using original sources. See also R. Evans, *In Defence of History* (New York: W. W. Norton, 1999); C. Gray, *The Irving Judgement* (Harmondsworth: Penguin, 2000).

17 BBC News, 20 February 2006.

18 ABC News Report, USA, 22 December 2006, written by Nasser Karimi.

● **Notes to Chapter 6: The Historical Debate**

1 Z. Baumann, *Modernity and the Holocaust* ([1978], Cambridge: Polity Press, 2000), p. 13.

2 K. Hildebrand, *The Third Reich* (London: Allen & Unwin, 1984), p. 141.

3 The most well known intentionalists are: Karl Dietrich Bracher, Klaus Hildebrand, Eberhard Jäckel, Richard Breitman, Daniel Goldhagen, Lucy Dawidowicz and Andreas Hillgruber. The most important functionalists are Christopher Browning, Hans Mommsen, Martin Broszat and Götz Aly. Those favouring a synthesis between the intentionalist–functionalist debate are Ian Kershaw, Richard Evans, Yehuda Bauer, Michael Marrus and Saul Friedländer.

4 See L. Dawidowicz, *The War against the Jews* (New York: Holt, Rinehart & Wilson, 1975); *The Holocaust and the Historians* (Cambridge, MA: Harvard University Press, 1981).

5 A. Mayer, *Why did the Heavens not Darken? The Final Solution in History* (New York: Pantheon, 1990).

6 See Hildebrand, *The Third Reich*.

7 See R. Breitman, *The Architect of Genocide: Himmler and the Final Solution, 1941–1942* (New Haven, CT: Holmes and Meier, 1985).

8 See K. Schleunes, *The Twisted Road to Auschwitz. Nazi Policy towards the Jews* (University of Illinois, 1970).

9 I. Kershaw, *The Nazi Dictatorship: Problems and Perspectives of Interpretation*, 4th edn (London: Edward Arnold, 2000).

10 See M. Broszat, *The Hitler State* (London: Longman, 1981); 'Hitler and the Genesis of the Final Solution', *Yad Vashem Studies*, 13, (1979).

11 See H. Mommsen, 'The Realisation of the Unthinkable: the Final Solution of the Jewish Question in the Third Reich', in G. Hirschfeld (ed.), *The Policies of Genocide: Jews and Soviet Prisoners of War in Nazi Germany*

(London: Allen & Unwin, 1986), pp. 97–144; H. Mommsen, *From Weimar to Auschwitz:. Essays in German History* (Oxford, 1991).

12   See G. Aly and S. Heim, *Architects of Annihilation: Auschwitz and the Logic of Destruction* (Princeton, NJ: Princeton University Press, 2002).

13   See G. Aly, *'Final Solution': Nazi Population Policy and the Murder of the European Jews* (London: Edward Arnold, 1999), pp. 243–63. See also, Interview with Christopher Browning, Shoah Research Centre, March 1997.

14   There had been two other major studies in the 1950s, Leon Poliakov's, *Bréviaire de la haine* (Breviary of Hate), which came out in France in 1951, and Gerald Reitlinger's *The Final Solution*, published in 1953 (2nd edn, 1968).

15   See R. Hilberg, *The Destruction of European Jews* (New Haven, CT: Yale University Press, 2003 edn); R. Hilberg, *The Holocaust Today* (Syracuse, NY: Syracuse University Press, 1988); R. Hilberg, *The Politics of Memory: The Journey of a Holocaust Historian* (Ivan R. Dee, 1996); R. Hilberg, *Perpetrators, Victims, Bystanders: The Jewish Catastrophe, 1933–1945* (New York: Aaron Asger, 1992).

16   R. Hilberg, *The Destruction of the Jews*, vol. 1 (London: Holmes and Meier, 1985), pp. 216–20; G. Corni, *Hitler's Ghettos: Voices from a Beleaguered Society, 1939–1944* (London: Edward Arnold, 2003), pp. 106–18; I. Trunk, *Judenrat: The Jewish Councils in Eastern Europe under Nazi Occupation* (University of Nebraska Press, 1972), pp. 570–4.

17   H. Arendt, *Eichmann in Jerusalem: A Report in the Banality of Evil* ([1963]; Harmondsworth: Penguin, 1994), p. 117.

18   Y. Bauer, 'The Judenräte: Some Conclusions', *Yad Vashem Studies*, 13 (1979); Y. Bauer, *They Chose Life: Jewish Resistance in the Holocaust* (New York: New York Institute of human Relations, 1973); Y. Bauer, *Rethinking the Holocaust* (New Haven, CT: Yale University Press, 2002), pp. 119–42; J. Glass, *Jewish Resistance during the Holocaust: Moral Uses of Violence and Will* (Basingstoke: Palgrave Macmillan, 2004); Y. Suhl, *They Fought Back: The Story of Jewish Resistance in Nazi Europe* (New York: Schocken Press, 1976).

19   R. Breitman, *Himmler, Architect of Genocide* (New York: Grafton, 1992), p. 97.

20   C. Browning, *The Origins of the Final Solution: The Evolution of Nazi Jewish Policy, 1939–1942* (London: Heinemann, 2004), pp. 356–73.

21   P. Burrin, *Hitler and the Jews. The Genesis of the Holocaust* (London: Edward Arnold, 1994), pp. 151–2.

22   M. Broszat, 'Hitler and the Genesis of the Final Solution: an Assessment of David Irving's Theses', *Yad Vashem Studies*, 13 (1979), and in H. Koch (ed.), *Aspects of the Third Reich* (Basingstoke: Macmillan, 1987), p. 405.

23 See P. Longerich, *The Unwritten Order: Hitler's Role in the Final Solution* (London: Tempus, 2003 edn). Longerich's eagerly awaited study is published in 2008 by Oxford University Press, entitled *Holocaust: Nazi Persecution of the Jews*.

24 See C. Dieckmann, 'Der Krieg und die Ermordung der litauschen Juden', in U. Herbert (ed.), *Nationalsozialistische Vernichtungspolitik, 1939–1945. Neue Forschungen und Kontroversen* (Frankfurt, 1998), pp. 292–329. See also C. Gerlach, *Kalkulierte Morde. Die deutsche Wirtschafts- und Vernichtungspolitik in Weissrussland 1941 bis 1944* (Hamburg, 2000).

25 M. Roseman, 'Shoot First and Ask Questions Afterwards: Wannsee and the Unfolding of the Final Solution', in N. Gregor (ed.), *Nazism, War and Genocide: Essays in Honour of Jeremy Noakes* (Exeter: University of Exeter, 2005), pp. 131–46.

26 G. Gerlach, 'The Wannsee Conference: the Fate of the German Jews and Hitler's Decision in Principle to Exterminate all European Jews', in O. Bartov, *The Holocaust: Origins, Implementation, Aftermath* (London: Routledge, 2000), p. 133.

27 The term 'working towards the Führer' is frequently mentioned in Nazi documents and was later adopted by Noakes and Pridham to describe how Nazi officials implemented policy at the local level. The term was also adopted by Sir Ian Kershaw in his major two-volume biography of Hitler.

28 See S. Friedländer, 'From Anti-Semitism to Extermination: a Historiographical Study of Nazi Policies towards the Jews and an Essay of Interpretation', *Yad Vashem Studies*, 16 (1984), and in M. Marrus (ed.), *The Nazi Holocaust*, vol. 3 (Munich: Meckler, 1989), pp. 301–50; S. Friedländer, *Probing the Limits of Representation: Nazism and the 'Final Solution'* (Cambridge, MA: Harvard University Press, 1992). See also S. Friedländer, *Nazi Germany and the Jews: The Years of Persecution, 1933–1939* (London: HarperCollins, 1997).

29 See Kershaw, *The Nazi Dictatorship*, pp. 93–133.

30 See P. Levi, *If This is a Man* (London: Abacus, 1987), published in 1958 as *Survival in Auschwitz: The Nazi Assault on Humanity*.

31 A. Pawełczyńska, *Values and Violence in Auschwitz* (University of Carolina Press, 1973).

32 I. Strzelecka, 'Women', in Y. Gutman and M. Berenbaum (eds.), *Anatomy of the Auschwitz Death Camp* (Indiana University Press, 1994), pp. 393–411.

33 See C. Koonz, *Mothers in the Fatherland: Women and the Family in Nazi Politics* (London: Methuen, 1988), p. 5.

34 See J. Stephenson, *Women in Nazi Germany* (Longman, 2001).

35 P. Phillips, *The Tragedy of Nazi Germany* (London: Routledge, Kegan & Paul, 1969), p. 173.

36 See H. Kubica, 'Children', in Y. Gutman and M. Berenbaum (eds), *Anatomy of the Auschwitz Death Camp*, pp. 412–27.

37   D. Dwork, *Children with a Star: Jewish Youth in Nazi Europe* (New Haven, CT: Yale University Press, 1991), p. xi.

38   J. Marks, *Hidden Children: Secret Survivors of the Holocaust* (New York: Random House, 1993), pp. 1–81; F. Weinstein, *A Hidden Childhood: A Jewish Girl's Sanctuary in a French Convent, 1942–1945* (New York: Farrar, Straus, Giroux, 1986); N. Tec, *Dry Tears: The Story of a Lost Childhood* (Oxford: Oxford University Press, 1984).

39   See G. Eisen, *Children at Play in the Holocaust* (Amherst, 1988).

40   See U. Herbert (ed.), *National Socialist Extermination Policies: Contemporary German Perspectives and Controversies* (Oxford: Berghahn, 2000).

41   T. Sandkühler, 'Anti-Jewish Policy and the Murder of Jews in Galicia, 1941–1942', in Herbert, *Extermination*, pp. 105–27.

42   M. Dean, *Collaboration in the Holocaust: Crimes of the Local Police in Byelorussia and the Ukraine, 1941–1944* (Basingstoke: Macmillan, 2000).

43   See R. Lere-Cohen, *The Holocaust in Lithuania* (Gefen, Israel, 2002); A. Tory, *Surviving the Holocaust: The Kovno Ghetto Diary*, ed. M. Gilbert (London: Pimlico, 1991).

44   R. Hilberg, *Persecutors, Victims and Bystanders: The Jewish Catastrophe, 1933–1945* (London: Harper, 1992, 2003), p. 78.

45   M. Gilbert, *Auschwitz and the Allies* (London: Michael Joseph, 1981), pp. 299–322; D. Wyman, 'Why Auschwitz was never bombed', *Commentary*, 65 (1978), and in Y. Gutman and Berenbaum, *Anatomy of the Auschwitz Death Camp*, pp. 569–87.

46   R. Breitman, *Official Secrets: What the Nazis Planned. What the British and Americans Knew* (New York: Hill and Wang, 1998), pp. 88–109. See also R. Lewin, *Ultra Goes to War: The Secret Story* (Harmondsworth: Penguin, 2001).

47   B. Wasserstein, *Britain and the Jews of Europe, 1933–1945* (New York: Continuum Press, 1999).

48   Breitman, *Official Secrets*, pp. 207–11. See also T. Kushner, 'Different Worlds: British Perceptions of the Final Solution' in D. Cesarani (ed.), *The Final Solution: Origins and Implementation* (London: Routledge, 1994), pp. 246–67.

49   A. Morse, *While Six Million Died: A Chronicle of American Apathy* (New York: Hart, 1975).

50   See R. Levy, 'The Bombing of Auschwitz Revisited: a Critical Analysis', in J. Neufeld and M. Berenbaum (eds), *The Bombing of Auschwitz: Should the Allies have Attempted it?* (New York: St Martins's Press, 2000), pp. 101–26.

51   See D. Cesarani, *Genocide and Rescue: The Holocaust in Hungary, 1944* (New York: Berg, 1997).

52   G. Lewy, *The Catholic Church and Nazi Germany* (New York: DaCapo Press, 2000).

53 D. Goldhagen, *A Moral Reckoning: The Role of the Catholic Church in the Holocaust and its Unfulfilled Duty of Repair* (New York: Little Brown, 2002), p. 107.

54 See A. Rhodes, *The Vatican in the Age of the Dictators, 1922–1945* (London: Hodder & Stoughton, 1973).

55 See J. Cornwall, *Hitler's Pope: The Secret History of Pius XII* (Harmondsworth: Penguin, 1999); S. Zuccotti, *Under his Very Windows: The Vatican and the Holocaust in Italy* (New Haven, CT: Yale University Press, 2002); J. K. Roth and C. Rittner (eds), *Pope Pius XII and the Holocaust* (Continuum, Pinter, 2002). For studies defending the role of Pope Pius XII see M. Marchione, *Consensus and Controversy: Defending Pope Pius XII* (Paulist Press, 2002); D. Dalin, *The Myth of Hitler's Pope: Pope Pius XII and his Secret War against Germany* (London: Regnery, 2005).

56 S. Milgram, *Obedience to Authority: An Experimental View* (new York: Pinter and Martin, 1995 edn; originally published in 1974).

57 See C. Browning, *Ordinary Men: Reserve Battalion 101 and the Final Solution in Poland* (New York: HarperCollins, 1992; Harmondsworth: Penguin, 2001); C. Browning, *The Path to Genocide: Essays on the Launching of the Final Solution* (Cambridge: Cambridge University Press, 1995); C. Browning, *Nazi Policy, Jewish Workers, German Killers* (Cambridge: Cambridge University Press, 2000); C. Browning, *The Origins of the Final Solution: The Evolution of Nazi Jewish Policy, 1939–1942* (London: Heinemann, 2004).

58 D. Goldhagen, *Hitler's Willing Executioners: Ordinary Germans and the Holocaust* (London: Abacus, 1996). For a full discussion of the impact of the book see G. Eley (ed.), *The 'Goldhagen Effect': History, Memory, Nazism – Facing the German Past* (Ann Arbor, MI: University of Michigan Press, 2000).

59 See N. Finkelstein, 'Daniel Jonah Goldhagen's "Crazy" Thesis: a Critique of *Hitler's Willing Executioners*', in N. Finkelstein and R. Birn (eds), *A Nation on Trial: The Goldhagen Thesis and Historical Truth* (New York: Holt, 1998).

60 Kershaw, *The Nazi Dictatorship*, p. 255.

61 See N. G. Finkelstein and R. Birn (eds), *A Nation on Trial: The Goldhagen Thesis and Historical Truth* (New York: Holt, 1998). Goldhagen responded to this criticism quite strongly and even threatened to sue Birn. See D. Goldhagen, 'Daniel Jonah Goldhagen Comments on Birn', *German Society and Politics*, vol. 16 (1998), pp. 80–91.

62 See Y. Bauer, *Rethinking the Holocaust* (New Haven, CT: Yale University Press, 2002).

63 E. Jäckel, 'Simply a Bad Book', in R. Shandley (ed.), *Unwilling Germans? The Goldhagen Debate* (University of Minnesota Press, 1998), pp. 87–92.

64 G. Eley, 'Ordinary Germans, Nazism and Judeocide', in Eley, *The 'Goldhagen Effect'*, pp. 1–31.

65   *Die Zeit*, 24 May 1996.

66   K. P. Fischer, *The History of an Obsession: German Judeophobia and the Holocaust* (London: Constable, 1998), pp. 397–403. See also A. Mierzejewski, *Hitler's Trains: The German National Railway and the Third Reich* (NIP Media, 2005); A. Gingrich (ed.), *Networks of Nazi Persecution: Business, Bureaucracy and the Organisation of the Holocaust* (Oxford: Berghahn, 2005); I. Haur and M. Fuhlbusch (eds), *German Scholars and Ethnic Cleansing, 1920–1945* (Oxford: Berghahn, 2005); M. Turda and P. Weindling (eds), *Blood and Homeland: Eugenics and Radical Nationalism in Central and South-east Europe, 1900–1940* (Central European University History Press, 2006); E. Black, *IBM and the Holocaust* (California: Three Rivers, 2002); E. Black, *War against the Weak: Eugenics and America's Campaign to Create a Master Race* (New York: Four Walls, Eight Windows, 2004).

67   R. Gellately, *Backing Hitler: Consent and Coercion in Nazi Germany* (Oxford: Oxford University Press, 2001), pp. 132–41; R. Gellately, *The Gestapo and German Society: Enforcing Racial Policy, 1933–1945* (Oxford: Clarendon Press, 1990, pp. 130–45; E. Johnson, *The Nazi Terror: The Gestapo, Jews and Ordinary Germans* (London: John Murray, 1999), pp. 253–375.

68   V. Klemperer, *I Shall Bear Witness: The Diaries of Victor Klemperer*, vol. 1: *1933–1941* (London: Weidenfeld and Nicolson, 1999), pp. 421–5.

69   G. Schafft, *From Racism to Genocide: Anthropology in the Third Reich* (Illinois: University of Illinois, 2005).

70   M. Kaplan, *Between Dignity and Despair: German Life in Nazi Germany* (Oxford: Oxford University Press, 1998), pp. 232–7.

71   K. P. Fischer, *History of an Obsession*, pp. 399–400.

72   See D. Welch (ed.), *Nazi Propaganda: The Power and the Limitations* (London: Beckenham, 1983); D. Welch, *The Third Reich: Politics and Propaganda* (London: Routledge, 1993); D. Welch, *Propaganda and the German Cinema, 1933-1945* ([1983], London: Tauris, 2001); J. Herf, *The Jewish Enemy: Nazi Propaganda during World War II and the Holocaust* (Cambride, MA: Belknap Press of Harvard University Press, 2006).

73   Kershaw, *The Nazi Dictatorship*, p. 264.

74   See M. Wildt, *Generation des Unbedingten* ('Generation of the Unbound') (Hamburg: Hamburger, 2003).

Who's Who in the Holocaust

Bormann, Martin (1900–45) became the second most powerful man in Nazi Germany during the Second World War. He was head of the Party Chancellery and Hitler's Private Secretary. During the First World War he had served in the German artillery and in the early post-war years was involved in paramilitary attacks on those suspected by the right-wing of 'stabbing Germany in the back'. He served a year in prison in 1924 for his involvement in a political murder (a co-conspirator was Rudolph Höss, the future Commandant of Auschwitz). He joined the Nazi Party in 1925. From 1928 to 1930 he was a senior figure in the SA and in late 1933 was made a Party 'Reich Leader' (*Reichsleiter*). At this time he became a Reichstag deputy and served Rudolf Hess, the Deputy Party Leader, as Personal Secretary. He then rose quietly through the Nazi bureaucracy to become an almost invisible power within the Party machinery. Totally loyal to Hitler, he was given increasing administrative responsibility. He controlled Hitler's finances and managed the huge 'Adolf Hitler Endowment Fund' (a slush fund of 'donations' from big business used by Bormann to grease palms and strengthen Nazi patronage systems). He bought the house in Obersalzberg used by Hitler as his mountain retreat. Bormann made the Party Chancellery the epicentre of policy making and silently acquired powers even the SS could not dilute. He was obsessively concerned with the promotion of Nazi racist ideology and his work strengthened the administration of the Final Solution, on which he composed hundreds of memoranda. His signature is on the decree of 9 October 1942 which required the 'permanent elimination of the Jews from the territory of Greater Germany'. He extended Eichmann's powers over Jewish policy and thus ensured the smooth working of the Final Solution. Always intriguing in the background, he was to control a raft of appointments in the Nazi bureaucracy and extend his tentacles of power throughout the system. At the end in 1945, he was Head of the *Volkssturm*, or makeshift Home Guard, that was all that was left of Germany's forces, a signatory of Hitler's last political testament and even a witness at the marriage of Hitler and Eva Braun. He escaped from the Berlin Führerbunker on 30 April 1945 after watching Hitler's body burn in its courtyard, and attempted to run through the flames as Berlin fell to the Russians. It was thought he had escaped but remains found beneath a Berlin street in 1973 were confirmed as Bormann's. Some historians remained unconvinced and there have been sightings of 'Bormann' in South America since the war.

Bouhler, Philipp (1899–1945) was born in Munich and joined the Nazi Party in the early 1920s. He was the party's head of business affairs and became the Head of the Chancellery of the Führer in 1934, and Police President of Munich. He was a senior SS officer (*Gruppenführer* or Lieutenant-General), a Reich Leader and member of the Reichstag. He was a key figure, with Dr Karl Brandt, in the organisation of the 'T4' euthanasia programme. Adult euthanasia campaigns started in 1939 with Hitler's letter to Bouhler and Brandt, dated 1 September 1939 (but written in October), authorising the 'mercy killings'. Bouhler and Himmler, from 1941, applied the euthanasia policy to the camps themselves; the programme was called 'Action 14f 13' (14f indicated the Concentration Camp Inspectorate, 13 the reason for killing the sick, i.e. 'special treatment'). In May 1945, Bouhler committed suicide.

Brack, Victor (1904–48) was a bureaucrat who worked in Hitler's Chancellery. He first joined the Nazi Party in 1929. He later became a Colonel in the SS. He was concerned with the administration of the sterilisation of concentration camp inmates and prepared a report for Himmler on the uses of X-Rays for the purposes of castration. He was central to the euthanasia campaign (or 'T4 programme' from 1940) as the deputy of Bouhler. He led Amt II (Office II) of the Chancellery, which administered the killings. Mobile gassing vans, which carried out the first of the executions at Chełmno extermination camp, were called 'Brack Aids'. During the 'Doctors' Trial' at Nuremberg (American Military Tribunal No. 1) in December 1946 at which 23 SS doctors were indicted for medical experiments on live camp inmates, he was implicated in the killing programmes. He was convicted and executed at Lansberg Prison in 1948.

Czerniakow, Adam (1880–1942) was the chairman of the Warsaw ghetto's Jewish Council or *Judenrat*. He had been on the Warsaw City Council before September 1939 and a member of the Polish Senate. The ghetto was formed in October 1940 and was to contain 380,000 people, a third of the city's population, in just over 2 per cent of its area. In July 1942, the Nazis demanded the deportation of the ghetto's Jews to the Treblinka death camp. Czerniakow had the task of organising this tragedy. He tried to protect as many Jews as he could but knew it was impossible. The Nazis demanded that 6000 Jews a day be selected and he found his position intolerable: the last straw for Czerniakow was his failure to keep the orphans from being put on the trains destined for the death camp. He committed suicide in the ghetto on 23 July 1942.

Eichmann, Adolf (1906–62) was born in the Rhineland, but brought up in Linz, Austria. He did not do well at school and then worked for his father in the oil business. Later his father pulled strings to get him work in the electricity industry. When the Depression destroyed his father's business he joined the Austrian Nazis in 1932. When the Nazis were outlawed in Austria in 1933, he went to Germany at the suggestion of Ernst Kaltenbrunner, who later succeeded Heydrich as head of the SD (SS Intelligence) and the RSHA (the Nazi Security Main Office). His first work was at Dachau concentration camp, near Munich. All his life he had been an able assistant to those in authority, carrying out orders punctiliously. By 1938, he was employed by the SD in Vienna. After the Nazi takeover in March 1938 (the 'Anschluss') he showed his administrative abilities again by streamlining the ejection of Jews. He repeated the process in Prague in 1939 and was then promoted to RSHA Department IVd 4 in Berlin. His job continued to be the acceleration of Jewish emigration. After the German invasion of Russia in June 1941, Eichmann's Office (now 'IVb 4') was given responsibility for the administrative aspects of the 'Final Solution'. He was also central to the organisation of the Wannsee Conference (January 1942), chaired by Heydrich. He went to Hungary in 1944 and personally ensured the deportation to Auschwitz, in two months, of the entire Hungarian Jewish population of over 400,000. Eichmann was not a murderous psychopath but a cog, if an important one, in the Nazi machine. In 1945 he was captured by the US Army, but, unrecognised, he escaped to Argentina where he was arrested by Israeli agents. He was tried in 1961 in Jerusalem and executed on 1 June 1962 after his appeal was turned down. His last words summed up the defence of many Nazis implicated in the Holocaust: 'I had to obey the rules of war and my flag. I am ready.' It was Eichmann's career that led Hannah Arendt to coin the phrase 'banality of evil' to describe the unthinking, pitiless automatons of the Nazi bureaucracies, who made the killing machines work with ruthless efficiency.

Eicke, Theodor (1892–1943) was a former Inspector of Police from Thuringia who became the first Commandant of Dachau concentration camp near Munich in 1933. From 1934, he became Germany's first Inspector of Concentration Camps and Chief of the SS Guards in the camps (the 'Death's Head Formations'). He had joined the Nazi Party in 1928 and soon was a member of the SA and the SS, in which he became a Major General (or *Gruppenführer*) and later a full General in the Waffen-SS. His meteoric rise in the SS was the result of his support for Himmler in the takeover of the Camp System and his role as an executioner in the 'Night of the Long Knives'. Eicke personally murdered Röhm, the SA Commander. In 1939, he commanded the first of the SS Death's Head Divisions and controlled the Death's Head Formations in the concentration camps in occupied Poland. He was shot down and killed on the Eastern Front in February 1943 while on air reconnaissance.

Frank, Hans (1900–46) was the Nazi Governor-General of Poland. A member of an irregular right-wing army unit (*Freikorps*) after the First World War, he joined the Nazi SA Brownshirts in 1923 and took part in Hitler's 'Munich Putsch' in the same year. He was a qualified lawyer and before 1933 defended Hitler, and many other Nazis, in countless actions, and became Hitler's personal lawyer. After Hitler's coming to power, he was given many senior appointments including the Bavarian and Reich Justice portfolios and the Presidency of the Academy of German Law. He was also Reich Minister without Portfolio in 1934. Yet it was in Poland that Frank became notorious for his determination to enslave and then destroy both Poles and Jews according to Nazi racial theories. Millions were killed and those who survived were slowly and inexorably crushed by starvation and exploitation. By 1942, over 80 per cent of Poland's Jews had perished in its death camps. He was increasingly ignored by other Nazi officials in Poland and, in 1942, was removed from all his posts, except that of Polish Governor-General, following his critical comments on the execution of a colleague. He was executed in Nuremberg Prison in October 1946 after conviction as a war criminal.

Globocnik, Odilo (1904–44) was born in Austro-Hungarian Trieste. He pursued a career in the building industry in the 1920s and was prominent in proto-Nazi groups in Austria before joining the Austrian Nazis in 1931. Between 1933 and 1935 the Austrian authorities arrested him on numerous occasions for his Nazi activities. In 1933 he was made Deputy Gauleiter of Austria and the following year he was inducted into the SS. After his effective work to ensure the Nazi takeover of Austria in March 1938 (the 'Anschluss') he was rewarded with the post of Gauleiter of Vienna in 1938. His Nazi career was interrupted in 1939 when Göring, following revelations of corruption, removed him from his posts. Himmler restored his fortunes following the German invasion of Poland in 1939, where 'Globus', as he was affectionately known in the SS elite, served with distinction in the Waffen-SS. He was made SS Police Leader (SSPF) in Lublin, in occupied Poland. In this role he was a key figure in the prosecution of the Holocaust. He set up the notorious killing camps at Belzec, Majdanek, Treblinka and Sobibór and was overseer of Operation Reinhard, the Nazi campaign of genocide. It is estimated that under his authority, 1.5 million people were killed. He was captured by the British and committed suicide in custody.

Goebbels, Josef (1897–1945) was the master 'spin doctor' of the Nazi Party and force behind the Nazification of German culture in the Nazi regime. He joined the Nazi Party in 1922. He was unusual in that he had a doctorate, in English literature, an academic qualification despised by most Nazis who preferred war medals and battle experience as evidence of strength and character. He suffered from polio in childhood and had a clubfoot. He did not measure up as an ideal member of the 'master race'. He was acutely aware of these shortcomings and consequently became a particularly ardent and radical follower of Hitler. His brilliant oratory, propaganda skills and ideological passion for Nazism made him a central figure in the party. He created the myth of Hitler as the Führer of the movement and the saviour of Germany. Using newspapers (he had his own called *Der Angriff*, 'The Attack'), publishing, radio, film, posters and set-piece choreographed mass rallies he galvanised Nazi Germany and focused attention particularly on the Jew as a threat. From 1933 he was Reich Minister of Propaganda and Public Enlightenment. He organised the infamous May 1933 burning of books by Jews, Marxists and other authors considered 'anti-German', in Berlin. He was a violent anti-Semite and spoke regularly on the Jews as a malignancy behind a world conspiracy: their sinister infiltration into German life had to be rooted out. He was the instigator of the November 1938 pogrom ('Kristallnacht') which destroyed many Jewish lives and property. He gave his last, most memorable speech in the Sportspalatz in February 1943 calling for 'Total War'. He remained deeply committed to Hitler and committed suicide in Hitler's bunker in April 1945. His wife committed suicide with him after supervising the poisoning of their six children.

Göring, Hermann (1893–1946) was the second most powerful political figure in the Third Reich. A highly decorated First World War pilot, he was an early Nazi Party member and took part in the 1923 Munich Putsch. He played a crucial role in Hitler's rise to power through his close links with the army and big business. After 1933 he helped to create the Gestapo, the Nazi Secret Police, was Prussian Minister of the Interior and later President of the Reichstag and Commander of the Luftwaffe. He was instrumental in setting up the first concentration camps and used his powers to complete the elimination of the SA leadership in the 'Blood Purge' of June 1934. In 1936 he was in charge of the economic 'Four Year Plan', the Nazi preparation of the economy for war. He was responsible for fining the Jewish community a billion marks for the damage caused on 'Kristallnacht', and the removal of Jews from the German economy, through the process of 'Aryanisation', which gave businesses and property to non-Jewish Germans at knock-down prices, and excluded Jews from schools, universities and public places. His letter of 31 July 1941 commissioning Heydrich for the 'General Solution of the Jewish Question' is regarded as a 'Holocaust Order'. He was captured by the US Army in May 1945 and brought before the Nuremberg Tribunal in 1946. He was found guilty of 'crimes against humanity' and sentenced to be hanged. He swallowed a cyanide pill just hours before the execution.

Griese, Irma (1921–46) was known at Auschwitz variously as 'the Angel of Hell' and 'Queen of Auschwitz'. She had been a member of the BDM, the Nazis' youth organisation for girls, and in 1939 she joined the SS. She was sent to Auschwitz as a camp guard and soon became the most senior female officer. She was particularly feared and her exceptionally brutal treatment of the prisoners and murderous psychopathy have become legendary. Instantly recognisable in her special sky blue uniform, she regularly beat, whipped and shot prisoners on a whim and was always involved in the 'selections' for the gas chambers. She was arrested by the Allies while attempting to flee Auschwitz as the Russians approached. She was brought before the Nuremberg Tribunal and accused of war crimes, specifically the execution of 45,000 women at Auschwitz. Many former prisoners could not fail to remember her. She was hanged in 1946.

Grynszpan, Herschel (1921–45) assassinated Ernst vom Rath, a Nazi official at the German Embassy in Paris, on 7 November 1938. This act was used by the Nazis to justify 'Kristallnacht'. He was born in Hanover but his parents were Polish Jews who had immigrated to Germany before the 1914–18 war. In 1938, as part of the growing assault on the Jews in Germany, Herschell's parents were forced by the Gestapo to hand over all their possessions and deported to Poland. Along with 12,000 other Jews, they were pushed into a no-man's-land at the Polish border but refused permission to enter Poland. They sent a letter to their son pleading for help: they had little food and no shelter. Enraged by this, Herschell blamed the Nazis and went to a gun shop in Paris, bought a revolver and contrived an interview at the German Embassy where he shot vom Rath. He was imprisoned in Paris and taken by the Nazis after the capital's fall in June 1940. He was accused of high treason but his trial was never instigated: there is evidence he was still alive in January 1945 but it is likely the Nazis executed him. His parents survived the war.

Heydrich, Reinhard (1904–42) was second only to Himmler in the SS, and dubbed the 'blond beast'. He was head of the RSHA, the Reich Security Service, and the SD, the SS intelligence branch. He joined the Nazi Party and the SS in 1931. Himmler saw him as his Aryan golden boy and he was made an SS Lieutenant-General in 1934. He Nazified the German police and became chief of the Berlin Gestapo before claiming command of all secret police operations throughout Germany in 1936. It was Heydrich who organised the Holocaust. He had initial responsibility as Administrator of Concentration Camps, and established the first ghettos and their Jewish Councils, but it was his position at the centre of the terrifying and ubiquitous terror machinery of the Nazi security system and secret police (the RSHA) that gave him unrivalled power to advance the Final Solution. He had received Göring's commission for the 'Final Solution', of 31 July 1941, and organised and chaired the crucial Wannsee Conference of 20 January 1942, which coordinated the full range of state agencies and resources the Final Solution required. He was made Deputy Reich Protector of Bohemia and Moravia (the rump of Czechoslovakia) in 1941 and his stewardship as 'Reich Protector' was exceptionally brutal. Czech partisans, parachuted into Prague by the British SOE (Special Operations Executive), attacked Heydrich on 27 May 1942 and he died of his wounds on 4 June 1942. German reprisals were murderous: over 1200 Czechs were condemned to death and the village of Lidice was razed to the ground; all its men and boys were executed. Heydrich was the epitome of the cold-hearted SS killer ordering the deaths of millions without compunction. After his death the killing of the Jews in the extermination camps increased and the campaign was appropriately entitled 'Operation Reinhard'.

Himmler, Heinrich (1900–45) was Hitler's enforcer and ruthless Chief of the SS, the Waffen-SS and the German police. He participated in Hitler's Munich Putsch of 1923 and later became Gauleiter (District Head) of Lower Bavaria. He was a poultry farmer who became head of the fledgling SS in 1929. He developed his own intelligence service (the SD) in 1934. After the 'Night of the Long Knives', which purged the SA, the SS under Himmler became the most powerful organisation in Nazi Germany. In 1933, as Chief of Police in Munich and then all Bavaria, he set up the first concentration camp at Dachau, near Munich. In April 1934 he was made Chief of the German Secret Police (Gestapo). By 1936, he was 'Reichsführer-SS' and leader of the combined forces of the entire German police system. In this capacity, and as Minster of the Interior and Commissar for the Consolidation of German Nationhood, he became chiefly responsible for the operation of the concentration camps and the carrying out of the Final Solution. He pioneered the *Lebensborn* project, an experiment in breeding designed to procreate 'Nordic supermen' by selecting racially screened women to have children by pure Aryan SS men, and by 1939 was appointed 'Reich Commissar for the Strengthening of Germandom'. After the subjugation of Poland he had the task of removing the Jews and bringing Germans (the *Volksdeutsche*) into the space so created. This required the elimination of millions of Jews. It is assumed that Hitler gave the order for the 'Final Solution' to Himmler sometime in 1941. Himmler was the overlord of the Final Solution: from the ghettos to the gas chambers, the mass shootings, medical experiments, sterilisation, abortion, euthanasia and the enslavement of millions. As the Allies closed in, Himmler attempted to make a separate peace and was expelled from the Nazi Party by an enraged Hitler who demanded his arrest. He was caught by the British disguised, clean-shaven and wearing an eye patch, as an ex-Gestapo agent called Heinrich Hitzinger. He committed suicide, swallowing a cyanide capsule while in British custody at Luneburg on 23 May 1945.

Hitler, Adolf (1889–1945) was Chancellor and Führer of the Third Reich and leader of the Nazi Party. He was Dictator of Germany from 1933 and Commander-in-Chief of the German Armed Forces from 1938. He was born in Austria but fought in the German army, being awarded the Iron Cross. Germany's defeat, what he saw as the vindictive Treaty of Versailles, and the Socialist uprisings of the 'German Revolution' of 1918, came as a shock to him. This 'Stab-in-the-Back' myth Hitler attributed to Communists and Jews and he entered right-wing nationalist politics in order to fight for the rehabilitation of Germany. He spied for the post-war German army (the *Reichswehr*) on right-wing splinter parties after the 1918 revolution and he joined the 'German Workers' Party' in 1919. He became its leader and changed its name to the NSDAP or National Socialist German Workers' Party (the Nazi Party). He soon developed an aggressive if popular oratorical style and established the SA, or Stormtroopers, as his bodyguard. Hitler's first attempt at power was the abortive 'Munich Beer Hall Putsch' of 1923. With Ludendorff, a leading Commander of German forces in the First World War, and Göring, he attempted to overthrow the Bavarian state government but was defeated by armed police, tried and convicted. He spent the next nine months in Landsberg Prison where he composed his political testament, *Mein Kampf* ('My Struggle'). Historians debate whether such a rambling thesis can be seen as evidence for an intention to carry out the 'Final Solution' but the book does contain a clear anti-Jewish stance that he maintained consistently to the end of his life. After 1923, Hitler developed more conventional political strategies and began to fight elections but by 1928 his party had only managed to win 12 seats in the Reichstag, the German Parliament. After 1930, the Nazi Party rose dramatically. In July 1932, the Nazis, with 230 seats, had become the largest party in the Reichstag, and Hitler had also made a most respectable showing in the elections for President of Germany. Hitler was offered the Chancellorship in January 1933, after much backstairs intrigue involving President Hindenburg. He swiftly established dictatorial rule after the Reichstag Fire. In 1934, the SA leadership was destroyed in the June 'Night of the Long Knives' and following the death of the old President Hindenberg, in August 1934 Hitler combined the offices of President and Chancellor to call himself 'Führer' or 'Leader' of Germany. He enjoyed remarkable foreign policy success in the 1930s: reparations were abandoned, occupied territory in the Rhineland reclaimed, Austria and most of Czechoslovakia incorporated into the Reich by 1939. By the time of Hitler's successful invasion of Poland in September 1939, the governments of Britain and France, who had vainly attempted to appease him, decided to go to war. The Nazi regime defeated France in 1940 and after – or before – the invasion of Russia in June 1941 Hitler gave the orders for the Final Solution. No 'Führer Order' has survived but the death camps in the east were at work by the end of 1941 and special killing units, the SS 'Einsatzgruppen', had killed hundreds of thousands. Following Hitler's failure to remove Britain from the war in 1940, a huge strategic blunder, Hitler's declaration of war on the USA in December 1941, meant that it was only a matter of time before the superiority of the Allies in men and resources would tell. This, and the incompetence of Hitler's war leadership, enabled the British and the Americans to defeat the Nazis in North Africa and advance on the Third Reich from France after D-Day, 6 June 1944. The Soviet Army attacked from the east as it recovered from the initial defeats of 1941. Bombarded mercilessly from the air by British and US aircraft and losing significant battles to the Russians at Stalingrad and Kursk, the Germans faced total defeat. In the Ardennes in 1944, the 'Battle of the Bulge' was a doomed, last Nazi assault and Germany was soon occupied. Remarkably, whilst facing Armageddon, Hitler continued to sanction the use of men, munitions, railway capacity, money and administrative resources for the Final Solution. As defeat neared, Hitler in his bunker in Berlin had long lost contact with the reality of the war, refusing to believe the inevitability of his downfall. He wrote his political testament as his regime's last rites, proclaiming to the end that 'international Jewry was the universal poisoner of peoples'. He then married his mistress Eva Braun and committed suicide with her on 30 April 1945.

Höss, Rudolf (1900–47) was born in Baden-Baden, Germany, and fought with distinction in the First World War, winning the Iron Cross 1st class. He was to become infamous as Commandant of Auschwitz death camp from May 1940 to November 1943. He joined the Nazis in 1922. He was imprisoned for five years, with Martin Bormann, who received a lighter sentence, for his involvement in a politically inspired murder. He joined the SS in 1934 and worked at Dachau from November 1934, but was soon promoted and sent to Sachsenhausen concentration camp, near Berlin. He joined the Waffen-SS in 1939 and was then given the responsibility for the establishment and development of the largest death camp of all, at Auschwitz, where he pioneered the use of Zyklon B gas. From December 1943, Höss was a senior official in the SS Economic and Administrative Central Office (SS-WVHA), which administered all concentration camps and death camps. By 1945 he was deputy to Richard Glücks, the Chief of the Concentration Camp Inspectorate. He was not an aloof bureaucrat: he was an innovator forever seeking new, more efficient ways to kill, and increase Auschwitz's appetite for corpses. At the end of his working day he led a quiet, simple family life with his wife and children in the Auschwitz grounds just yards from one of the crematoria. He was captured by the British in March 1946, and later executed.

Jäger, Karl (1888–1959) commanded the Security Police (Sipo) and SS Intelligence (SD) in Lithuania. In May 1940 he was placed in command of *Einsatzkommando* 3 as a section of *Einsatzgruppe* A attached to Army Group North under Dr Franz Stahlecker, operating in the Baltic states. He was born in Switzerland and after war service in Germany joined the Nazi Party in 1923 and was in the SS by 1932. However, his notoriety is as author of one of the most damning documents to survive the war: his December 1941 'Jäger Report' on the activities of his 'kommando', detailing every single killing of 137,346 Lithuanian Jews over a five-month period. In the report he claimed the 'solving the Jewish problem in Lithuania'. In a later report of February 1942, Jäger listed the executions of 136,421 Jews, 1064 Communists, 653 mentally ill and 134 'others'. The death toll included over 55,000 women and 35,000 children. In late 1943, he was transferred as Police Chief in Reichenberg in the Sudetenland, formerly part of Czechoslovakia. He avoided arrest by the Allies in 1945 and lived under an assumed name until April 1959 when he was exposed: he committed suicide in prison before he could be arraigned as a war criminal.

Kaltenbrunner, Ernst (1903–46) was leader of the Austrian SS and worked with the Germans to complete the Anschluss of 1938. He had joined the Nazi Party and the SS in Austria in 1932. He was even implicated in the assassination of the Austrian Chancellor, Dollfuss, in 1934. By 1941, he was a Major-General in the German police and the SS. Kaltenbrunner replaced Heydrich as Chief of the Reich Security Service, the RSHA, after the latter's assassination in June 1942, and he also led the SS Intelligence unit, the SD. He became a powerful figure at the centre of the Nazi machine and worked with Martin Bormann to secure a position very close to Hitler. His powerful position placed him at the heart of the prosecution of the Final Solution. He directed the Einsatzgruppen actions on the Eastern Front, and controlled the Gestapo as well as the concentration camps and their slave labour and routines of annihilation. He advised on methods of execution in the camps, was at the core of the Nazi administration of death and a key figure in carrying forward the Holocaust discussed by Heydrich at the Wannsee Conference in January 1942. He was arrested by the Allies and arraigned at Nuremberg. Found guilty, he was executed in October 1946.

Mengele, Josef (1911–79) was the infamous SS doctor called the 'angel of death' at Auschwitz. He performed medical experiments on live inmates without anaesthesia and had a particular interest in the physiology and morbidity of twins and dwarves. Subjects had their blood removed, were injected with disease, had limbs amputated, and suffered a wide range of invasive surgery and sterilisation procedures from which many subsequently died. In some cases his patients were deliberately killed in order to provide dissection material. He had a prominent role in the 'selections' of Jews for the gas chambers upon their arrival at Auschwitz and was renowned for his brutal treatment of those who fell into his hands at the camp. He was always ready to condemn hundreds to the gas chambers. He came from a middle-class family and in 1930 gained a doctorate in Anthropology. He later obtained a medical doctorate (1938), thus adding to the high proportion of the Nazi elite who had held doctorates. For example, three out of the four commanders of *Einsatzgruppen* had doctorates: these were Otto Rasch who had two doctorates, Otto Ohlendorf and Franz Stahlecker. Mengele joined the 'Stahlhelm' (a right-wing veterans' paramilitary organisation) in 1930, and the SA Brownshirts in 1933. He became a Nazi Party member in 1937 and an SS man in 1938. After service on the Russian Front he was invalided out and sent to Auschwitz where he was promoted to Chief Medical Officer in the camp hospital. In 1945, he was captured by the British but remained unrecognised and fled to Argentina. He also lived in Paraguay and Brazil and he remained at large until his death from a stroke in 1979.

Müller, Heinrich ('Gestapo Müller') (1901–45) was Gestapo Chief during the war and effectively Eichmann's superior officer. He was head of 'Amt IV' of the RSHA, the Reich Security Main Office, and in charge of the implementation of the Final Solution. Before the war, he had served as a policeman in Bavaria with responsibility for the surveillance of communists. He worked with Heydrich in the Gestapo but did not join the Nazi Party until 1939. A ruthless operator, he was admired by Heydrich and Himmler for his blind obedience and willingness to use violence against the regime's opponents, whether inside or outside the party. By 1941 he was an SS-*Obergruppenführer* (Lieutenant-General) and Chief of Police with responsibility for destroying resistance to the Nazis. In this capacity he ruthlessly hunted down the assassins of Heydrich and the army officers in the 'July Plot' who failed to kill Hitler in 1944. He was present at the Wannsee Conference in January 1942 that developed the administration of the Holocaust, and his name appears on the many orders requiring the deportation of Jews to Auschwitz. His energetic driving of the administration of the Final Solution rendered his contribution to the Holocaust greater than that of almost any other member of the Nazi elite, including Himmler, Heydrich and Eichmann. He went to Rome to demand that the Italians increased the transportation of Jews to Auschwitz. He is known to have ordered the execution of Russian and even British prisoners of war. He was in Hitler's bunker in the last days of the war but disappeared: his fate has never been explained.

Naumann, Erich (1905–51) was an SS Brigadier and Commander of *Einsatzgruppe* B, one of the four special killing units sent to Russia to operate behind German lines from June 1941. Naumann commanded his group from November 1941 and reported to Berlin his responsibility for the killing of 17,256 people, including children from a children's home, in the Smolensk area in that month alone. Naumann was from Meissen and had joined the Nazi Party in 1929. He was also in the SA Brownshirts from 1933, a police officer and, from 1935, an SD (the SS Security Service) operative. He was captured and placed on trial at Nuremberg. When asked whether the killing of thousands of defenceless men, women and children was justified he answered immediately, 'Yes'. He saw nothing wrong in carrying out orders with which he agreed. He was sentenced to death for war crimes and was executed in June 1951.

Nebe, Artur (1894–1945) joined the police after the First World War and was a detective during the Weimar period. In the Gestapo (Secret Police) from 1933, he became Berlin Police Chief and head of the *Kriminalpolizei* (or 'Kripo') by 1936. This was later to be SS Amt V (Office V) of the SS Reich Security Main Office (RSHA). He was a Major-General SS and Amt V Chief from 1941 to 1945. He led *Einsatzgruppe* B, which operated towards Moscow and in the Minsk area, from May to November 1941 and was responsible for 45,476 victims. He was replaced as its leader by Erich Naumann. Nebe's friends claimed he exaggerated the activities of his Einsatzgruppe to please his superiors, and found the work sufficiently distasteful for him to contact General Oster and other army officers involved in the 1944 July Plot to assassinate Hitler. He was caught and sentenced to death by the Nazi 'People's Court'. He was hanged with piano wire with other conspirators on 21 March 1945.

Ohlendorf, Otto (1907–51) was the notorious commander of the mobile execution unit Einsatzgruppe D, which operated on the Eastern Front, in the Ukraine, after the Nazi invasion of Russia in June 1941. Born in Berlin, he had joined the SA (Nazi Party Brownshirts or Stormtroopers) in 1925 and the SS a year later. He became an economic adviser in the SD (SS Intelligence) in 1936 and throughout the Second World War was chief of SS Amt III (Office III), charged with assessing the impact of Nazi laws in Germany. From 1943 to 1945 he was Under-State Secretary in the Reich Ministry of Economics. In 1945, with Germany on the brink of defeat, he was an economic adviser to the stillborn Doenitz government which tried to negotiate with the Allies as Hitler's successor. He was captured by the US Army and brought to trial in 1947 at Nuremberg. His leadership of an Einsatzgruppe was exposed in the 'Einsatzgruppen Case' (Military Tribunal Case No. 9) that began on 3 July 1947. Ohlendorf was the chief defendant and freely admitted to being responsible for the execution of 90,000 people, and confirmed that the German army was complicit in these murders. He was hanged in 1951.

Pohl, Oswald (1892–1951) served in the German navy in the First World War. After the war he dropped out of university to become a *Freikorps* (right-wing paramilitary formations) member, mainly in Berlin. He joined the SA (Nazi Brownshirts or 'Stormtroopers') in 1925 and the Nazi Party itself in 1926. His career sponsored by Heinrich Himmler, he rose to lead the new SS Inspectorate of Concentration Camps in 1935. By 1939 he was leading the SS Department responsible for the economy, which was, by 1943, the SS-WVHA (Economic and Welfare Office with responsibility for the concentration camps). Pohl's Office supervised the handling of forced labour in the camps and in effect ran the camp system. He was also at the head of the Waffen-SS administration. Eventually captured by the British in 1946, he was sentenced to death at a Nuremberg Tribunal (the 'Pohl' or 'WVHA' Trial conducted by the United States) in 1947. He was hanged at Landsberg in June 1951.

Rasch, Otto (1891–1948) commanded *Einsatzgruppe* C, the special killing squad attached to Army Group South and operating in northern and central Ukraine. Rasch's group was responsible for one of the most horrific mass murders of the Second World War, that at Babi-Yar, the ravine near Kiev where in September 1941, over 30,000 Jews were machine-gunned into pits in two days. Under Rasch, *Einsatzgruppe* C killed hundreds of thousands. He was born in East Prussia, had served in the German navy in the First World War and joined the Nazi party in 1931. He had two doctorates, in Law and Politics, and was known as 'Dr. Dr. Rasch' to distinguish him from other highly educated senior SS staff. He was mayor of Wittenberg and in 1936 was working for the RSHA, the Reich Security Main Office run by Heydrich. In 1938, he was Police Chief in Frankfurt and also Head of Security in Upper Austria, and the following year led the Security Police (Sipo) and SS Intelligence (SD) in Prague. He also held such senior police and security posts in Königsberg, East Prussia. He commanded *Einsatzgruppe* C from May until October 1941. Rasch was imprisoned and arraigned before the Nuremberg Military Tribunal (the '*Einsatzgruppen* Case' of July 1947 to April 1948) but died of natural causes before the trial ended.

Rosenberg, Alfred (1893–1946) was born in Estonia and was the so-called 'philosopher' of the Nazi Party. He was a strong proponent of the idea that the Nazis should establish a 'master race'. His main work was *The Myth of the Twentieth Century* (1925), which purported to expose the dangers of 'lower races', especially Jews, and celebrate the splendours of Aryan/Nordic man. He was also the author of anti-Semitic pamphlets and in 1934 he was given the grand title 'the Führer's Delegate for the Entire Intellectual and Philosophical Education and Instruction of the National Socialist Party'. During the war, he played a key part in the confiscation of Jewish property in the occupied territories. In July 1941, he was made Minister for the Eastern Occupied Territories and was thus heavily involved in the organisation of slave labour and the administration of the 'Final Solution'. He was found guilty at Nuremberg and hanged in 1946.

Rumkowski, Mordechai Chaim (1877–1944) was a Jewish businessman and Zionist, appointed by the Nazis as head of the Jewish Council or *Judenrat* in the Lodz or 'Litzmannstadt' ghetto. This was the second biggest ghetto in Poland after Warsaw and the last to be destroyed by the Nazis. Rumkowski ensured that the Nazis' demands were accommodated by imposing the harsh discipline of the ghetto's Jewish Police. He was responsible for ensuring the smooth running of regular deportations of Jews, which were selected by the *Judenrat* itself, to Chełmno and Auschwitz. He was notorious for his 1942 'give me your children' speech, calling for the children to be deported so that the ghetto could survive, and he has been dismissed as 'King Chaim', a megalomaniac whose conceit was that he was his people's father and that only he stood between his Jews and immolation. The Lodz ghetto was liquidated in stages from July 1944. On the last transport to the Auschwitz gas chambers were Rumkowski and his family, who were executed in August 1944.

Schindler, Oskar (1908–74) was a German businessman who saved over 1000 of his Jewish workforce from the Final Solution. Initially, his activities did not indicate such a role. He had ties with the German *Abwehr*, the army's Counter-Intelligence Service, and it is likely he helped plan the German invasion of Poland in September 1939. He then took advantage of the profits to be made from exploiting the Jews, taking over an 'Aryanised' Jewish business in Krakow, using slave labour to make enamelware. Eventually he ran three businesses, two in Poland, one making vodka bottles, and one in Bohemia. He employed many non-Jewish Polish workers but it is his famous 'Schindler's List' of protected Jewish employees that has ensured his lasting fame. He protested to the Nazi authorities that his Jews were vital to the economy and went to extraordinary lengths to protect his workforce. He smuggled children out of the Kracow ghetto and indulged in black market activities, and succeeded in saving Jewish property. He also bribed SS guards to protect his workers. As the Red Army advanced, he evacuated his workforce to Bohemia and safety. After the war, Schindler went to Argentina but failed in business, a trend he repeated upon his return to Germany in 1958. He died in 1964 and is buried in Jerusalem. His life was the subject of Thomas Keneally's book *Schindler's Ark*, turned by Steven Spielberg into the 1993 film *Schindler's List* starring Liam Neeson as Schindler. He was a man of dubious reputation who nevertheless saved over a thousand Jews from the Holocaust.

Stahlecker, Franz Walther (1900–42) was leader of *Einsatzgruppe* A, regarded as one of the most ruthless of the four 'Special Groups' of killing machines attached to the German Army Group following the invasion of Russia in June 1941. He joined the Nazi Party in 1932 and rose to lead the Württemberg Gestapo. Appointed to the SS intelligence organisation, the SD, he became their Chief in the Danube District of Vienna after the Anschluss of 1938. He later worked in the Foreign Office, in the Protectorate of Bohemia and Moravia (the former Czechoslovakia) and in Norway after the Nazi invasion of 1940. He became leader of *Einsatzgruppe* A, attached to Army Group North, in June 1941 and supervised the mass murders in the Baltic states and in occupied Russia before the siege of Leningrad. In November 1941, Stahlecker reported the annihilation of 250,000 Jews, Communists, prisoners of war and Gypsies and he was rewarded with the post of HSSPF (Higher SS and Police Leader) for 'Reichskommissariat Ostland' (covering the Baltic states and Belarus). He died on the Eastern Front in March 1942 while fighting Russian partisans.

Stangl, Franz (1908–71) was born in Austria and worked as a weaver before joining the Austrian police in 1931. After the Nazi takeover in 1938 (the 'Anschluss') he was promoted by Himmler and supervised killings at the Hartheim Asylum under the euthanasia 'T4' programme. At Hartheim he worked with Christian Wirth. By 1942 he was working for Globocnik in Poland and soon was Commandant of his own extermination camp at Sobibór, from March to September 1942. He ran the Treblinka death camp until August 1943. Always immaculately dressed in white riding clothes, he was the typical unemotional bureaucrat, regarding the Jews being sent to the gas chambers as merely 'baggage' or 'cargo' to be processed, and he never questioned the legitimacy of mass murder. He was only concerned with efficiency and turnover. At Treblinka it is estimated he was responsible for the efficient murder of over 900,000 people, and 99 per cent of people arriving at Treblinka were dead within two hours. He personally stole about 140kg of gold and thousands of diamonds from those he drove to the gas chambers. He eluded arrest after the war, with the help of the Vatican, and hid in Syria for three years. He was found in Brazil by Nazi-hunter Simon Wiesenthal in 1967 and given a life sentence after trial in West Germany.

Streicher, Julius (1885–1946) was the Nazis' Jew-baiter-in-chief. He ran the scandalous weekly newspaper *Der Stürmer* and was responsible for the popularisation of anti-Semitism in Nazi Germany. A schoolteacher by profession, he had joined the Nazi Party early in 1921. As a Bavarian he was an early intimate of Hitler. His anti-Semitic newspaper *Der Stürmer* depicted Jews as dangerous, animal-like, repulsive creatures. By 1937, it sold 500,000 copies a day. Streicher was appointed to Nazi organisations such as the Central Committee for the Defence against Jewish Atrocity and Boycott Propaganda, and became a member of the Reichstag and an SS Major-General. He was eventually removed from all his Party positions in 1940 because of a common revulsion at his coarseness, his rudeness, his outrageous immorality and Göring's anger at Streicher's public attack on his virility. He continued to edit *Der Stürmer* until the end of the war, until arrested by the Allies and executed following the Nuremberg Trials in 1946.

Stroop, Jürgen (1895–1951) was skilled in the imposition of Nazi control in the occupied territories of Czechoslovakia, Greece, Poland and Russia. He was an SS Brigadier and particularly infamous for his leadership of the Nazi troops that ruthlessly put down the Warsaw ghetto uprising of April–May 1943. The Warsaw operation resulted in the slaughter of 14,000 Jews with another 42,000 sent to the death camps (mainly Treblinka) and slave labour facilities. The 'Stroop Report' was his summary of his use of the SS and Wehrmacht and contains gratuitously graphic descriptions and photographs of the brutality used by his troops against the Jewish defenders. He was later HSSPF (Higher SS and Police Leader), where he was involved in the shooting of American prisoner-of-war pilots. In 1947 he was sentenced to death by a US Military Tribunal (at Dachau) but subsequently retried in Poland for war crimes and executed in September 1951.

Stuckart, Wilhelm (1902–51) was a Nazi lawyer whose most important work was the drafting of the 'Nuremberg Laws' of 1935, which provided the legal foundation for Nazi anti-Semitic legislation. With Hans Globke he continued to write legal commentaries on the racist/*volkisch* meaning of the 'Nuremberg Laws'. By 1944 he had been promoted to SS Lieutenant-General after proving his importance to the development of the Final Solution by advocating sterilisation for 'non-Aryans' and his chairmanship of the Commission for the Protection of German Blood. He attended the Wannsee Conference of January 1942. The Allies caught him in 1945 but he protested ignorance of the death camps. Astonishingly, his claim was accepted and he was given four years' imprisonment in 1949 and released immediately because he had already served this term. He was killed in a suspicious car crash in 1953, probably the work of an anti-Nazi retribution cell.

Wirth, Christian (1885–1944) was a key figure in the operation of the extermination camps in Poland after 1939 and was the first Commandant of Belzec concentration camp. He had worked as a joiner and sometime police officer and joined the Nazi Party in 1931. By 1939 he was a member of the Nazi SA (Brownshirts), the SS and its intelligence arm, the SD. When war began, he was a police officer in Stuttgart working alongside the Gestapo. He had an important role in the Nazis' euthanasia (T4) programme. In 1941, he was involved in the first gassing of Jews at Chełmno, where gas vans were used. In December 1941, Wirth was Commandant at Belzec, the first of the 'Action Reinhard' camps designed to intensify the 'Final Solution', and was renowned for his brutal treatment of both prisoners and SS guards. Called 'Christian the savage' he beat his own men mercilessly and personally attacked and screamed at Jews when they arrived at Belzec. He beat them with whips and drove them into the gas chambers. In 1942, Wirth was Inspector of the Reinhard Camps and was to be central to the 'Harvest Festival' killings of Jewish forced labour in 1943. The Reinhard Programme killed over 1.7 million people, mostly Jews, and Wirth ensured its efficiency. He was transferred to Italy in 1944 and set up gas chambers for the Jews of Trieste. He was killed fighting partisans in Yugoslavia in May 1944.

Select Bibliography

Place of publication is London, UK, unless otherwise stated.

● Books

Adam, U., *Judenpolitik im Dritten Reich* (Düsseldorf: Droste Verlag, 1972; 2nd edn, 1979).

Adelsberger, L., *Auschwitz: A Doctor's Story* (Robson, 1996).

Adelson, A. and Lapides, G., *Lodz Ghetto: Inside a Community under Siege* (New York: Viking, 1989).

Adler, H-G., *Der verwaltete Mensch. Studien zur Deportation der Juden aus Deutschland* (Tübingen: Mohr, 1974).

Adorno, T. et al., *The Authoritarian Personality* (New York: Harper, 1950).

Allen, M. T., *The Business of Genocide: The SS, Slave Labor and the Concentration Camps* (Chapel Hill, NC: University of North Carolina Press, 2002).

Almond, M., *Europe's Backyard War: War in the Balkans* (Mandarin, 1994).

Aly, G., *Aktion T4: 1939–1945. Die 'Euthansie'-Zentrale in der Tiergartenstrasse 4* (Berlin: Edition Heinrich, 1989).

Aly, G., *'Final Solution': Nazi Population Policy and the Murder of the European Jews* (Edward Arnold, 1999).

Aly, G., *Hitler's Beneficiaries: Plunder, Racial War and the Nazi Welfare State* (New York: Henry Holt, 2007).

Aly, G. and Heim, S., *Vordenker der Vernichtung, Auschwitz und die Pläner für eine neue europäische Ordnung* (3rd edn, Frankfurt a.M.: Fischer Taschenbuch Verlag, 1994).

Aly, G. and Heim, S., *Architects of Annihilation: Auschwitz and the Logic of Destruction* (Weidenfeld and Nicolson, 2002).

Aly, G., Chroust, P. and Pross, C., *Cleansing the Fatherland: Nazi Medicine and Racial Hygiene* (Baltimore, MD: Johns Hopkins University Press, 1994).

Angrick, A., *Besatzungspolitik und Massenmord. Die Einsatzgruppe D in der Sowjetunion 1941–1943* (Hamburg, 2003).

Annisimov, M., *Primo Levi: Tragedy of an Optimist* (Aurum Press, 1998).

Arad, Y., *Ghetto in Flames: The Struggle and Destruction of the Jews in Vilna in the Holocaust* (Jerusalem: Yad Vashem, 1980).

Arad, Y., *Belzec, Sobibór, Treblinka. The Operation Reinhard Death Camps* ([1987] Bloomington, IN: Indiana University Press, 1999).

Arad, Y., Krakowski, S. and Spector, S. (eds), *The Einsatzgruppen Reports: Selections from the Dispatches of the Nazi Death Squads* (Washington, DC: US Holocaust Museum, 1990).

Arendt, H., *The Origins of Totalitarianism* (André Deutsch, 1951).

Arendt, H., *Eichmann in Jerusalem: A Report on the Banality of Evil* (Penguin, 1994).

Arendt, H., *Eichmann and the Holocaust* (Penguin Books, 2006).

Aroneanu, E. (ed.), *Inside the Concentration Camps: Eyewitness Accounts of Life in Hitler's Death Camps* (Westport, CT: Greenwood Press, 1996).

Aronson, S., *Hitler, the Allies and the Jews* (Cambridge: Cambridge University Press, 2004).

Ayçoberry, P., *The Social History of the Third Reich, 1933–1945* (New York: New Press, 1999).

Bajohr, F., *'Aryanisation' in Hamburg: The Economic Exclusion of the Jews and the Confiscation of their Property in Nazi Germany* (Oxford: Berghahn, 2002).

Baldwin, P. (ed.), *Reworking the Past: Hitler, the Holocaust and the Historians' Debate* (Boston, MA: Beacon Press, 1990).

Bankier, D., *The Germans and the Final Solution: Public Opinion under Nazism* (Oxford: Blackwell, 1996).

Bankier, D. (ed.), *Probing the Depths of German Anti-Semitism: German Society and the Persecution of the Jews, 1933–1941* (Yad Vashem, the Leo Baeck Institute, Oxford: Berghahn Books, 2000).

Barkai, A., *From Boycott to Annihilation: The Economic Struggle of German Jews, 1933–1945* (Dartmouth College, NH: University Press of New England, 1989).

Barnet, V., *For the Soul of the People: Protestant Protest against Hitler* (Oxford: Oxford University Press, 1992).

Barnett, V., *Bystanders: Conscience and Complicity during the Holocaust* (Westport, CT: Greenwood Press, 2000).

Bartov, O., *Murder in our Midst: The Holocaust, Industrial Killing and Representation* (New York: Oxford University Press, 1996).

Bartov, O. (ed.), *The Holocaust: Origins, Implementation, Aftermath* (Routledge, 2000).

Bartov, O., *The Eastern Front, 1941–45: German Troops and the Barbarization of War* (Basingstoke: Macmillan, 2001).

Bartov, O., *Germany's War and the Holocaust: Disputed Histories* (New York: Cornell University Press, 2003).

Bar-Zohar, M., *Beyond Hitler's Grasp: The Heroic Rescue of Bulgaria's Jews* (Chicago, IL: Adams, 1998).

Bau, J., *Dear God: Have You Ever Gone Hungry?* (Boston, MA: Little, Brown, 2000).

Bauer, Y., *They Chose Life: Jewish Resistance in the Holocaust* (New York: New York Institute of Human Relations, 1973).

Bauer, Y., *The Holocaust in Historical Perspective* (Seattle: University of Washington Press, 1978).

Bauer, Y., *A History of the Holocaust* (New York: Franklin Watts, 1982).

Bauer, Y., *Rethinking the Holocaust* (New Haven, CT: Yale University Press, 2002).

Bauer, Y. and Rotenstreich, N., *The Holocaust as Historical Experience: Essays and a Discussion* (New York: Holmes and Meier, 1981).

Baumann, Z., *Modernity and the Holocaust* ([1978] Cambridge: Polity Press, 2000).

Baumann, Z. and Tester, K., *Conversations with Zygmunt Baumann* (Cambridge: Polity Press, 2001).

Baynes, N. H., *The Speeches of Adolf Hitler* ([Oxford, 1942]; New York: Howard Vertag, 2006).

Benz, W. (ed.), *Dimension des Völkermords. Die Zahl der jüischen Opfer des Nationalsozialismus* (Munich: Oldenbourg, 1991).

Benz, W., *The Holocaust: A German Historian Examines the Holocaust* (New York: Columbia University Press, 1999).

Berenbaum, M. (ed.), *A Mosaic of Victims: Non-Jews Persecuted and Murdered by the Nazis* (New York: New York Press, 1992).

Berenbaum, M., *The World Must Know: The History of the Holocaust as Told in the United States Holocaust Memorial Museum* (Boston, MA: Little, Brown, 1993).

Berenbaum, M. (ed.), *Anatomy of the Auschwitz Death Camp* (Bloomington, IN: Indiana University Press, 1994).

Berenbaum, M., *Witness to the Holocaust* (New York: HarperCollins, 1997).

Berenbaum, M. and Peck, A. J. (eds), *The Holocaust and History: The Known, the Unknown and the Re-Examined* (Bloomington, IN: Indiana University Press, 1998).

Bergen, D. L., *War and Genocide: A Concise History of the Holocaust* (New York: Rowman & Littlefield, 2003).

Berghahn, V., *Modern Germany: Society, Economy and Politics in the Twentieth Century* (Cambridge: Cambridge University Press, 1982).

Berkley, G. E., *Hitler's Gift: The Story of Theresienstadt* (Boston, MA: Branden, 2002).

Bernstein, R. J., *Hannah Arendt and the Jewish Question* (Cambridge: Polity Press, 1996).

Bettelheim, B., *Surviving the Holocaust* ([1952] London: Fontana, 1986).

Binion, R., *Hitler Among the Germans* (Champaign, IL: Illinois University Press, 1984).

Bitton-Jackson, L., *Elli: Coming of Age in the Holocaust* (HarperCollins, 1984).

Bitton-Jackson, L., *I Have Lived a Thousand Years* (New York: Simon & Schuster, 2000).

Black, E., *IBM and the Holocaust: The Strategic Alliance between Nazi Germany and America's Most Powerful Corporation* (Boston, MA: Little, Brown, 2001).

Black, E., *War Against the Work of Eugenics and America's Campaign to Create a Master Race* (New York: Four Walls, Eight Windows, 2004).

Blass, T., *The Man who Shocked the World: The Life and Legacy of Stanley Milgram* (Perseus, 2004).

Bloxham D., *Genocide on Trial: War Crimes Trials and the Formation of Holocaust History and Memory* (Oxford: Oxford University Press, 2001).

Bloxham, D. and Kushner, T., *The Holocaust: Critical Historical Approaches* (Manchester: Manchester University Press, 2005).

Bock, G., *Zwangssterilisation im Nationalsozilaismus. Studien zur Rassenpolitik und Frauenpolitik* (Opladen: Westdeutscher Verlag, 1986).

Borowski, T., *This Way for the Gas, Ladies and Gentlemen* (Penguin, 1976).

Bosworth, R. J. B., *Explaining Auschwitz and Hiroshima: History Writing and the Second World War, 1945–90* (Routledge, 1993).

Bower, T., *Blind Eye to Murder* (André Deutsch, 1981).

Bracher, K. D., *The German Dictatorship: The Origins, Structures, and Effects of National Socialism* (New York: Praeger, 1970; Pelican University Books, 1973).

Braham, R. L., *The Politics of Genocide: The Holocaust in Hungary* (New York: Columbia University Press, 1981).

Braham, R. and Miller, S. (eds), *The Nazis' Last Victims: The Holocaust in Hungary* (Detroit, MI: Wayne State University Press, 1998).

Breitman, R., *The Architect of Genocide: Himmler and the Final Solution* (New York: Grafton, 1992).

Breitman, R., *Official Secrets: What the Nazis Planned, What the British and Americans Knew* (New York: Hill & Wang, 1998).

Bridenthal, R., Grossmann, A. and Kaplan, M. (eds), *When Biology Became Destiny: Women in Weimar and Nazi Germany* (New York: Monthly Review Press, 1984).

Broszat, M. (ed.), *Kommandant in Auschwitz. Autobiographische Aufzeichnungen des Rudolf Höss* (Stuggart: Deutsche Verlags-Anstalt, 1958).

Broszat, M., *The Hitler State* (Longman, 1981).

Browning, C. R., *The Final Solution and the German Foreign Office: A Study of Referat III of Abteilung Deutschland, 1940–43* (New York: Holmes & Meier, 1978).

Browning, C. R., *Fateful Months: Essays on the Emergence of the Final Solution* (New York: Holmes & Meier, 1985).

Browning, C. R., *The Path to Genocide: Essays on Launching the Final Solution* (Cambridge: Cambridge University Press, 1995).

Browning, C. R., *Nazi Policy, Jewish Workers, German Killers* (Cambridge: Cambridge University Press, 2000).

Browning, C. R., *Ordinary Men: Reserve Police Battalion 101 and the Final Solution in Poland* (Penguin, 2001).

Browning, C. R., *Collected Memories: Holocaust History and Postwar Testimony* (Madison, WI: University of Wisconsin Press, 2003).

Browning, C. R., *The Origins of the Final Solution: The Evolution of Nazi Jewish Policy, 1939–1942* (Heinemann, 2004).

Brustein, W. I., *Roots of Hate: Anti-Semitism in Europe before the Holocaust* (Cambridge: Cambridge University Press, 2003).

Bullock, A., *Hitler: A Study in Tyranny* (Penguin, [1952, 1962] 1990).

Burleigh, M., *Death and Deliverance: 'Euthanasia' in Germany, 1900–1945* (Cambridge: Cambridge University Press, 1994).

Burleigh, M. (ed.), *Confronting the Nazi Past: New Debates on Modern German History* (Collins and Brown/History Today, 1996).

Burleigh, M., *Ethics and Extermination: Reflections on Nazi Genocide* (Cambridge: Cambridge University Press, 1997).

Burleigh, M., *The Third Reich: A New History* (Basingstoke: Macmillan, 2000).

Burleigh, M., *Germany Turns Eastwards: A Study of* Ostforschung *in the Third Reich* (Basingstoke: Pan, 2002).

Burleigh, M., *Sacred Causes: Religion and Politics from the European Dictators to Al Qaeda* (HarperPress, 2006).

Burleigh, M. and Wippermann, W., *The Racial State: Germany 1933–1945* (Cambridge: Cambridge University Press, 1991).

Burrin, P., *Hitler and the Jews: The Genesis of the Holocaust* (Edward Arnold, 1994).

Burrin, P., *Nazi Anti-Semitism: From Prejudice to the Holocaust* (New York: New Press, 2005).

Caracciolo, N. et al., *Uncertain Refuge: Italy and the Jews during the Holocaust* (Champaign, IL: University of Illinois Press, 1995).

Cesarani, D. (ed.), *The Final Solution: Origins and Implementation* (Routledge, 1994).

Cesarani, D. (ed.), *Genocide and Rescue: The Holocaust in Hungary, 1944* (Oxford: Berg, 1997).

Cesarani, D., *Eichmann: His Life and Crimes* (William Heinemann, 2004).

Cesarani, D., *Becoming Eichmann: Rethinking the Life, Crimes and Trial of a Desk Murderer* (Jackson, TN: Da Capo Press, 2006).

Chapin, D. A., *The Road from Letichev: The History and Culture of a Forgotten Jewish Community in Eastern Europe*, 2 vols (B. Weinstock Writers' Co-operative, 2000).

Charny, I. W. (ed.), *The Encyclopedia of Genocide* (Santa Barbara, CA: ABC-CLIO, 1999).

Chary, F. B., *The Bulgarian Jews and the Final Solution, 1940–1944* (Pittsburgh University Press, 1972).

Chêne, E. le, *Mauthausen: The History of a Death Camp* (Methuen, 1971).

Childers, T. and Caplan, J., *Re-Evaluating the Third Reich* (New York: Holmes and Meier, 1993).

Choumov, P. S., Kogon, E., Langbein, H. and Ruckerl, A. (eds), *Nazi Mass Murder: A Documentary History* (New Haven, CT: Yale University Press, 1914).

Clendinnen, I., *Reading the Holocaust* (Cambridge: Cambridge University Press, 1999).

Cohen, E. A., *Human Behaviour in the Concentration Camp* (Jonathan Cape, [1954] Free Association Books, 1988).

Cohen, S., *States of Denial: Knowing about Atrocities and Suffering* (Cambridge: Polity Press, 2001).

Cole, T., *Selling the Holocaust: From Auschwitz to Schindler – How History is Bought, Packaged and Sold* (Routledge, 2000).

Cole, T., *Holocaust City: The Making of a Jewish Ghetto* (Routledge, 2003).

Coppa, F. J., *The Papacy, the Jews and the Holocaust* (Washington, DC: Catholic University of America Press, 2006).

Corni, G., *Hitler's Ghettos: Voices from a Beleaguered Society, 1939–1944* (Edward Arnold, 2003).

Cornwell, J., *Hitler's Pope: The Secret History of Pius XII* (Penguin, 1999).

Cornwell, J., *Hitler's Scientists: Science, War and the Devil's Pact* (New York: Penguin/Viking, 2003).

Crankshaw, E., *Gestapo: Instrument of Tyranny* (New York: Four Square, 1966).

Crew, D., *Nazism and German Society, 1933–1945* (Routledge, 1994).

Crowe, D., *A History of the Gypsies of Eastern Europe an Russia* (New York: St Martins Press, 1996).

Crowe, D. and Kolsti, J. (eds), *The Gypsies of Eastern Europe* (New York: Sharpe, 1992).

Czech, D., *Das Kalendarium von Auschwitz* (Reinbeck: Rowohlt, 1989).

Dalin, D. G., *The Myth of Hitler's Pope: Pope Pius XII and his Secret War against Germany* (Washington, DC: Regnery, 2005).

Dallin, A., *German Rule in Russia, 1941–1945: A Study of Occupation Policies* (Basingstoke: Macmillan, 2nd edn, 1981).

Davies, N., *Rising '44: The Battle for Warsaw* (New York: Viking, 2004).

Dawidowicz, L. (ed.), *A Holocaust Reader* (New York: Behrman House, 1976).

Dawidowicz, L., *The War against the Jews, 1933–45* (Pelican, 1979).

Dawidowicz, L., *The Holocaust and the Historians* (Cambridge, MA: Harvard University Press, 1981).

Dean, M., *Collaboration in the Holocaust: Crimes of the Local Police in Belorussia and the Ukraine, 1941–1944* (New York: Macmillan/US Memorial Holocaust Museum, 2000).

Dedencks, M., *Heydrich: The Face of Evil* (Greenhill, 2006).

De Felici, R., *The Jews in Fascist Italy: A History* (New York: Enigma Books, 2001).

Deschner, G., *Heydrich: The Pursuit of Total Power* (Orbis, 1981).

Des Pres, T., *The Survivor: An Anatomy of Life in the Death Camps* (Oxford: Oxford University Press, 1980).

Diefendorf, J. (ed.), *Lessons and Legacies*, vol. VI: *New Currents in Holocaust Research* (Evanston, IL: Northwestern University Press, 2005).

Diner, D., *Beyond the Conceivable: Studies on Germany, Nazism and the Holocaust* (Berkeley, CA: University of California Press, 2000).

Dobrowski, L. (ed.), *The Chronicle of the Lodz Ghetto* (New Haven, CT: Yale University Press, 1987).

Dwork, D., *Children with a Star: Jewish Youth in Nazi Europe* (New Haven, CT: Yale University Press, 1991).

Dwork, D. (ed.), *Voices and Views: A History of the Holocaust* (Madison, WI: University of Wisconsin Press, 2003).

Dwork, D. and van Pelt, J., *Auschwitz* (New York: W. W. Norton, 2002).

Dwork, D. and van Pelt, J., *Holocaust: A History* (John Murray, 2002).

Eaglestone, R., *Post-Modernism and Holocaust Denial* (Cambridge: Icon Books, 2001).

Eisen, G., *Children and Play in the Holocaust* (Amerst, MA: Amherst, 1988).

Eisenberg, A. L., *The Lost Children of the Holocaust* (Ohio: Pilgrim Press, 1982).

Eley, G. (ed.), *The 'Goldhagen Effect': History, Memory, Nazism – Facing the German Past* (Ann Arbor, MI: University of Michigan Press, 2000).

Engel, D., *The Holocaust: The Third Reich and the Jews* (Longman, 2000).

Evans, R., *In Defence of History* (New York: W. W. Norton, 1999).

Evans, R. J., *Telling Lies about Hitler: The Holocaust, History and the David Irving Trial* (Verso, 2002).

Fahlbusch, M. and Haar, I. (eds), *German Scholars and Ethnic Cleansing, 1920–1945* (Oxford: Berghahn, 2004).

Feig, K., *Hitler's Death Camps: The Sanity of Madness* (New York: Holmes and Meier, 1981).

Fein, H., *Accounting for Genocide: National Responses and Jewish Victimization during the Holocaust* (Chicago, IL: University of Chicago Press, 1984).

Feingold, H., *The Politics of Rescue: The Roosevelt Administration and the Holocaust, 1938–1945* (New York: Rutgers University Press, 1986).

Feingold, H., *Bearing Witness: How America and its Jews Responded to the Holocaust* (New York: Syracuse University Press, 1995).

Feldman, G. D. and Seibel W., *Networks of Nazi Persecution: Division of Labour in Implementing the Holocaust* (Oxford: Berghahn Books, 2004).

Felice, R. de, *The Jews in Fascist Italy: A History* (New York: Enigma Books, 2001).

Finkelstein, N. G., *The Holocaust Industry: Reflections on the Exploitation of Jewish Suffering* (Verso, 2001).

Finkelstein, N. G. and Birn, R. B., *A Nation on Trial: The Goldhagen Thesis and Historical Truth* (New York: Holt, 1998).

Fischer, K. P., *Nazi Germany: A New History* (Constable, 1995).

Fischer, K. P., *The History of an Obsession: German Judeophobia and the Holocaust* (Constable, 1998).

Fischler-Martinho, J., *Have You Seen My Little Sister?* (Vallentine Mitchell, 2003).

Fleming, G., *Hitler and the Final Solution* (Oxford: Oxford University Press, 1986).

Fox, F. (ed.), *Am I a Murderer? Testament of a Jewish Ghetto Policeman* (Boulder, CO: Westview Press, 1996).

Frei, N., *National Socialist Rule in Germany* (Blackwell, 1993).

Frei, N. et al. (eds), *Standort- und Kommandanturbefehle des Konzentrationslagers Auschwitz 1940–1945* (Munich: Saur, 2000).

Fried, H., *Fragments of a Life: The Road to Auschwitz* (Robert Hale, 1990).

Friedlander, A. H., *Out of the Whirlwind: A Reader of Holocaust Literature* (New York: Schocken Books, 1976).

Friedlander, H., *The Origins of Nazi Genocide: From Euthanasia to the Final Solution* (Chapel Hill, NC: University of North Carolina Press, 1995).

Friedländer, S., *Pius XII and the Third Reich: A Documentation* (New York: Alfred A. Knopf, 1966).

Friedländer, S., *No Haven for the Oppressed: United States Policy towards Jewish Refugees, 1938–1945* (Detroit, MI: Wayne State University Press, 1973).

Friedländer, S., *Probing the Limits of Representation: Nazism and the 'Final Solution'* (Cambridge, MA: Harvard University Press, 1992).

Friedländer, S., *Memory, History and the Extermination of the Jews of Europe* (Bloomington, IN: Indiana University Press, 1993).

Friedländer, S., *Nazi Germany and the Jews: The Years of Persecution, 1933–39*, vol. 1 (Weidenfeld and Nicolson, 1997).

Friedländer, S., *The Extermination of the Jews*, vol. 2: *Nazi Germany and the Jews* (HarperCollins, 2007).

Friedman, I., *The Other Victims: First Person Stories of Non-Jews Persecuted by the Nazis* (New York: Houghton Mifflin, 1990).

Friedman, S., *A History of the Holocaust* (Vallentine Mitchell, 2002).

Friedrich, O., *The Kingdom of Auschwitz* (Penguin Putnam, USA, 1996).

Fröhlich, E. (ed.), *Die Tagebücher von Joseph Goebbels. Sämtliche Fragmente*, vol. 1: *1924–1941* (London and Munich, 1987).

Fromer, R. C., *The Holocaust Odyssey of Daniel Bennahmias, Sonderkommando* (Tuscaloosa, AL: University of Alabama Press, 1993).

Fulbrook, M., *German National Identity after the Holocaust* (Cambridge: Polity Press, 1999).

Furet, F. (ed.), *Unanswered Questions: Nazi Germany and the Genocide of the Jews* (New York: Schocken Books, 1989).

Gallo, P. J. (ed.), *Pius XII, the Holocaust and the Revisionists* (New York: McFarland, 2006).

Gellately, R., *The Gestapo and German Society: Enforcing Racial Policy, 1933–1945* (Oxford: Clarendon Press, 1990).

Gellately, R., *Backing Hitler: Consent and Coercion in Nazi Germany* (Oxford: Oxford University Press, 2001).

Gerlach, C., *Krieg, Ernährung, Völkermord: Forschungun zur deutschen Vernichtungspolitik im Zweiten Weltkrieg* (Hamburg HIS Verlag, 1998).

Gerlach, C., *Kalkulierte Morde: Die deutsche Wirtschaft- und Vernichtsungspolitik in Wiessrussland 1941 bis 1944* (Hamburg: Hamburger, 2000).

Gerlach, W., *And the Witnesses were Silent: The Confessing Church and the Persecution of the Jews* (Lincoln, NB: University of Nebraska Press, 2000).

Gigliotti, S. and Lang, B. (eds), *The Holocaust: A Reader* (Oxford: Blackwell, 2004).

Gilbert, M., *Auschwitz and the Allies* (Michael Joseph, 1981).

Gilbert, M., *The Holocaust: A History of the Jews of Europe during the Second World War* (New York: Rinehart & Winston, 1985).

Gilbert, M., *The Holocaust: The Jewish Tragedy* (Collins, 1986).

Gilbert, M., *The Boys: Triumph over Adversity* (Weidenfeld and Nicolson, 1996, 1997).

Gilbert, M., *Never Again: A History of the Holocaust* (HarperCollins/Imperial War Museum, 2001).

Gilbert, M., *The Routledge Atlas of the Holocaust* (Routledge, 2002).

Gilbert, M., *Final Journey: The Fate of the Jews in Nazi Europe* (ibooks, 2006).

Gilbert, M., *Kristallnacht: Prelude to Destruction* (HarperCollins, 2006).

Gill, A., *The Journey Back from Hell: Conversations with Concentration Camp Survivors* (HarperCollins, 1989).

Gingrich, A. (ed.), *Networks of Nazi Persecution: Business, Bureaucracy and the Organization of the Holocaust* (Oxford: Berghahn, 2005).

Gitelman, Z. Y. (ed.), *Bitter Legacy: Confronting the Holocaust in the USSR* (Bloomington, IN: Indiana University Press, 1997).

Glass, J., *Life Unworthy of Life: Racial Phobia and Murder in Hitler's Germany* (New York: Basic Books, 1997).

Glass, J., *Jewish Resistance during the Holocaust: Moral Uses of Violence and Will* (Basingstoke: Palgrave Macmillan, 2004).

Goldhagen, D. J., *Hitler's Willing Executioners: Ordinary Germans and the Holocaust* (Abacus, 1996).

Goldhagen, D. J., *A Moral Reckoning: The Role of the Catholic Church in the Holocaust and its Unfulfilled Duty of Repair* (Boston, MA: Little Brown, 2002).

Gordon, H., *The Shadow of Death: The Holocaust in Lithuania* (Lexington, KY: University of Kentucky, 1992).

Gordon, S., *Hitler, Germans and the Jewish Question* (Princeton, NJ: Princeton University Press, 1984).

Graber, G. S., *History of the SS* (Robert Hale, 1978).

Graml, H., *Anti-Semitism and its Origins in the Third Reich* (Oxford: Oxford University Press, 1992).

Grau, G. (ed.), *Hidden Holocaust? Gay and Lesbian Persecution in Germany, 1933–45* (New York: Continuum, 1995).

Gray, C., *The Irving Judgement* (Penguin, 2000).

Greenman, L., *An Englishman in Auschwitz* (Vallentine Mitchell, 2001).

Greenspan, H., *On Listening to Holocaust Survivors: Recounting and Life History* (Westport: Praeger, 1998).

Gregor, N. (ed.), *Nazism, War and Genocide: Essays in Honour of Jeremy Noakes* (Exeter: University of Exeter Press, 2005).

Grode, W., *Die 'Sonderbehandlung 14f13' in den Konzentrationslagern des Dritten Reiches. Ein Beitrag zur Dynamik der faschisischen Vernichtungpolitik* (Frankfurt, Bern and New York: Peter Lang, 1987).

Gross, J. T., *Polish Society under German Occupation: The Generalgouvernement, 1939–1944* (Princeton, NJ: Princeton University Press, 1979).

Gross, L., *The Last Jews of Berlin* (New York: Simon & Schuster, 1988).

Grunberger, R., *A Social History of the Third Reich* (Penguin, 1971).

Grynberg, M. (ed.), *Words to Outlive Us: Eyewitness Accounts from the Warsaw Ghetto* (London: Granta Books, 2003).

Gurewitsch, M. (ed.), *Mothers, Resisters, Sisters: Oral Histories of Women who Survived the Holocaust* (University of Alabama Press, 1998).

Gutman, Y., *The Jews of Warsaw, 1939–43: Ghetto, Underground, Revolt* (Bloomington, IN: Indiana University Press, 1982).

Gutman, Y., *Resistance: The Warsaw Ghetto Uprising* (New York: Mariner Books, 1994).

Gutman, Y. (ed.), *Encyclopaedia of the Holocaust* (New York: Macmillan Reference Library, 1995).

Gutman, Y. and Berenbaum, M. (eds), *Anatomy of the Auschwitz Death Camp* (Bloomington and Indianapolis: Indiana University Press, 1994).

Gutman, Y. and Krakowski, S., *Unequal Victims: Poles and Jews during World War Two* (New York: Holocaust Library, 1987).

Gutman, Y., Arad, Y. and Margaliot, A., *Documents on the Holocaust* (Jerusalem: Yad Vashem Publications, 1999).

Guttenplan, D. D., *The Holocaust on Trial: History, Justice and the David Irving Libel Case* (Granta Books, 2001).

Haffner, S., *The Meaning of Hitler* (Phoenix, 2000).

Halamish, A., *The Exodus Affair: Holocaust Survivors and the Struggle for Palestine* (New York: Syracuse University Press, 1998).

Harvey, E., *Women in the Nazi East: Agents and Witnesses of Germanization* (New Haven, CT: Yale University Press, 2003).

Hatheway, J., *In Perfect Formation: SS Ideology and the SS-Junkerschule-Tolz* (Atglen, PA: Aschiffer Military History, 1999).

Hauer, I. and Fuhlbusch, D. (ed.), *German Scholars and Ethnic Cleansing 1920–1945* (Oxford: Berghahn, 2005).

Headland, R., *Messages of Murder: The Study of the Reports of the Einsatzgruppen of the Security Police and Security Service, 1941–43* (Fairleigh Dickinson University Press, 1992).

Heer, H., *The German Army and Genocide: Crimes against War Prisoners, Jews and Other Civilians in the East, 1939–44* (New York: New Press, 1999).

Heer, H. and Naumann, K. (eds), *War of Extermination: The German Military in World War II, 1941–44* (Oxford: Berghahn Books, 2000).

Heger, H., *The Men with the Pink Triangle: The True Life and Death Story of Homosexuals in the Nazi Death Camps* (Boston, MA: Alyson Press, 1994).

Heinemann, I., *Rasse, Siedlung, deutsches Blut: Das Rasse- und Siedlungshauptamt der SS und die rassenpolitische Neuordnung Europas* (Göttingen: Wallstein Verlag, GmbH, 2003).

Hellig, J., *The Holocaust and Anti-Semitism: A Short History* (Oxford: Blackwell, 2003).

Herbert, U., *Best. Biographische Studien über Radikalismus, Weltanschauung und Vernunft 1903–1989* (Bonn: Dietz, 1996).

Herbert, U., *Hitler's Foreign Workers* (Cambridge: Cambridge University Press, 1997).

Herbert, U. (ed.), *National Socialist Extermination Policies: Contemporary German Perspectives and Controversies* (Oxford: Berghahn Books, 2000).

Herf, J., *Divided Memory: The Nazi Past in the Two Germanys* (Cambridge, MA: Harvard University Press, 1997).

Herf, J., *The Jewish Enemy: Nazi Propaganda during World War II and the Holocaust* (Cambridge, MA: Belknap Press of Harvard University Press, 2006).

Hilberg, R., *The Destruction of the European Jews*, 3 vols (New York: Holmes & Meier, 1985).

Hilberg, R., *The Holocaust Today* (New York: Syracuse University Press, 1988).

Hilberg, R., *The Politics of Memory: The Journey of a Holocaust Historian* (Chicago, IL: Ivan R. Dee, 1996).

Hilberg, R., *Perpetrators, Victims, Bystanders: The Jewish Catastrophe, 1933–1945* (New York: Harper, 1992, 2003).

Hilberg, R., Staron, S. and Kermisz, J. (eds), *The Warsaw Diary of Adam Czerniakow: Prelude to Doom* (New York: Scarborough Books, 1982).

Hildebrand, K., *The Third Reich* (Allen & Unwin, 1984).

Hillgruber, A., *Staatsmänner und Diplomaten bei Hitler. Vertrauliche Aufzeichnungen über Unterredungen mit Vertretern des Auslandes 1942–1944* (Frankfuurt a.M.: Bernard and Graefe Verlag, 1970).

Hillgruber, A., *Germany and the Two World Wars* (Cambridge, MA: Harvard University Press, 1981).

Hirschfeld, G., *The Policies of Genocide: Jews and Soviet Prisoners of War in Nazi Germany* (German Historical Institute/Allen & Unwin, 1986).

HMSO, *Documents on German Foreign Policy*, Series D, vol. XIII: *The War Years June 23 1941–December 11 1941* (London, 1964).

Höhne, H., *The Order of the Death's Head: The Story of Hitler's SS* (Penguin, [1969] 2000).

Höss, R., *Death Dealer: Memoirs of the Kommandant at Auschwitz* (New York: Da Capo Press, 1992).

Howsden, M., *Hans Frank, Lebensraum and the Holocaust* (Basingstoke: Palgrave Macmillan, 2003).

Ioanid, R., *The Holocaust in Romania: The Destruction of Jews and Gypsies under the Antonescu Regime, 1940–1944* (Chicago: Chicago University Press, 2000).

Jäckel, E., *Hitler's Weltanschauung: A Blueprint for Power* (New Haven, CT: Yale University Press, 1972).

Jäckel, E., *Hitler in History* (Brandeis, NH: Brandeis University Press, 1984).

Jäckel, E. and Kuhn, A. (eds), *Hitler: Sämtliche Aufzeichnungen 1905–24* (Stuttgart, 1980).

Jäckel, E. and Rohwer, J. (eds), *Der Mord an den Juden im Zweiten Weltkrieg. Entschlussbildung und Verwirklichung* (Frankfurt a.M.: Fischer Taschenbuch Verlag, 1987).

Jäger, H., *Verbrechen unter totalitärer Herrschaft. Studien zur nationalsozialistischen Gewaltkriminalität* (Frankfurt a.M.: Suhrkamp, 1967).

Jarausch, K. H., *The Unfree Professions: German Lawyers, Teachers and Engineers, 1900–1950* (Oxford: Oxford University Press, 1990).

Johnson, E. A., *The Nazi Terror: The Gestapo, Jews and Ordinary Germans* (John Murray, 1999).

Johnson, E. and Reuband, K.-H., *What We Knew: Terror, Mass Murder and Everyday Life in Nazi Germany* (John Murray, 2005).

Kagan, J. and Coven, D., *Surviving the Holocaust with the Russian Jewish Partisans* (Vallentine Mitchell, 2001).

Kansteiner, W., *In Pursuit of German Memory: History, Television and Politics after Auschwitz* (Athens, OH: Ohio University Press, 2005).

Kaplan, M. A., *Between Dignity and Despair: Jewish Life in Nazi Germany* (Oxford: Oxford University Press, 1998).

Kater, M. H., *Doctors under Hitler* (Chapel Hill, NC: University of North Carolina Press, 1989).

Katz, R., *Fatal Silence: The Pope, the Resistance and the German Occupation of Rome* (Weidenfeld and Nicolson, 2003).

Katz, S. T., *The Holocaust in Historical Context*, vol. 1 (Oxford: Oxford University Press, 1994).

Katzburg, N., *Hungary and the Jews: Policy and Legislation, 1920–1943* (Israel: Bar-Ilan University Press, 1981).

Kautz, F., *The German Historians: Hitler's Willing Executioners and Daniel Goldhagen* (Montreal: Black Rose Books, 2003).

Keneally, T., *Schindler's Ark* (Hodder and Stoughton, 1982).

Kenrick, D. and Puxon, G., *The Destiny of Europe's Gypsies* (Basic Books, 1972).

Kershaw, I., *Popular Opinion and Political Dissent in the Third Reich: Bavaria, 1933–1945* (Oxford: Oxford University Press, 1983).

Kershaw, I., *The Hitler Myth: Image and Reality in the Third Reich* (Oxford: Oxford University Press, 1987).

Kershaw, I., *The Nazi Dictatorship: Problems and Perspectives of Interpretation* (4th edn; Edward Arnold, 2000).

Kirkpatrick, C., *Women in Nazi Germany* (Jarrold, 1939).

Klee, E., *'Euthanasie' im NS-Staat. Die 'Vernichtung lebensunwerten Lebens'* (Frankfurt a.M.: Fischer Verlag, 1983).

Klee, E., Dressen, W. and Reiss, V., *The Good Old Days: The Holocaust as Seen by its Perpetrators and Bystanders* (New York: Free Press, 1991).

Klemperer, V., *I Shall Bear Witness: The Diaries of Victor Klemperer*, vol. 1: *1933–41* (Weidenfeld and Nicolson, 1998).

Klemperer, V., *To the Bitter End: The Dairies of Victor Klemperer*, vol. 2: *1942–45* (Weidenfeld and Nicolson, 1999).

Klemperer, V., *The Language of the Third Reich: LTI – Lingua Tertii Imperii. A Philologist's Notebook* (Athlone Press, 2000).

Knowlton, J. and Cates, T. (eds), *Forever in the Shadow of Hitler? The Dispute about the German Understanding of History: Original Documents of the Holocaust, the Controversy concerning the Singularity of the Holocaust* (New Jersey: Humanities International Press, 1993).

Koch, H. W. (ed.), *Aspects of the Third Reich* (Basingstoke: Macmillan, 1987).

Koch, H. W., *In the Name of the Volk: Political Justice in Hitler's Germany* (I. B. Tauris, 1997).

Koehl, R. L., *RKFDV: German Resettlement and Population Policy, 1939–1945: A History of the Reich Commission for the Strengthening of Germandom* (Harvard University Press, 1957).

Koehl, R. L., *The Black Corps: The Structure and Power Struggles of the Nazi SS* (Madison, WI: University of Wisconsin, 1983).

Kogon, E., *The Theory and Practice of Hell: The German Concentration Camps and the System Behind Them* ([1950] New York: Time Warner, 1998).

Koonz, C., *Mothers in the Fatherland: Women, the Family and Nazi Politics* (Methuen, 1988).

Koonz, C., *The Nazi Conscience* (Cambridge, MA: Belknap Press, 2005).

Krakowski, S., *The War of the Doomed: Jewish Armed Resistance in Poland, 1942–44* (New York: Holmes & Meier, 1984).

Krakowski, S., *A Small Village in Europe: Chełmno (Kulmhof), the First Nazi Mass Execution Camp* (Jerusalem: Yad Vashem, 2001).

Krausnick, H., *Hitlers Einsatzgruppen. Die Truppen des Weltanschauungskrieges 1938–1942* (Frankfurt a.M.: Fischer Taschenbuch Verlag, 1985).

Krausnick, H. and Broszat, M., *Anatomy of the SS State* (Paladin, 1973).

LaCapra, D., *History and Memory after Auschwitz* (New York: Cornell University Press, 1998).

Lagnado, L. et al., *Children of the Flames: Dr Josef Mengele and the Untold Story of the Twins of Auschwitz* (Penguin, 1992).

Landau, R. S., *Studying the Holocaust* (Routledge, 1998).

Landau, R. S., *The Nazi Holocaust: Its History and Meaning* (I. B. Tauris, [1992] 2006).

Lang, B., *Post-Holocaust: Interpretation, Misinterpretation and the Claims of History* (Bloomington, IN: Indiana University Press, 2005).

Lang, J. von and Sibyll, C., *Eichmann Interrogated: Transcripts from the Archives of the Israeli Police* (New York: Da Capo Press, 1999).

Langer, L., *Holocaust Testimonies: The Ruins of Memory* (New Haven, CT: Yale University Press, 1991).

Laqueur, W., *The Terrible Secret: The Suppression of the Truth about the Final Solution* (New York: Holt, 1998).

Laqueur, W. and Breitman, R., *Breaking the Silence. The German who Exposed the Final Solution* ([1986] Waltham, MA: Brandeis University Press, 1994).

Leitz C. (ed.), *The Third Reich: The Essential Readings* (Oxford: Blackwell, 1999).

Lengyel, O., *Five Chimneys* (Chicago: Academy, [1947] 1993).

Lere-Cohen, R., *The Holocaust in Lithuania, 1941–1945* (Jerusalem: Gefen, 2002).

Levenden, I., *Not the Germans Alone: A Son's Search for the Truth of Vichy* (Evanston, IL: Northwestern University Press, 2000).

Levi, N. and Rothberg, M., *The Holocaust: Theoretical Readings* (Edinburgh: Edinburgh University Press, 2003).

Levi, P., *If This is a Man* (Abacus, 1987).

Levi, P., *The Drowned and the Saved* (Abacus, 1989).

Levi, P., *Survival in Auschwitz: The Nazi Assault on Humanity* ([1958] Touchstone, 1996).

Levi, P., *The Black Hole of Auschwitz* (Cambridge: Polity Press, 2006).

Levi, P. et al., *Auschwitz Report* (Verso, 2006).

Levin, D., *Fighting Back: Lithuanian Jewry's Armed Resistance to the Nazis, 1941–1945* (New York: Holmes & Meier, 1985).

Lewin, R., *Ultra goes to War: The Secret Story* (Penguin, 2001).

Lewy, G., *The Catholic Church and Nazi Germany* (New York: DaCapo Press, 2000).

Lewy, G., *The Nazi Persecution of the Gypsies* (Oxford: Oxford University Press, 2000).

Lifton, R. J., *The Nazi Doctors: A Study of the Psychology of Evil* (Basingstoke: Macmillan, 1986).

Lindemen, Y. (ed.), *Shards of Memory: Narratives of Holocaust Survival* (New York: Praeger Press, 2007).

Lipstadt, D., *Denying the Holocaust: The Growing Assault on Truth and Memory* (Penguin, 1994).

Lipstadt, D., *History on Trial: My Day in Court with David Irving* (New York: HarperCollins, 2005).

Lochner, P. (ed.), *The Goebbels Diaries, 1942–1943* (New York: Doubleday, 1948).

London, L., *Whitehall and the Jews, 1933–1948: British Immigration Policy and the Holocaust* (Cambridge: Cambridge University Press, 2000).

Longerich, P. (ed.), *Die Erdmordung der europäischen Juden. Eine umfassende Dokumentation des Holocaust 1941–1945* (Munich, Zurich: Piper, 1989).

Longerich, P., *Politik der Vernichtung. Eine Gesamtdarstellung der Nationalsozialistische Judenverfolgung* (Munich: Piper Verlag, 1998).

Longerich, P., *The Unwritten Order: Hitler's Role in the Final Solution* (Tempus, 2003).

Loshitzky, Y., *Spielberg's Holocaust: Critical Perspectives on 'Schindler's List'* (Bloomington, IN: Indiana University Press, 1997).

Lower, W., *Nazi Empire-building and the Holocaust in the Ukraine* (Chapel Hill, NC: University of North Carolina Press, 2005).

Lozowick, Y., *Hitler's Bureaucrats: The Nazi Security Police and the Banality of Evil* (Continuum, 2000).

Lukas, R. C., *Forgotten Holocaust: The Poles under German Occupation, 1939–1944* (New York: Hippocrene Books, 2001).

McKale, D. M., *Hitler's Shadow War: The Holocaust and World War II* (Lanham, MD: Taylor, 2006).

MacLean, F., *The Cruel Hunters: SS-Sonderkommando Dirlewanger, Hitler's Most Notorious Anti-Partisan Unit* (Atglen, PA: Schiffer Books, 1998).

MacLean, F., *The Field Men: The SS Officers who Led the Einsatzkommandos – The Nazi Mobile Killing Units* (Atglen, PA: Schiffer Books, 1999).

MacMaster, N., *Racism in Europe* (Basingstoke: Macmillan, 2001).

Madajczyk, C., *Die Okkupationspolitik Nazideutschlands in Polen, 1939–1945* (Berlin: Akademie, 1987).

Madayczyk, C. et al. (eds), *Vom Generalplan Ost zum Generalsiedlungsplan* (Munich: Saur, 1994).

Maier, C. S., *The Unmasterable Past: History, Holocaust and German National Identity* (Cambridge, MA: Harvard University Press, 1997).

Mann, M., *The Dark Side of Democracy: Explaining Ethnic Cleansing* (Cambridge, MA: Harvard University Press, 2005).

Marchione, M., *Consensus and Controversy: Defending Pope Pius XII* (Mahweh, NJ: Paulist Press, 2002).

Marks, J., *The Hidden Children: Secret Survivors of the Holocaust* (New York: Random House, 1993).

Markusen, E. and Kopf, D., *The Holocaust and Strategic Bombing, Genocide and Total War in the Twentieth Century* (Boulder, CO: Westview Press, 1995).

Marrus, M. (ed.), *The Nazi Holocaust: Historical Articles on the Destruction of the European Jews*, 9 vols (Westport, CT: Meckler, 1989).

Marrus, M., *Perspectives on the Holocaust* (Westport, CT: Meckler, 1989).

Marrus, M., *The Nuremberg War Crimes Trial of 1945–46: A Documentary History* (Boston, MA: Bedford Books, 1997).

Marrus, M., *The Holocaust in History* (Toronto: Key Porter, 2000).

Marrus, M. and Paxton, R., *Vichy France and the Jews* (Stanford, CA: Stanford University Press, 1995).

Martel, G. (ed.), *Modern Germany Reconsidered, 1870–1945* (Routledge, 1992).

Märthesheimer, P. and Frenzel, I. (eds), *Im Kreuzfeuer: Der Fernsehfilm 'Holocaust'. Eine Nation ist betroffen* (Frankfurt a.M.: Fischer-Taschenbuch Verlag, 1979).

Marton, K., *Wallenberg: Missing Hero* (New York: Arcade, 1995).

Mayer, A., *Why did the Heavens not Darken? The Final Solution in History* (New York: Pantheon, 1990).

Mazower, M., *Inside Hitler's Greece, 1941–1944* (New Haven, CT: Yale University Press, 1993).

Medoff, R., *The Deafening Silence: American Jewish Leaders and the Holocaust* (New York: Shapolsky Press, 1986).

Meinecke, F., *The German Catastrophe: Reflections and Recollections* ([1946] Boston, MA: Beacon Press, 1950).

Mendelsohn, D., *The Lost: A Search for Six of the Six Million* (New York: HarperCollins, 2007).

Michaelis, M., *Mussolini and the Jews: German–Italian Relations and the Jewish Question in Italy* (Oxford: Oxford University Press, 1978).

Michelson, M., *City of Life, City of Death: Memories of Riga* (Boulder, CO: Colorado University Press, 2001).

Mierzejewski, A., *Hitler's Trains: The German National Railway and the Third Reich* (Stroud: Tempus, 2005).

Milgram, S., *Obedience to Authority: An Experimental View* ([1974] Pinter & Martin, 1995).

Millu, L., *Smoke over Birkenau* (Evanston, IL: Northwestern University Press, 1998).

Moeller, R. G., *War Stories: The Search for a Usable Past in the Federal Republic of Germany* (Berkeley, CA: University of California Press, 2001).

Mommsen, H., *From Weimar to Auschwitz: Essays in German History* (Oxford, 1991).

Mommsen, H. and Willems, S. (eds), *Herrschaftsalltag im Dritten Reich. Studien und Texte* (Düsseldorf: Schwann, 1988).

Moore B., *Victims and Survivors: Nazi Persecution of the Jews in the Netherlands, 1940–1945* (Hodder-Arnold, 1997).

Morse, A., *While Six Million Died: A Chronicle of American Apathy* (New York: Random House, 1968).

Mosse, G. L., *The Crisis of German Ideology* (New York: Grosset & Dunlop, 1964).

Mosse, G. L., *Towards the Final Solution: A History of European Racism* (New York: Howard Fertig, 1978).

Mueller-Hill, B., *Murderous Science: Elimination by Scientific Selection of Jews, Gypsies and Others in Germany, 1933–45* (Oxford: Oxford University Press, 1997).

Müller, F., *Eyewitness Auschwitz: Three Years in the Gas Chambers* (Dee, Chicago: US Holocaust Museum, 1979).

Müller, R.-D., *Hitlers Ostkrieg und die deutsche Siedlungspolitik. Die Zusammenarbeit von Wehrmacht, Wirtschaft und SS* (Frankfurt: Fischer Taschenbuch Verlag, 1991).

Mulligan, T. P., *The Politics of Illusion and Empire: German Occupation Policy in the Soviet Union, 1942–43* (New York: Praeger Press, 1988).

Neave, A., *Nuremberg: A Personal Record of the Trial of the Major Nazi War Criminals* (Hodder & Stoughton, 1978).

Neufeld, M. J. and Berenbaum, M. (eds), *The Bombing of Auschwitz: Should the Allies have Attempted it?* (New York: St Martin's Press, 2000).

Neumann, F., *Behemoth: The Structure and Practice of National Socialism* (Victor Gollancz, 1942).

Noakes, J. and Pridham, G., *Nazism, 1919–1945: A Documentary Reader*, vol. 3: *Foreign Policy, War and Racial Extermination* (Exeter: University of Exeter Press, 1997).

Nolte, E., *The Three Faces of Fascism* (Weidenfeld and Nicolson, 1965).

Nolte, E., *The European Civil War, 1917–1945: National Socialism and Bolshevism* (1987).

Nomberg-Przytyk, S., *Auschwitz: True Tales from a Grotesque Land* (Chapel Hill, NC: University of North Carolina Press, 1985).

Novick, P., *The Holocaust and Collective Memory: The American Experience* (Bloomsbury, 2001).

Nyiszli, M., *Auschwitz: A Doctor's Eyewitness Account* (New York: Arcade, 1993).

Ofer, D. and Weitzman, L. J. (eds), *Women in the Holocaust* (New Haven, CT: Yale University Press, 1998).

Owings, A., *Frauen: German Women Recall the Third Reich* (Penguin, 1995).

Padfield, P., *Himmler: Reichsführer-SS* (New York: H. Holt, 1990).

Paris, E., *Genocide in Satellite Croatia, 1941–1945: A Record of Racial and Religious Persecution and Massacre* (Chicago: American Institute for Balkan Affairs, 1961).

Paris, E., *Long Shadows: Truth, Lies and History* (Bloomsbury, 2000).

Pätzold, K. (ed.), *Verfolgung, Vertreibung, Vernichtung. Dokumente des faschistischen Antisemtismus* (Leipzig: Verlag Philip, 1987).

Pätzold, K. and Schwartz, E., *Tagesordung Judenmord. Die Wannsee-Konferenz am 20. Januar 1942* (Berlin: Metropol, 1992).

Pawełczyńska, A., *Values and Violence in Auschwitz* ([1973] Berkeley, CA: University of California Press, 1979).

Paxton, R. O., *Not the Germans Alone: A Son's Search for the Truth of Vichy* (Levendel: Northwestern University Press, 2000).

Pehle, W. H. (ed.), *November 1938: From 'Kristallnacht' to Genocide* (Oxford: Blackwell, 1991).

Pendas, D. O., *The Frankfurt Auschwitz Trial, 1963–65: Genocide, History and the Limits of Law* (Cambridge: Cambridge University Press, 2006).

Penkower, M., *The Jews were Expendable: Free World Diplomacy and the Holocaust* (Detroit, MI: Wayne State University Press, 1988).

Phayer, M., *The Catholic Church and the Holocaust* (Bloomington, IN: Indiana University Press, 2000).

Phillips, P., *The Tragedy of Nazi Germany* (Routledge & Kegan Paul, 1969).

Pine, L., *Nazi Family Policy, 1933–1945* (Oxford: Berg, 1997).

Piotrowski, T., *Poland's Holocaust: Ethnic Strife, Collaboration with Occupying Forces and Genocide in the Second Republic, 1918–1947* (New York: McFarland, [1997] 2007).

Piper, F., *Auschwitz Prisoner Labor: The Organisation and Exploitation of Auschwitz Concentration Camp Prisoners as Laborers* (Auschwitz-Birkenau State Museum, 2002).

Piper, F. and Swiebocka, T. (eds), *Auschwitz: Nazi Death Camp* (Auschwitz-Birkenau State Museum, 1996).

Plant, R., *The Pink Triangle: Nazi War against Homosexuals* (New York: Holt, 1996).

Pohl, D., *Von der 'Judenpolitik' zum Judenmord. Drer Distrikt Lublin des Generalgouvernements 1939–1944* (Frankfurt a.M.: Peter Lang, 1993).

Poliakov, L., *Harvest of Hate: The Nazi Program for the Destruction of the Jews of Europe* (New York: Syracuse University Press, 1954).

Poliakov, L., *Bréviaire de la haine. Le IIIe Reich et les Juifs* ([1951] Brussels: Complexe, 1985).

Porat, D., *Israeli Society, the Holocaust and its Survivors* (Vallentine Mitchell, 2007).

Posner, G. L. and Berenbaum, M., *Mengele: The Complete Story* (New York: Cooper Square Press, 2000).

Poznanski, N., *Jews in France during World War II* (New York: Brandeis University Press, 2001).

Pressac, J.-C., *Les Crématoires d'Auschwitz: La Machinerie du Meurtre de Masse* (Paris: CNRS Editions, 1993).

Pringle, H., *The Master Plan: Himmler's Scholars and the Holocaust* (New York: Harper Perennial, 2006).

Proctor R. N., *Racial Hygiene: Medicine under the Nazis* (Cambridge, CT: Harvard University Press, 1988).

Pulzer, P., *Jews and the German State: The Political History of a Minority* (Oxford: Blackwell, 1992).

Rees, L., *Auschwitz, the Nazis and the Final Solution* (BBC Books, 2005).

Rees, L., *Auschwitz: A New History* (New York: Public Affairs, USA, 2006).

Reiter, A., *Narrating the Holocaust* (Continuum/EJPS, 2000).

Reitlinger, G., *The Final Solution: The Attempt to Exterminate the Jews, 1939–1945* (Vallentine Mitchell, 1953; 2nd edn, 1968).

Reitlinger, G., *The House Built on Sand: The Conflicts of German Policy in Russia, 1939–1945* (New York: Viking Press, 1960).

Reitlinger, G., *The SS: Alibi of a Nation, 1922–1945* (Arms and Armour Press, 1981).

Reuth, R. G. (ed.), *Joseph Goebbels' Tagebücher 1924–1945*, 5 vols (Munich and Zurich: Piper, 1992).

Rhodes, A., *The Vatican in the Age of the Dictators, 1922–45* (Hodder & Stoughton, 1973).

Rhodes, R., *Masters of Death: The SS Einsatzgruppen and the Invention of the Holocaust* (Oxford: Perseus Press, 2002).

Rieger, B., *Creator of Nazi Death Camps: The Life of Odilo Globocnik* (Vallentine Mitchell, 2007).

Ritter, G., *The German Problem: Basic Questions of German Political Life, Past and Present* ([1948] Berkeley, CA: University of California Press, 1962).

Rohrlich, R. (ed.), *Resisting the Holocaust* (Oxford: Berg, 1998).

Roland, C. G., *Courage under Siege: Starvation, Disease and Death in the Warsaw Ghetto* (Oxford: Oxford University Press, 1992).

Roseman, M., *The Villa, the Lake, the Meeting: Wannsee and the Final Solution* (Allen Lane, Penguin Books, 2002).

Rosenbaum, A. S. (ed.), *Is the Holocaust Unique? Perspectives on Comparative Genocide* (Boulder, CO: Westview Press, 2001).

Rosenberg, A. and Myers, G. E. (eds), *Echoes from the Holocaust: Philosophical Reflections on a Dark Time* (Philadelphia, PA: Temple University Press, 1988).

Roth, J. K. and Rittner, C. (eds), *Pope Pius XII and the Holocaust* (Continuum/Pintner, 2002).

Rubinstein, R. L. and Roth, J. K., *Approaches to Auschwitz: The Holocaust and its Legacy* (Atlanta, GA: John Knox Press, 1987).

Rubinstein, W. D., *The Myth of Rescue: Why the Democracies could Not have Saved More Jews from the Nazis* (Routledge, 1997).

Rückerl, A., *Nationalsozialistische vernichtungslager im Spiegel deutscher Strafprozesse. Belzec, Sobibór, Treblinka, Chelmno* (Munich: Deutscher Taschenbuch, 1977).

Russell of Liverpool, Lord, *The Scourge of the Swastika* (Cassell, 1954).

Ryan, D. F., *The Holocaust and the Jews of Marseille: The Enforcement of Anti-Semitic Policies in Vichy France* (Champaign, IL: University of Illinois Press, 1996).

Safrian, H., *Die Eichmann-Manner* (Vienna: Europa Verlag, 1993).

Safrian, H., *Eichmann und seine Gehilfen* (Frankfurt a.M.: Fischer Verlag, 1995).

Samelson, W., *Warning and Hope: Nazi Murder of European Jewry* (Vallentine Mitchell, 2003).

Sandkühler, T., *'Endlösung' in Galizien: Der Judenmord in Ostpolen und die Rettungsinitiativen von Berthold Beitz 1941–1944* (Kempton: J. H. W. Dietz, 1996).

Schafft, G., *From Racism to Genocide: Anthropology in the Third Reich* (Champaign, IL: University of Illinois Press, 2005).

Scheffler, W., *Judenverfolgung im Dritten Reich 1933 bis 1945* (Frankfurt a.M.: Büchergilde Gutenberg, 1961).

Schelvis, J., *Sobibor: A History of a Nazi Death Camp* (Oxford: Berg, 2006).

Schlant, E., *The Language of Silence: West German Literature and the Holocaust German History* (Routledge, 1999).

Schleunes, K. A., *The Twisted Road to Auschwitz* (Champaign, IL: University of Illinois, 1970).

Schneider, W. (ed.), *Vernichstungspolitik. Eine Debatte über den Zusammenhang von Sozialpolitik und Genocid im nationalsozialistischen Deutschland* (Hamburg: Junius, 1991).

Schoenbaum, D., *Hitler's Social Revolution: Class and Status in Nazi Germany, 1933–39* (Weidenfeld and Nicolson, 1966).

Schulte, T. J., *The German Army and Nazi Policies in Occupied Russia* (Oxford: Berg, 1989).

Schulze, H., *Germany: A New History* (Cambridge, MA: Harvard University Press, 1998).

Schumann, W. and Nestler, L. (eds), *Europa unterm Hakenkreuz. Die Okkupationspolitik des deutschen Faschismus*, 8 vols (Berlin: Huthig Press, 1989).

Sereny, G., *Into that Darkness: From Mercy Killing to Mass Murder* ([1974]; Pimlico, 1995).

Sereny, G., *The German Trauma: Experiences and Reflections, 1938–2000* (Allen Lane, 2000).

Shandley, R. R., *Unwilling Germans? The Goldhagen Debate* (Minneapolis, MN: University of Minnesota Press, 1998).

Shermer, M. and Grobman, A., *Denying History: Who Says the Holocaust Never Happened and Why Do They Say It?* (Stanford, CA: University of California Press, 2002).

Shepherd, B., *War in the Wild East: The German Army and Soviet Partisans* (Cambridge, MA: Harvard University Press, 2004).

Sliwowska, W., *The Last Eyewitnesses: Children of the Holocaust Speak* (Northwestern University Press, 1998).

Smith, L., *Forgotten Voices of the Holocaust: A New History in the Words of Men and Women who Survived* (Ebury Press, 2006).

Smith, M. J., *Dachau: The Harrowing Hell* (State University of New York Press, 1995).

Sofsky, O., *The Order of Terror: The Concentration Camp* (Princeton, NJ: Princeton University Press, 1993).

Stackelberg, R., *Hitler's Germany: Origins, Interpretations, Legacies* (Routledge, 1999).

Stein, G. H., *The Waffen SS: Hitler's Elite Guard at War, 1939–1945* (New York: Cornell University Press, 1966).

Steinbacher, S. and Whiteside, S., *Auschwitz: A History* (Penguin, 2005).

Steinberg, J., *All Or Nothing: The Axis and the Holocaust, 1941–43* (Routledge, 1991).

Steiner, J.-F., *Treblinka* (Meridian, 1994).

Steinweis, A. E., *Studying the Jew: Scholarly Anti-Semitism in Nazi Germany* (Cambridge, MA: Harvard University Press, 2006).

Stephenson, J., *Women in Nazi Society* (New York: Croom Helm, 1975).

Stephenson, J., *Women in Nazi Germany* (Longman, 2001).

Stolleis, M., *The Law under the Swastika* (Chicago: University of Chicago Press, 1998).

Stolleis, M., *A History of Public Law in Germany, 1914–45* (Oxford: Oxford University Press, 2004).

Stone, D., *Constructing the Holocaust: A Study in Historiography* (Vallentine Mitchell, 2003).

Stone, D. (ed.), *The Historiography of the Holocaust* (Basingstoke: Palgrave Macmillan, 2004).

Stone, D., *History, Memory and Mass Atrocity: Essays on the Holocaust and Genocide* (Vallentine Mitchell, 2006).

Streim, A., *Die Behandlung sowjetischer Kriegsgefangener im 'Fall Barbarossa'* (Heidelberg: Juristischer Verlag, 1981).

Streit, C., *Keine Kameraden: Die Wehrmacht und die sowjetischen Kriegsgefangenen 1941–1945* (Verlag J. H. W. Dietz Nachf, 1997).

Stroop, J., *The Stroop Report* ([1943] Secker & Warburg, 1980).

Styron, W., *Sophie's Choice* (London, 2000).

Suhl, Y. (ed.), *They Fought Back: The Story of Jewish Resistance in Nazi Europe* (New York: Schocken, 1976).

Sydnor, C. W., *Soldiers of Destruction: The SS Death's Head Division, 1933–1945* (Princeton, NJ: University of Princeton Press, 1990).

Tanner, M., *Croatia* (New Haven, CT: Yale university Press, 1997).

Tec, N., *Dry Tears: The Story of a Lost Childhood* (Oxford: Oxford University Press, 1984).

Tec, N., *When Light Pierced the Darkness: Christian Rescue of Jews in Nazi-occupied Poland* (Oxford: Oxford University Press, 1986).

Tec, N., *Defiance: The Bielski Partisans* (Oxford: Oxford University Press, 1996).

Tec, N., *Jewish Resistance: Facts, Omissions and Distortions* (Washington, DC: Miles Lerman Centre for the Study of Jewish Resistance, 1997).

Tenebaum, J., *Race and Reich: The Story of an Epoch* (New York: Twayne, 1956).

Thalmann, R. and Feinermann, E., *Crystal Night: 9–10 November 1938* (Thames & Hudson, 1974).

Tittmann, H. H. T., *Inside the Vatican of Pius XII: The Memoir of an American Diplomat during World War II* (New York: Image Books, Doubleday, 2004).

Todorov, T., *Facing the Extreme: Moral Life in the Concentration Camps* (Weidenfeld & Nicolson, 1999).

Toland, J., *Adolf Hitler* (New York: Doubleday, 1976).

Tomasevich, J., *War and Revolution in Yugoslavia, 1941–1945* (Standord, CA: Stanford University Press, 2001).

Tory, A., *Surviving the Holocaust: The Kovno Ghetto Diary*, ed. Martin Gilbert (Pimlico, 1991).

Traverso, E., *Understanding Nazi Genocide: Marxism after Auschwitz* (Pluto Press, 1999).

Trevor-Roper, H., *The Goebbels Diaries: The Last Days* (Secker & Warburg: 1978).

Trunk, I., *Judenrat: The Jewish Councils in Eastern Europe under Nazi Occupation* (Lincoln, NB: University of Nebraska Press, 1972).

Trunk, I., *Jewish Responses to Nazi Persecution* (New York: Stein & Day, 1979).

Trunk, I., *Lodz Ghetto: A History* (Indiana University Press, 2006).

Turdar, M. and Weindling, P. (ed.), *Blood and Homeland: Eugenics and Radical Nationalism in Central and South-Eastern Europe* (New York: Central European History Press, 2006).

Van Pelt, R. J., *The Case for Auschwitz: Evidence from the Irving Trial* (Indiana University Press, 2002).

Vidal-Naquet, P., *Assassins of Memory: Essays on the Denial of the Holocaust* (New York: Columbia University Press, 1992).

Von Lang, J. and Sibyll, C. (eds), *Eichmann Interrogated: Transcripts from the Archives of the Israeli Police* (New York: DaCapo Press, 1999).

Vrba, R., *I Escaped from Auschwitz* (Robson Books, [1964] 2006).

Wachsmann, N., *Hitler's Prisons: Legal Terror in Nazi Germany* (New Haven, CT: Yale University Press, 2004).

Wasser, B., *Himmlers Raumplanung im Osten. Der General Plan Ost in Polen 1940–1944* (Basel: Birkhäuser, 1993).

Wasserstein, B., *Britain and the Jews of Europe, 1939–1945* (New York: Continuum Press, 1999).

Webster, P., *Pétain's Crime: The Full Story of French Collaboration in the Holocaust* (Pan Books, 1990).

Weindling, P., *Health, Race and German Politics between National Unification and Nazism, 1870–1945* (Cambridge: Cambridge University Press, 1993).

Weinreich, M., *Hitler's Professors: The Part of Scholarship in Germany's Crimes against the Jewish People* ([1946] New Haven, CT: Yale University Press, 1999).

Weinstein, F., *A Hidden Childhood: A Jewish Girl's Sanctuary in a French Convent* (New York: Farrar, Straus & Giroux, 1986).

Weiss, J., *Ideology of Death: Why the Holocaust Happened in Germany* (New York: Dee, 1997).

Weitz, E. D., *A Century of Genocide: Utopias of Race and Nation* (Princeton, NJ: Princeton University Press, 2003).

Welch, D. (ed.), *Nazi Propaganda: The Power and the Limitations* (Beckenham: Croom Helm, 1983).

Welch, D., *Nazi Germany: Politics and Propaganda* (Routledge, 1993).

Welch, D., *Propaganda and the German Cinema, 1933–1945* ([1983] I. B. Tauris, 2006).

Werner, H. and Werner, M., *Fighting Back: A Memoir of Jewish Resistance in World War II* (New York: Columbia University Press, 1994).

Westermann, E. B., *Hitler's Police Battalions: Enforcing Racial War in the East* (Lawrence, KS: University of Kansas, 2005).

Wiesel, E., Dawidowicz, L., Rabinowitz, D. and Brown, R. M., *Dimensions of the Holocaust: Lectures at Northwestern University* (Evanston, IL: Northwestern University Press, [1977] 1990).

Wildt, M., *Generation des Unbedingten. Das Führungskorps des Reichssicherheitshauptamtes* (Hamburg: Kartoniert/Broschiert, 2002).

Wilhelm, H.-H., *Rassenpolitik und Kriegsführung. Sicherheitspolizei und Wehrmacht in Polen und der Sowjetunion* (Passau, Bavaria: Wissenschaftsverlag Richard Rothe, 1991).

Wistrich, R., *Anti-Semitism: The Longest Hatred* (Methuen, 1991).

Wistrich, R. S., *Hitler and the Holocaust* (Phoenix, 2002).

Wittmann, R., *Beyond Justice: The Auschwitz Trial* (Cambridge, MA: Harvard University Press, 2005).

Wyman, D., *Paper Walls: America and the Refugee Crisis, 1938–1941* (Amherst, MA: University of Massachusetts Press, 1968).

Wyman, D., *The World Reacts to the Holocaust* (Baltimore, MD: Johns Hopkins University Press, 1996).

Wyman, D., *The Abandonment of the Jews: America and the Holocaust, 1941–45* (New York: New Press, 1998).

Zeman, Z. A. B., *Nazi Propaganda* (Oxford: Oxford University Press, 1973).

Zertel, I., *From Catastrophe to Power: Holocaust Survivors and the Emergence of Israel* (Berkeley, CA: University of California Press, 1998).

Zimmerman, J. C., *Holocaust Denial: Demographics, Testimonies and Ideologies* (Pennsylvania, PA: University Press of America, 2000).

Zuccotti, S., *The Holocaust, the French and the Jews* (New York: Basic Books, 1994).

Zuccotti, S., *The Italians and the Holocaust: Persecution, Rescue, Survival* (Lincoln, NB: University of Nebraska, 1996).

Zuccotti, S., *Under his Very Windows: The Vatican and the Holocaust in Italy* (New Haven, CT: Yale University Press, 2002).

● **Articles**

Adam, U., 'An Overall Plan for Anti-Jewish Legislation in the Third Reich', *Yad Vashem Studies*, 11 (1976).

Allen, M. T., 'Not just a "Dating Game": Origins of the Holocaust at Auschwitz in the Light of Witness Testimony', *German History*, 25 (2007).

Aly, G., 'Hinweise für die weitere Erforschung der NS- Gesundheitspolitik und der "Euthanasie"-Verbrechen', *Arbeitsmigration und Flucht. Vertreibung und Arbeitskräfteregulierung im Zwischenkriegseuropa*, 11 (1993).

Aly, G. and Heim, S., 'The Economics of the Final Solution: a Case Study from the General Government', *Simon Wiesenthal Center Annual*, 5 (1988).

Bankier, D., 'Hitler and the Policy-Making Process on the Jewish Question', *Holocaust and Genocide Studies*, 3 (1988).

Barkai, A., 'Die deutschen Unternehmer und die Judenpolitik im Dritten Reich', *Geschichte und Gesellschaft*, 15 (1989).

Bauer, Y., 'The Judenräte: Some Conclusions', *Yad Vashem Studies*, 13 (1979).

Bauer, Y., 'The Place of the Holocaust in History', *Holocaust and Genocide Studies*, 2 (1987).

Bauer, Y., 'The Impact of the Holocaust', *Annals of the American Academy of Political and Social Science*, 548 (1996).

Benedict, S., 'Nurses' Participation in the Nazi Euthanasia Programme', *Western Journal of Nursing*, 21 (1999).

Bergen, D. L., 'The Nazi Concept of "Volksdeutsche" and the Exacerbation of Anti-Semitism in Eastern Europe, 1939–45', *Journal of Contemporary History*, 29 (1994).

Birn, R. B., 'Revising the Holocaust', *Historical Journal*, 40 (1997).

Breitman, R., 'The Allied War Effort and the Jews', *Journal of Contemporary History*, 20 (1985).

Breitman, R., 'Himmler and the "Terrible Secret" among the Executioners', *Journal of Contemporary History*, 26 (1991).

Broszat, M., 'Hitler and the Genesis of the "Final Solution": an Assessment of David Irving's Theses', *Yad Vashem Studies*, 13 (1979). Also in H. Koch (ed.), *Aspects of the Third Reich* (Basingstoke: Macmillan, 1987).

Browning, C. R., 'Zur Genesis der "Endlösung". Eine Antwort an Martin Broszat', *Vierteljahrshefte für Zeitgeschichte* [hereafter *VZG*], 29 (1981). For English translation: 'A Reply to Martin Broszat Regarding the Origins of the Final Solution', *Simon Wiesenthal Center Annual*, 1 (1984).

Browning, C. R., 'Nazi Ghettoization Policy in Poland: 1939–1941', *Central European Studies*, 19 (1986).

Browning, C. R., 'Nazi Resettlement Policy and the Search for a Solution to the Jewish Question, 1939–1941', *German Studies Review*, 9 (1986).

Browning, C. R., 'A Reply to Martin Broszat Regarding the Origin of the Final Solution', in M. Marrus (ed.), *The Nazi Holocaust: Historical Articles on the Destruction of the European Jews*, vol. 3 (Meckler, 1989), pp. 168–87.

Browning, C. R., 'Hitler and the Euphoria of Victory', in D. Cesarani (ed.), *The Final Solution: Origins and Implementation* (London: Routledge, 1994).

Browning, C. R., 'Genocide and Public Health: German Doctors and Polish Jews, 1939–1941', *Holocaust and Genocide Studies*, 3 (1988). Also in idem., *The Path to Genocide: Essays on Launching the Final Solution* (Cambridge: Cambridge University Press, 1995).

Browning C. R., 'A Final Decision for the "Final Solution"? The Riegner Telegram Reconsidered', *Holocaust and Genocide Studies*, 10 (1996).

Büchler, Y., 'Kommandostab Reichsführer-SS: Himmler's Personal Murder Brigades in 1941', *Holocaust and Genocide Studies*, 1 (1986).

Connolly, J., 'Nazis and Slavs: from Racial Theory to Racist Practice', *Central European History*, 32 (1999).

Dieckmann, C., 'Der Krieg und die Ermordung der litauschen Juden', in U. Herbert, *Nationalsozialistische Vernichtungspolitik, 1939–1945. Neue Forschungen und Kontroversen* (Frankfurt, 1998). See English translation: U. Herbert, *National Socialist Extermination Policies: Contemporary German Perspectives and Controversies* (Berghahn Books, 2000).

Dietrich, D. J., 'Holocaust as Public Policy: the Third Reich', *Human Relations*, 34 (1981).

Drobisch, K., 'Die Judenreferate des Geheimen Staatspolizeiamtes und des Sicherheitsdienstes der SS 1933 bis 1939', *Jarbuch für Antisemitismusforschung*, 2 (1993).

Eley, G., 'Ordinary Germans, Nazism and Judeocide', in G. Eley (ed.), *The 'Goldhagen Effect': History, Memory, Nazism – Facing the German Past* (Ann Arbor: University of Michigan Press, 2000).

Ezard, J., 'The Germans Knew of the Holocaust Horror about Death Camps', *Guardian*, 17 February 2001.

Feldman, G., 'The Economics of the Final Solution', *Australian Journal of Politics and History*, 53 (2007).

Forster, J., 'The Relation between Operation Barbarossa as an Ideological War of Extermination and the Final Solution', in D. Cesarani (ed.), *The Final Solution: Origins and Implementation* (London: Routledge, 1994).

Friedländer, S., 'From Anti-Semitism to Extermination: a Historiographical Study of Nazi Policies toward the Jews', *Yad Vashem Studies*, 16 (1984). Also in M. Marrus (ed.), *The Nazi Holocaust: Historical Articles on the Destruction of the European Jews*, vol. 3 (New York: Meckler, 1989).

Friedländer, S., 'From Anti-Semitism to Extermination: a Historical Study of Nazi Policies towards the Jews and an Essay of Interpretation', in M. Marrus (ed.), *The Nazi Holocaust*, Part 3, Vol. 1: *'The Final Solution': The Implementation of Mass Murder* (New York: Meckler, 1989).

Friedman, P., 'The Jewish Ghettoes of the Nazi Era', *Jewish Social Studies*, 16 (1954).

Gerlach, C., 'Die Wannsee-Konferenz, das Schicksal der deutschen Juden und Hitlers politische Grundsatzentschieden, alle juden Europas zu morden', *Werkstattgeschichte*, 18 (1997).

Gerlach, C., 'The Wannsee Conference: the Fate of the German Jews and Hitler's Decision in Principle to Exterminate all European Jews', in O. Bartov (ed.), *The Holocaust: Origins, Implementation, Aftermath* (London: Routledge, 2000).

Gigliotti, S., 'History's Dark Sides: Writing Genocide and Post-Holocaust Obligations', *Journal of Contemporary History*, 41 (2006).

Goeschel, C., 'Suicides of German Jews in the Third Reich', *German History*, 25 (2007).

Goldhagen, D., 'Daniel Joseph Goldhagen Comments on Birn', *German Society and Politics*, 16 (1998).

Goshen, S., 'Eichmann und die Nisko-Aktion im November 1939', *VZG*, 29 (1981).

Griech-Pollele, B., 'Image of a Churchman Resister: Bishop von Galen, the Euthanasia Project and the Sermons of Summer 1941', *Journal of Contemporary History*, 36 (2001).

Gruchmann, L., '"Blutscgutgesetz" und Justiz. Zur Entstehung und Auswirkung des Nürnberger Gesetzes vom 15. September 1935', *VZG*, 31 (1983).

Hayes, P., 'Big Business and "Aryanization" in Germany', *Jahrbuch für Antisemitismusforschung*, 3 (1994).

Heer, H., 'Killing Fields: the Wehrmacht and the Holocaust in Belorussia, 1941–1942', *Holocaust and Genocide Studies*, 11 (1997).

Heiber, H., 'Der Generalplan Ost', *VZG*, 6 (1958).

Heilbronner, O., 'The Role of Nazi Anti-Semitism in the Nazi Party's Activity and Propaganda', *Leo Baeck Institute Year Book*, 35 (1990).

Heilbronner, O., 'From Anti-Semitic Peripheries to Anti-Semitic Centres: the Place of Anti-Semitism in German History', *Journal of Contemporary History*, 35 (2000).

Heinsohn, G., 'What Makes the Holocaust a Uniquely Unique Genocide?' *Journal of Genocide Research*, 2 (2000).

Herbert, U., 'Labor and Extermination: Economic Interest and the Primacy of "Weltanschauung" in National Socialism', *Past and Present*, 138 (1993).

Hillgruber, A., 'Die "Endlösung" und das deutsche Ostimperium als Kernstück das rassenideologischen Programms des Nationalsozialismus', *VZG*, 20 (1972).

Hillgruber, A., 'Die ideologisch-dogmatische Grundlage der nationalsozialistischen Politik der Ausrottung der Juden in den besetzten Gedieten der Sowjetunion und ihre Durchfürung 1941–44', *German Studies Review*, 2 (1979).

Huttenbach, H. H., 'Locating the Holocaust on the Genocide Spectrum', *Holocaust and Genocide Studies*, 3 (1988).

Jäckel, E., 'Simply a Bad Book', in R. Shandley, *Unwilling Germans? The Goldhagen Debate* (Minneapolis, MN: University of Minnesota Press, 1998).

Jick, L., 'The Holocaust and its Use and Abuse within the American Public', *Yad Vashem Studies*, 14 (1981).

Kansteiner, W., 'Nazis, Viewers and Statistics: Television History, Television Audience Research and Collective Memory in West Germany', *Journal of Contemporary History*, 39 (2004).

Kershaw, I., 'Improvised Genocide? The Emergence of the "Final Solution" in the "Wartegau"', *Transactions of the Royal Historical Society*, 6th Series, 2 (1992).

Kubica, H., 'Children', in Y. Gutman and M. Berenbaum (eds), *Anatomy of the Auschwitz Death Camp* (Bloomington and Indianapolis: Indiana University Press, 1994).

Kulka, O., 'Die Nürnberger Rassengesetze und die deutsche Bevölkerung im Lichte geheimer NS-Lage- und Stimmungsberichte', *VZG*, 32 (1984).

Kulka, O. D., 'Major Trends and Tendencies of German Historiography on National Socialism and the "Jewish Question", 1924–1984', *Year Book of the Leo Baeck Institute*, 30 (1985).

Kushner, T., 'Different Worlds: British Perceptions of the Final Solution', in D. Cesarani (ed.), *The Final Solution: Origins and Implementation* (London: Routledge, 1994).

Levine, H. S., 'Local Authority and the SS-State: The Conflict over Population Policy in Danzig-West Prussia', *Central European History*, 2 (1969).

Levine, M., 'Illumination and Opacity in Recent Holocaust Scholarship', *Journal of Contemporary History*, 37 (2002).

Levy, R., 'The Bombing of Auschwitz Re-Visited: a Critical Analysis', in J. Neufeld and M. Berenbaum (eds), *The Bombing of Auschwitz: Should the Allies have Attempted It* (New York: St Martin's Press, 2000).

Manchel, F., 'The Reel Witness: Steven Spielberg's Representation of the Holocaust in *Schindler's List*', *Journal of Modern History*, 67 (1995).

Mann, M., 'Were the Perpetrators of Genocide "Ordinary Men" or "Real Nazis"? Results from Fifteen Hundred Biographies', *Holocaust and Genocide Studies*, 14 (2000).

Marrus, M., 'Jewish Resistance and the Holocaust', *Journal of Contemporary History*, 30 (1995).

Marrus, M., 'The Holocaust at Nuremberg', *Yad Vashem Studies*, 26 (1998).

Meyers, O., 'The Sound-Track of Memory: Ashes and Dust and the Commemoration of the Holocaust in Israeli Popular Culture', *Media Culture and Society*, 24 (2002).

Milgram, S., 'Behavioural Study of Obedience', *Journal of Abnormal and Social Psychology*, 67 (1963).

Mommsen, H., 'Die Realisierung des Utopischen: Die "Endlösung der Judenfrage" im Dritten Reich', *Geschichte und Gesellschaft*, 9 (1983). English translation: 'The Realisation of the Unthinkable: the "Final Solution" of the Jewish Question', in G. Hirschfeld (ed.), *The Policies of Genocide: Jews and Soviet Prisoners of War in Nazi Germany* (German Historical Institute/Allen & Unwin, 1986).

Mommsen, H., 'Hitler's Reichstag Speech of 30th January 1933', *History and Memory*, 9 (1997).

Ofer, D., 'Everyday Life of Jews under Nazi Occupation: Methodological Issues', *Holocaust and Genocide Studies*, 9 (1995).

Pegelow, T., 'Determining "People of German Blood" and "Jews" and "Mischlinge": the Third Reich Kinship Office and the Competing Discourses and Powers of Nazism, 1941–43', *Contemporary European History*, 15 (2006).

Piper, F., 'Estimating the Number of Deportees to, and the Victims of, Auschwitz-Birkenau Camp', *Yad Vashem Studies*, 21 (1991).

Roseman, M., 'Recent Writing on the Holocaust', *Journal of Contemporary History*, 36 (2001).

Roseman, M., 'Shoot First and Ask Questions Afterwards? Wannsee and the Unfolding of the Final Solution', in N. Gregor (ed.), *Nazism, War and Genocide: Essays in Honour of Jeremy Noakes* (Exeter: University of Exeter Press, 2005).

Rothberg, M., 'Beyond Eichmann: Rethinking the Emergence of Holocaust Memory', *History and Theory*, 46 (2007).

Sandkühler, T., 'Anti-Jewish Policy and the Murder of the Jews in Galicia, 1941–1942', in U. Herbert (ed.), *National Socialist Extermination Policies: Contemporary German Perspectives and Controversies* (Oxford: Berghahn Books, 2000).

Scheffler W., 'Zur Entstehungsgeschichte der "Endlösung"', *APZ* (*Aus Politik und Zeitgeschichte* [Beilage zur Wochenzeitung das Parlament]), 30 October 1982).

Scheffler, W., 'The Forgotten Part of the "Final Solution": the Liquidation of the Ghettoes', *Simon Wiesenthal Center Annual*, 2 (1985).

Schoenfeld, G., 'Auschwitz and the Professors', *Commentary*, 105 (1998).

Steinberg, J., 'Types of Genocide: Croatians, Serbs and Jews, 1941–45', in D. Cesarani (ed.), *The Final Solution: Origins and Implementation* (Routledge, 1994).

Streim, A., 'The Tasks of the *Einsatzgruppen*', *Simon Wiesenthal Center Annual*, 6 (1989).

Strzelecka, I., 'Women', in Y. Gutman and M. Berenbaum (eds), *Anatomy of the Auschwitz Death Camp* (Bloomington and Indianapolis: Indiana University Press, 1994).

Volkmer, G. F., 'Die deutscher Forschung zu Osteuropa und zum osteuropäis-chen Judentum in den Jahren 1933 bis 1945', *Forschungen zur osteuropäis-chen Geschichte*, 42 (1989).

Westermann, E. B., '"Friend and Helper": German Uniformed Police Operations in Poland and the General Government, 1939–1941', *Journal of Military History*, 58 (1994).

Westermann, E. B., '"Ordinary Men" or "Ideological Soldiers"? Police Battalion 310 in Russia, 1942', *German Studies Review*, 21 (1998).

Witte, P. 'Two Decisions concerning the "Final Solution to the Jewish Question": Deportations to Łódź and Mass Murder in Chełmno', *Holocaust and Genocide Studies*, 9 (1995).

Wyman, D., 'Why Auschwitz was Never Bombed', *Commentary*, 65 (1978). Also see Y. Gutman and M. Berenbaum (eds), *Anatomy of the Auschwitz Death Camp* (Bloomington and Indianapolis: 1994).

Zimbardo. P. G., 'The Pathology of Imprisonment', *Society*, 9 (1972).

Index